CYBERCRIME

CYBERCRIME

THE INVESTIGATION, PROSECUTION AND DEFENSE OF A COMPUTER-RELATED CRIME

EDITED BY

RALPH D. CLIFFORD
PROFESSOR, SOUTHERN NEW ENGLAND
SCHOOL OF LAW

CAROLINA ACADEMIC PRESS
Durham, North Carolina

Copyright © 2001
Ralph D. Clifford
All Rights Reserved.

ISBN 0-89089-723-9
LCCN 2001091828

CAROLINA ACADEMIC PRESS
700 Kent Street
Durham, North Carolina 27701
Telephone (919) 489-7486
Fax (919) 493-5668
www.cap-press.com

Printed in the United States of America

Contents

Chapter One   Introduction
   Ralph D. Clifford   1

Chapter Two   Defining Cybercrime:
A Review of State and Federal Law
   Susan W. Brenner   11

  I. Introduction   11
  II. Cybercrimes: New Crimes or Old Wine in New Bottles?   12
  III. Federal Cybercrime Legislation   16
    A. Copyright Infringement   18
    B. Trademarks and Trade Secrets   29
    C. Hacking, Cracking, Fraud, Virus Dissemination and Extortion   32
    D. Mail Fraud and Wire Fraud   39
    E. Sexual Exploitation of Children   42
    F. Transporting Stolen Property   49
    G. Unauthorized Access to Stored Electronic Communications   49
    H. Sending Obscene, Abusive or Harassing Communications   50
    I. Sending Offensive Material to Minors   51
    J. Sending Commercial Communications Containing Material Harmful to Minors   53
    K. Transmitting Information about a Minor   55
    L. Online Stalking, Harassment and Threats   55
    M. Fraud in Connection with Access Devices   58

IV.	State Cybercrime Legislation	62
	A. Hacking/Cracking	62
	B. Disseminating Viruses and Other Harmful Programs	63
	C. Miscellaneous Computer-Related Offenses	63
	D. Offenses Involving Children	64
	E. Stalking and Harassment	65
	F. Fraud and Theft	66
	G. Forgery	67
	H. Crimes Against Government	68
V.	Conclusion	68

Chapter Three The Investigation and Prosecution of a Cybercrime
Ivan Orton — 71

I. Introduction — 71
II. Acquisition of Evidence — 73
   A. What Crimes? — 73
   B. What Computers? — 73
   C. Legal Limits on Searches — 74
      1. Constitutional Limits — 74
         a. Does the Fourth Amendment Apply to the Situation? — 74
            (1) Is There a Reasonable Expectation of Privacy? — 74
            (2) Is Government Action Involved? — 75
                (a) Searches by Non-forum, State Law Enforcement — 75
                (b) Searches by Private Citizens — 77
         b. Is There a Legal Warrant? — 77
            (1) The Application for the Warrant Must Demonstrate Probable Cause to Believe That Evidence of a Crime Will Be Found in the Place to Be Searched — 77
                (a) Evidence of a Crime — 77
                (b) Will Be Found in the Place to Be Searched — 78
            (2) Signed by a Neutral and Detached Magistrate — 79
            (3) Reasonably Precise in Describing the Place to Be Searched and the Items to Be Seized — 80

			(4) Knock and Announce	81
		c.	Take Items in Plain View	82
		d.	Good Faith	82
		e.	Take Computers off Premises to Search	83
		f.	Prompt Execution	83
	2.	If There Is Not a Legal Warrant Does the Search Fall Within the Exceptions to the Warrant Requirement?		83
		a.	Consent	84
			(1) Who May Consent?	84
			(a) Employer	85
			(b) Parent	86
			(c) Spouse	86
			(d) Co-user	86
			(2) Must the Consentor Be Advised of His/Her Right to Withhold Consent	87
			(3) Consent May Be Limited and May Be Withdrawn	88
		b.	Search Incident to Arrest	88
		c.	Exigent Circumstances	89
		d.	Inventory	90
		e.	Stop and Frisk	90
		f.	Mobility	90
		g.	Plain View	91
	3.	State Constitutional Considerations		92
D.	Statutes			92
	1.	Privacy Protection Act		92
		a.	Suppression	94
		b.	Civil liability	95
		c.	Good Faith	95
	2.	Electronic Communications Privacy Act		96
		a.	What Does the ECPA Cover?	96
		b.	What Does the ECPA Prohibit?	96
		c.	When Is a Disclosure to the Government Allowed?	96
			(1) Subscriber or Customer Records	96

		(2) Contents of Electronic Communications	97
	d.	What Is the Remedy for Violation of this Act?	97
		(1) Criminal Liability	97
		(2) Civil Liability	97
		(3) Suppression	98
		(4) Good Faith	98
E.	Court Rules and Magistrate Imposed Restrictions	98
	1.	Court Rules — Time Within Which Search Must Be Completed	98
	2.	Magistrate Imposed Restrictions	99

III. Analysis of Evidence 100
   A. At the Search Location 100
      1. Who Should Accompany the Officers Executing the Search? 100
         a. Should an Expert Accompany the Officers? ... 100
         b. Should a Representative of the Victim Accompany the Officers? But What If the Only Expert Is a Representative of the Victim? ... 101
      2. What Can Be Seized ... 103
      3. When to Get an Additional Warrant ... 104
   B. Offsite/Detailed Analysis ... 105
      1. Accurate Pristine Mirror ... 105
      2. Analysis Protocol ... 106
      3. What Must Be Returned and When ... 107
         a. Stipulation ... 108
         b. What If the Computer Owner Is Not the Suspect? ... 108
         c. Contraband on Computer ... 109
            (1) Obvious Contraband ... 109
            (2) Suspected Stolen Property — No Irreversible Harm in Returning ... 109
            (3) Suspected Stolen Property — Irreversible Harm in Returning ... 109
            (4) Other Types of Contraband — Passwords, Hacking Programs ... 110

IV. Presentation of Evidence at Trial ... 110
   A. Computer Printouts and Summaries ... 110

	B. Display Computer Contents on Screen/Demonstrations	110
	C. Animation	111
	D. Experts	112
	1. Expert as Educator	112
	2. Expert for Legal Validity	113
	3. Expert for Persuasion	113
V.	Unique Issues	113
	A. Dates and Times	114
	B. Authenticity	116
	C. How to Prove Authorship of Computer File	116
	D. Computer Trespass by Outsider Versus Exceeding Authority by Authorized User	117
	E. Knowledge/Intent	119
	1. Directory Structure	119
	2. File Names	120
	3. Date and Time	120
VI.	Conclusion	121

Chapter Four Defending Cybercrime Cases: Selected Statutes and Defenses
Joseph F. Savage, Jr. with Amanda J. Metts and Darlene DeMelo   123

I.	Computer Related Offenses in the New Economy	124
	A. Introduction	124
	B. The Computer Fraud and Abuse Act	126
	1. Substantive Prohibitions	126
	2. Defenses	128
	a. Jurisdiction	128
	b. Intent	129
	c. "Obtain Anything of Value"	130
	3. Lack of "Damage" Under the CFAA	131
	4. Penalties	131
	C. The Electronic Communications Privacy Act of 1986	132
	1. The Wiretap Statute — § 2511	132
	2. SWECTRA — § 2701	133
	D. The Economic Espionage Act	134
	1. Overview of the Statute	134

			2. The Wide Expansion of Trade Secret Prosecution	137
			3. Defending Against Liability Under the EEA	138
			a. The Prosecutors' Perspective on Defenses	139
			(1) Parallel Development	139
			(2) Reverse Engineering	139
			(3) General Knowledge	140
			(4) The First Amendment	140
			b. Practical Conclusions	141
	E.	The Copyright Act		142
		1.	Criminal Copyright Infringement and the NET Act	142
		2.	Defenses to Criminal Copyright Infringement	144
			a. Invalidate the Copyright	144
			b. No Infringement	144
			c. First Sale Doctrine	145
			d. Fair Use Doctrine	145
			e. Willfulness: The Use Was Authorized	146
			f. Copyright Misuse	147
		3.	Pseudo-Copyright Infringement	148
			a. Trafficking in Counterfeit Labels or Computer Program Documentation or Packaging	148
			b. Unauthorized Fixation of and Trafficking in Sound Recordings and Music Videos of Live Performance	149
			c. Digital Millennium Copyright Act	149
			d. Fraudulent Copyright Notice and Removal of Such Notices	150
			e. False Representation in Application to Register Copyright	150
II.	General Defenses to Cybercrime Allegations			151
	A.	Search and Seizure Issues		151
		1.	Introduction	151
		2.	Federal Statutory Protection	151
			a. The ECPA — Interception of Electronic Communication	152
			b. SWECTRA — Accessing Stored Electronic Communications	152

	3. The Fourth Amendment	153
	a. Scope of Searches	154
	b. Intermingled Documents	155
	c. Plain View Doctrine	156
	d. Consent Searches	157
	e. Privilege	158
B. Other Defenses		159
	1. Anonymity	159
	2. First Amendment as a Defense to Computer Crime	160
	3. Entrapment	161
III. Conclusion		162

Chapter Five   International Aspects of Cybercrime
Jessica R. Herrera   165

I. Introduction   165
II. What is Computer Crime?   167
III. The Challenges of Cybercrime   169
    A. Technical Challenges   170
    B. Meaningfully Enforcing National Laws   173
        1. Differing Definitions of Cybercrimes   173
        2. Differing Procedural Hurdles   175
    C. Operational Challenges   178
IV. Leadership and Education in the Private Sector   179
V. International Multilateral Efforts   182
    A. Organisation for Economic Cooperation
       and Development   182
    B. The Group of Eight Nations   182
    C. Council of Europe   185
        1. Substantive Laws   186
        2. Procedural Laws   187
        3. International Cooperation   187
    D. United Nations   188
    E. European Union   189
VI. Conclusion   189

Index   191

CHAPTER ONE

INTRODUCTION

RALPH D. CLIFFORD*

A book about cybercrime should start with the basics—defining what a "cybercrime" is. Using a lawyer's training, the first place to look for such a definition would be the case law. Unfortunately, no reported case has even used the term, much less defined it.[1] At the same time, the expression has become common among policy makers,[2] within the news media[3] and, in-

---

* Professor of Law, Southern New England School of Law. Member of the bars of Massachusetts, New York and Connecticut.

1. For example, a Westlaw search of the "ALLCASES" database performed on February 10, 2001, indicated that no case used the term "cybercrime" or the phrase "cyber crime." Similarly, a search of Findlaw's database, http://www.findlaw.com (visited Feb. 10, 2001), provided no matches for the terms. In contrast, the phrase "computer crime" occurs in ninety-four cases in the Westlaw ALLCASES database.

2. *See, e.g., Internet Denial of Service Attacks and the Federal Response: Hearing Before the Subcomm. on Crime of the House Comm. on the Judiciary and the Subcomm. on Criminal Oversight of the Senate Comm. on the Judiciary*, 106th Cong., 2d Sess. (Feb. 29, 2000) (statement of Eric Holder, Deputy Attorney General of the United States), http://www.cybercrime.gov/dag0229.htm; *Cybercrime: Hearing Before the Subcomm. for the Dept. of Commerce, Justice, State, the Judiciary, and Related Agencies of the Senate Comm. on Appropriations*, 106th Cong., 2d Sess. (Feb 16, 2000) (statement of Louis J. Freeh, Director of the F.B.I.), http://www.fbi.gov/pressrm/congress/congress00/cyber021600.htm.

3. *See, e.g.* Alison Gerber, *Police Perplexed in Dealing with Cybercrime*, USA TODAY, http://www.usatoday.com/life/cyber/tech/cti456.htm (Aug. 29, 2000); *NewsHour: Cybercrime and the Congress* (PBS television broadcast, Feb. 16, 2000) (transcript at http://www.pbs.org/newshour/bb/cyberspace/jan-june00/cybersec_2-16.html).

creasingly, among academicians.[4] To understand the term, the history[5] of computer technology and computer-related criminal law must be explored as its origins are found there.

Although "cybercrime" is a new term, "computer crime" has been recognized at least since the 1960s,[6] and it entered the legal mainstream in the 1970s.[7] This class of crimes included those that used computer technology to commit a violation; indeed, many times, the computer was merely the tool used by the criminal to commit a traditionally recognized crime.[8] But

---

4. John Schultz, *"The Substance of the Crime Was a State of Mind"—How a Mainstream, Middle Class Jury Came to War with Itself*, 68 U.M.K.C. L. REV. 637, 669–70 (2000); David L. Gripman, Comment, *The Doors Are Locked but the Thieves and Vandals Are Still Getting In: A Proposal in Tort to Alleviate Corporate America's Cyber-crime Problem*, 16 J. MARSHALL J. COMPUTER & INFO. L. 167 (1997); Walter A. Effross, *Hightech Heroes, Virtual Villains, and Jacked-in Justice: Visions of Law and Lawyers in Cyberpunk Science Fiction*, 45 BUFF. L. REV. 931 (1997); Susan W. Brenner, *Can There be Truly Virtual Crime?*, http://www.cybercrimes.net/Virtual/Virtual.html (1999).

5. To be addressing an historic issue associated with cybercrime, or any other computer-related law, seems unusual as the history of the field is measured in a handful of decades rather than millennia. *See* Brian Randell, *History of Digital Computers—Origins*, *in* ENCYCLOPEDIA OF COMPUTER SCIENCE 545, 549 (Anthony Ralston, Edwin D. Reilly & David Hemmendinger, eds., 4th ed., 2000) (ENIAC, the first "general-purpose" digital computer, was officially operational in 1946) [hereinafter ENCYCLOPEDIA OF COMPUTER SCIENCE]. The pace of "history" within the computer field is unlike that in other fields, however, as the pace of change of computer technology radically exceeds that which has been found in other disciplines. *Cf.* Haim Mendelson, *Computer Laws in* ENCYCLOPEDIA OF COMPUTER SCIENCE at 960, 960–61 ("Moore's Law" has accurately predicted that the processing power of a computer doubles every two years leading to a "computer revolution"). It is quite common, for example, for the products currently being sold to have been rendered obsolete already by the next generation of technology that has just begun to be manufactured.

Thus, even though there has only been fifty years of computer history, it has been a remarkably paced fifty years, easily comparable to several hundred years of history in other fields. As Robert X. Cringely expressed it, "[i]f the automobile had followed the same development cycle as the computer, a Rolls-Royce would today cost $100, [and] get one million miles to the gallon...." INFOWORLD (1996), *reprinted at* www.quoteland.com/qldb/author/48 (visited Feb. 21, 2001). Of course, Mr. Cringely finished his statement by noting that his hypothetical Rolls-Royce would "explode once a year, killing everyone inside." *Id.*

6. *See* Donn. B. Parker, *Computer Crime in* ENCYCLOPEDIA OF COMPUTER SCIENCE 349, 352 (the first federal computer law prosecution was in 1966).

7. *See* U.S. v. Jones, 553 F.2d 351, 353 (4th Cir.), *cert. denied*, 431 U.S. 968 (1977).

8. *See* TOM FORESTER & PERRY MORRISON, COMPUTER ETHICS 23–25 (2d Ed. 1994) (discussing the use of computers to commit "old" crimes such as theft and forgery as well as "new" crimes of ATM and EFT fraud).

the capabilities of a computer also allowed new forms of potentially criminal behavior that would not have been possible without the use of computer technology.[9]

An example of this computer-enabled impropriety was the appropriation by an employee of a bank of the round-off from bank interest calculations that occurred in New York in the late 1970s.[10] As a bank's computer calculated the interest earned by each deposit account in the bank, the result often included a fraction of a cent. For example, if an account earns 5% interest on a balance of $100.50, the amount of interest would be $5.015. As banks do not maintain fractional cents in the balance of an account—the ½¢ in the example above—the amount was typically discarded. A programmer working for the bank who recognized this, inserted his own code into the interest calculation program to accumulate all of the discarded fractions of cents and deposited the sum of them into his own account. While this crime of taking less than a penny may not seem like much, as the interest calculation was done daily for millions of accounts, he was able to misappropriate between $5,000 and $10,000 per day. By the end of the year, he had accumulated over $2,000,000 in his account.

Misconduct of this type provided significant challenges to the criminal justice system. Although the programmer's misappropriation was perceived as a theft of the bank's money, criminal laws existing at the time often made prosecution difficult or impossible.[11] This led to an initial round of amendments to state and federal criminal statutes to insure that the newly invented computer crimes would be considered illegal at

---

9. *See Id.* at 29–30 (discussing unauthorized use of another's computer and incremental crime in which the computer is used to commit numerous, but small crimes).

10. The author learned of this caper while he was working as a programmer for Citicorp in New York right after the caper occurred.

11. *See, e.g.*, Lund v. Virginia, 232 S.E.2d 745, 748 (Va. 1977) ("At common law, larceny is the taking and carrying away of the goods and chattels of another with intent to deprive the owner of the possession thereof permanently."). *See generally*, JAY JOSEPH BLOOMBECKER, COMPUTER CRIME LAWS § 2:2 (1993).

Another common problem was getting investigators and prosecutors to treat misuses of computer technology that were within the scope of a criminal statute as a crime. Often, whether because the misuse was not seen as particularly threatening or because the lack of knowledge about computer technology prevented understanding of the misconduct, neither the police nor the prosecutor would pursue complaints. *See* Michael Gemignani & Esther Roditte, *Legal Aspects of Computing in* ENCYCLOPEDIA OF COMPUTER SCIENCE 969, 973 ("Initially prosecutors and the courts were unwilling to treat computer crime seriously.").

law.¹² Consequently, legislatures amended the laws to remove impediments to prosecution including requirements that the crime involve tangible property.¹³ Additionally, the law recognized that computer services and time should not be subject to unpenalized misappropriation.¹⁴

Just as the state and federal legislatures had begun to successfully address this type of computer crime, however, a new technology began its exponential growth — the Internet. The idea of creating the Internet was developed in 1966 by the ARPA office of the Defense Department.¹⁵ Construction of its components began in 1969 and, by the end of that year, computer scientists established that networking computers of different types was practical by developing a network of four nodes.¹⁶ By the early 1970s, many more nodes had been added, a simple e-mail system had been coded to run on the network and the concept of linking multiple networks together — the "Internet" — was conceived.¹⁷ For the decade and a half that followed, the Internet was used mostly by academicians and computer scientists. This changed in the late 1980s when the control of the Internet backbone was transferred from the Defense Department to the National Science Founda-

---

12. *See, e.g.* N.J. REV. STAT. ANN. § 2C:20-1(g) (West 1982); BLOOMBECKER, COMPUTER CRIME LAWS § 1:1[b].

13. *E.g.*, Massachusetts v. Yourawski, 425 N.E.2d 298, 299 (Mass. 1981) ("the intellectual property which appears on the cassette tapes is not 'property' within the definition of property in G.L. c. 266, § 30(2)"). That section of the statue was amended on May 31, 1983 to include "electronically processed or stored data, either tangible or intangible, data while in transit" within the definition of property. 1983 MASS. ACTS ch. 147, § 1 (May 31, 1983).

14. *E.g.*, Lund v. Virginia, 232 S.E.2d 745, 748 (Va. 1977) ("services [can] not be the subject of the statutory crime of false pretense"); *id.* ("the unauthorized use of the computer is not the subject of larceny"). The Virginia legislature responded with three sections within the Virginia Computer Crimes Act, VA. CODE ANN. §§ 18.2-152.1–18.2-152.15 (1985): § 18.2-152.3 outlaws computer fraud, § 18.2-153.4 prohibits computer trespass, and § 18.2-152.6 outlaws the theft of computer services.

15. KATIE HAFNER & MATTHEW LYON, WHERE WIZARDS STAY UP LATE 40–41 (Touchstone Ed. 1998) [hereinafter HAFNER, WIZARDS]. Despite the common misconception, the incentive for developing the Internet was not to create a network that could survive nuclear war. *Id.* at 77. Instead, the early proponents of the Internet were seeking "to create a new public communications network [with] greater speed and efficiency than existing systems." *Id.* at 66. The military's interest in the network was to support research projects facing complex computations that would benefit from the use of multiple computers. *See* David H. Brandin & Daniel C. Lynch, *Internet in* ENCYCLOPEDIA OF COMPUTER SCIENCE 915, 916.

16. HAFNER, WIZARDS at 103, 151–54.

17. *Id.* at 191 & 223–24.

tion and private carriers,[18] and was radically accelerated in 1990 when the World Wide Web was created.[19] Since the early 1990s, private and commercial parties became the majority of the users of the Internet, replacing the earlier dominance of governmental academic users.[20]

The privatization and commercialization of the Web and Internet unfortunately triggered a new kind of computer crime. Previously, with most computers effectively operating in isolation from one another, there was very little opportunity for outsiders to readily manipulate another's computer in order to gain an illicit profit. Computer crimes of the 1970s and 1980s were predominately crimes committed by insiders. When the norm for computers changed from isolation to interconnection, however, the type of crime similarly changed. In the 1990s, the threats to a computer system were as likely to reside outside of the organization as within it, and now, external threats are perceived to be greater than those from the inside.[21]

Although this externalization of perpetrator explains some of the changes in the criminal law that took place in the 1990s, a more significant cause was the societal impacts of the Web and Internet. These technologies are widely recognized as being fundamentally transformational.[22] Society, itself, was radically altered because of the increasing use of these inventions. A term coined as science-fiction in 1984 was adopted to describe the exis-

---

18. *Id.* at 256.

19. *Id.* at 257–58. The "World Wide Web" is a collection of information that is made available over the Internet in a form that allows fairly easy browsing by individuals without sophisticated computer knowledge. It does this by standardizing the publication of information so that the specific computer used by the individual is irrelevant and by making the process of referring to another page within the collection trivial. Today, the Web is the largest single application executing on the Internet. *See generally*, Hal Berghel, *World Wide Web in* ENCYCLOPEDIA OF COMPUTER SCIENCE 1867.

20. *See* David H. Brandin & Daniel C. Lynch, *Internet in* ENCYCLOPEDIA OF COMPUTER SCIENCE 915, 916–21. The commercial dominance of the Internet has so radically altered its character that the academic community is developing its own private internet, usually termed "Internet II." *See Internet II*, http://www.fnc.gov/Internet_II.html (Oct. 11, 1996).

21. *See Cybercrime: Hearing Before the Subcomm. for the Dept. of Commerce, Justice, State, the Judiciary, and Related Agencies of the Senate Comm. on Appropriations*, 106th Cong., 2d Sess. (Feb 16, 2000) (statement of Louis J. Freeh, Director of the F.B.I.), http://www.fbi.gov/pressrm/congress/congress00/cyber021600.htm ("In short, even though we have markedly improved our capabilities to fight cyber intrusions, the problem is growing even faster and thus we are falling further behind.").

22. *See* Hal Berghel, *World Wide Web in* ENCYCLOPEDIA OF COMPUTER SCIENCE 1867, 1872–73.

tence of this new societal force—"cyberspace."[23] Cyberspace is defined by the virtual environment[24] created by computers in which humans interact. When the cyberspace defined in science-fiction in the 1980s became the cyberspace existing in reality in the 1990s, it is not surprising that a reexamination of the criminal law became necessary. Even if "there's no there, there,"[25] criminals have determined how to commit crimes within cyberspace. When they do so, particularly if the crime could only occur because of how cyberspace operates, the term "cybercrime" has been used to describe this behavior.

These cybercrimes are different from the computer crimes of the seventies and eighties. Cyberspace is not just a newer version of older computer technology. Before cyberspace, computer crimes looked like older crimes— finding the bank's money in a computer vault rather than a physical vault, for example. Within cyberspace, however, the nature of the technology allows fundamental changes in the nature of the misconduct being committed:

- Because of cyberspace's speed, transactions can occur that never would have been possible before its creation. Without the pervasive electronic communication brought by the existence of cyberspace, many business techniques such as just-in-time inventory processing would be impossible. Similarly, the speed of cyberspace allows a criminal to commit a crime remarkably quickly, often in less than a second.[26]

---

23. The source of the term is from William Gibson's science-fiction novel, NEUROMANCER 4–5 (1984). Gibson's best definition of cyberspace is found in his later novel, MONA LISA OVERDRIVE 48 (Bantam Paperback ed. 1989): "*There's no there, there.* They taught that to children, explaining cyberspace." Even if the first sentence was originally applied to Oakland, California by Gertrude Stein, it accuracy to the virtual neighborhood created by the Internet and Web is more apropos.

24. A "virtual" environment is one that "[a]ppears to be rather than actually being." WEBSTER'S NEW WORLD DICTIONARY OF COMPUTER TERMS 608 (5th ed. 1994). *See generally*, William R. Cockayne, *Virtual Reality in* ENCYCLOPEDIA OF COMPUTER SCIENCE 1835; Peter J. Denning, *Virtual Memory,* 2:2 ACM COMPUTING SURVEYS 153 (1970); Peter J. Denning, *Virtual Memory,* 28:4 ACM COMPUTER SURVEYS 213 (1996).

25. WILLIAM GIBSON, MONA LISA OVERDRIVE 48 (Bantam Paperback ed. 1989).

26. Donn. B. Parker, *Computer Crime in* ENCYCLOPEDIA OF COMPUTER SCIENCE 349, 350 ("The timing of some crimes is... different. Traditionally, the duration of criminal acts is measured in minutes, hours, days, weeks, months, and years. Today, some crimes are being perpetrated in less than 0.003 of a second (3 ms.).")

- Because of cyberspace's universality, interactions can occur among groups and individuals which would have been unthinkable in an earlier time. As many totalitarian societies are discovering, the Internet destroys the regime's ability to prevent "outside" ideas from being obtained by its citizens. When some of these ideas are considered to be illegal outside of cyberspace, the ease in which they can be spread within cyberspace triggers difficult legal issues.[27]
- Because of cyberspace's one-to-many nature, it allows individuals to more easily publish opinions that would have been publically ignored earlier. Speakers, whether positive or full of hate now have a broad audience.[28] But, as importantly, cyberspace has a many-to-one capability, also. This has allowed an increasingly common form of criminal attack—the "denial of service attack" where many computers, often at the direction of a single individual, simultaneously generate a flood of Web requests for the target site. When the target site cannot handle the crush of requests—as no site can—it either ceases operating or is so overwhelmed with bogus requests that it has no ability to process *bona fide* ones.[29] Cyberterrorism has been enabled.
- But most importantly, because of cyberspace's lack of physicality, fundamental legal concepts that have been used throughout history are crumbling. Of these concepts, the one causing the most difficulty

---

27. *See, e.g.,* Crispian Balmer, *Yahoo! Restricted,* http://abcnews.go.com/sections/world/DailyNews/yahoo001120.html (visited Feb. 16, 2001) (a French court orders Yahoo! to block access to its sites that auction Nazi memorabilia despite Yahoo! assertion that the sites were in the U.S. and the contents of the sites were protected by the First Amendment); Tony Smith, *Napster Partner Urged to Curb Nazi Song Swaps,* THE REGISTER, http://www.theregister.co.uk/content/6/15598.html (visited Feb. 16, 2001) (The German government pressures Bertelsmann, as Napster's partner, to prevent Napster from being used to exchange neo-Nazi songs).

See also, http://www.cyber-rights.org/isps/somm-dec.htm (visited Feb. 16, 2001). (Felix Somm, the CompuServe managing director in Germany, was convicted of failing to block access to pornographic materials within Germany from CompuServe's U.S. servers. The material in the U.S. would be constitutionally protected speech. Ultimately, the German courts reversed the conviction holding that there were no technologically feasible means for blocking access.).

28. *See* previous footnote, *supra.*

29. *See* Ellen Messmer and Denise Pappalardo, *One Year after DoS Attacks, Vulnerabilities Remain,* http://www.cnn.com/2001/TECH/internet/02/08/ddos.anniversary.idg/index.html (Feb. 8, 2001) (pessimistically asserting that "[a] year after distributed denial-of-service attacks blasted the likes of Yahoo!, eBay, CNN.com and eTrade offline, no one has found an easy way to defend against a flood of unwanted IP packets.").

within the criminal justice system is the decreased importance of a nation's borders (or, similarly, a state's borders). Although the edges of a country are of great significance in the physical society, in cyberspace, they are practically invisible. Often, it is impossible to determine from where a cyberspace message originated. Equally, it is impossible to prevent a message from traveling throughout cyberspace, regardless of any intervening borders.

As all of these changes were, and are, occurring, the societies involved have been required to reexamine many aspects of their criminal laws. The responses to these challenges that have been enacted into criminal law have served to define "cybercrimes." The purpose of this book is to discuss these cybercrimes as they have been defined, and to address the practicalities of investigating, prosecuting and defending them.

In the next chapter, therefore, Professor Susan Brenner, an expert in criminal law, discusses the misconduct that has been defined to be a cybercrime. She starts her discussion by examining the nature of cyber-misconduct to determine how novel this misconduct is when compared to traditional criminal conduct. Then, she examines the cybercrime laws of the United States at both the federal and state levels, discussing their elements and limitations.

In Chapter III, the practical issues associated with investigating and prosecuting a cybercrime case are addressed. Prosecuting Attorney Ivan Orton discusses all aspects of the preparation and presentation of a cybercrime. Based on his experience prosecuting cybercrimes, he addresses investigatory issues such as appropriate training standards, computer forensics, and warrant requirements, as well as trial presentation techniques for a cybercrime prosecution.

Chapter IV, written by Defense Attorney Joseph Savage, also addresses these practical issues, but from the perspective of an attorney who is defending someone who has been accused of a cybercrime. Not surprisingly, many of the same issues are covered in Attorney Savage's chapter as were discussed in Chapter III, but the defense rather than prosecutorial perspective on the issues creates a significantly different understanding of them.

In the final chapter, Attorney Jessica Herrera, based on her experience as an attorney who works on cybercrime issues in the U.S. Department of Justice, discusses the increasing international recognition of cybercrimes and the attempts by various international groups to address the problems caused by cyberspace's lack of clear national borders. Her chapter, especially, attempts to forecast where cybercrime prevention efforts will be directed in the immediate future.

These presentations differ greatly in style and emphasis, based on each author's unique perspective. The appreciation of cybercrimes will differ if they are examined from the police officer's, prosecutor's or defense attorney's orientation and is different again when approached from the point of view of an academician or of a legislative, executive or judicial policy maker. To obtain a comprehensive understanding of cybercrimes, perspectives different from the reader's own are important.[30] The legal system's responses to cybercrimes have been multifaceted. As a consequence, a book discussing them must be also.

---

30. For example, a police officer should be aware of a defense attorney's likely consideration of cybercrime issues to be able to better investigate the occurrence and to adequately prepare the evidence for trial.

CHAPTER TWO

DEFINING CYBERCRIME: A REVIEW OF STATE AND FEDERAL LAW

SUSAN W. BRENNER[*]

There is disagreement nationally and globally as to what exactly constitutes a computer crime. The term "computer crime" covers such a wide range of offenses that unanimity has been an elusive goal. For example, if a commercial burglary takes place and a computer is stolen, does this constitute a computer crime, or is it merely another burglary? Does copying a friend's Microsoft Excel disks constitute a computer crime? What about sending obscene pictures over the Internet? The answers to each of these questions may depend entirely upon the jurisdiction in which one finds oneself.[1]

I. INTRODUCTION

This chapter, which uses the term "cybercrime" instead of the phrase "computer crime" to refer to the phenomenon under consideration, reviews

---

[*] Associate Dean and Professor of Law, University of Dayton School of Law. Member of the bars of Indiana and Illinois.

1. Marc D. Goodman, *Why the Police Don't Care About Computer Crime*, 10 HARV. J. L. & TECH. 465 § I(C) (1997), http://jolt.law.harvard.edu/low/articles/10hjolt465.html (footnotes omitted) [hereinafter Goodman, *Why the Police Don't Care*].

the legal definitions of "cybercrime" that have been developed at the federal and state levels. It is divided into four substantive sections: Section II examines the concept of cybercrime as representing the emergence of new kinds of criminal offenses which require the adoption of new substantive criminal legislation. Section III describes and analyzes the federal statutes which address cybercrimes, while section IV does the same thing for cybercrime legislation adopted at the state level. Section V is a brief conclusion, which summarizes the state of the substantive law governing cybercrimes.

II. Cybercrimes: New Crimes or Old Wine in New Bottles?

Cybercrimes are often described as falling into three categories: crimes in which the computer is the target of the criminal activity, crimes in which the computer is a tool used to commit the crime, and crimes in which the use of the computer is an incidental aspect of the commission of the crime.[2]

---

2. *See, e.g.* Id. *See also* U.S. Department of Justice—Computer Crime and Intellectual Property Section, *Federal Guidelines for Searching and Seizing Computers* § I(C), http://www.usdoj.gov/criminal/cybercrime/search_docs/sect1.htm#C (visited Jan. 14, 2001) [hereinafter *Federal Searching Guidelines*].

These categories are not impermeable. Assume, for example, that someone hacks into a bank's computer system and uses the system to commit theft by transferring funds to an account in another bank. *See, e.g.,* LivingInternet.com, *Vladimir Levin*, http://www.livinginternet.com/i/ia_hackers_levin.htm (visited Jan. 14, 2001); RICHARD POWER, TANGLED WEB 92–96 (2000) [hereinafter TANGLED WEB]. Here, the bank's computer system is simultaneously the victim of the crime, an instrument used to commit the crime and a source of evidence about the crime. *See, e.g., Federal Searching Guidelines* § I(C).

For a slightly different categorization of cybercrimes, *see* Laura J. Nicholson, Tom F. Shebar & Meredith R. Weinberg, *Computer Crimes,* 37 AM. CRIM. L. REV. 207, 211 (2000) [hereinafter Nicholson, *Computer Crimes*] (footnotes omitted):

> First, a computer may be the 'object' of a crime: the offender targets the computer itself. This encompasses theft of computer processor time and computerized services. Second, a computer may be the 'subject' of a crime: a computer is the physical site of the crime, or the source of, or reason for, unique forms of asset loss. This includes the use of 'viruses,' 'worms,' 'Trojan horses,' 'logic bombs,' and 'sniffers.' Third, a computer may be an 'instrument' used to commit traditional crimes in a more complex manner. For example, a computer might be used to collect credit card information to make fraudulent purchases.

While this categorization was developed for use in drafting warrants to search and seize computer equipment,[3] it also provides a useful framework for thinking about the ways in which criminal activity can be carried out in and via cyberspace.[4]

When a computer is the target of criminal activity, the perpetrator attacks an innocent user's computer or computer system either by breaking into it or by bombarding it from outside.[5] Cybercrimes that fall into this category and that require breaking into the target include hacking (breaking into a computer system to which one does not have lawful access or breaking into parts of a computer system to which one does not have lawful access),[6] cracking (breaking into a computer system or parts of a computer system to which one does not have lawful access in order to commit another crime such as illegally copying information contained in that system)[7] or sabotage (breaking into or using one's lawful access to a computer system to damage the system and/or information contained in it).[8] It is also possible to attack an innocent system from outside, as evidenced by the

---

3. *See, e.g., Federal Searching Guidelines* §I(C).

4. For a different, less structured characterization of the roles computers can play in the commission of crimes, *see* U.S. Department of Justice—Computer Crime and Intellectual Property Section, *Prosecuting Crimes Facilitated by Computers and by the Internet* §A, http://www.usdoj.gov/criminal/cybercrime/crimes.html (visited Jan. 14, 2001).

5. Goodman, *Why the Police Don't Care* §I(C).

6. For example, in 1994 two young criminals "hacked" into the computer systems at the U.S. Air Force's Rome Air Development Center in New York. *See, e.g.,* TANGLED WEB 66–75 (2000). In addition to exploring the Rome computer systems, the hackers used that system to hack into computers around the world, including South Korea's Atomic Research Institute. *Id. See also Security in Cyberspace, U.S. Senate Permanent Subcomm. on Investigations, App. B* (Minority Staff Statement, June 5, 1996), http://www.fas.org/irp/congress/1996_hr/s960605b.htm.

7. For example, in the mid-1990's, a gang known as the Phonemasters routinely broke into various computer system belonging to telephone companies, credit-reporting services, Dun & Bradstreet and Lexis-Nexis to steal information which they then sold. *See, e.g.,* TANGLED WEB 102–113. *See also* D. Ian Hopper & Richard Stenger, *Large-scale Phone Invasion Goes Unnoticed by All But FBI,* SIGNALTONOISE.NET LIBRARY, http://www.signaltonoise.net/library/phonemasters.htm (visited Jan. 14, 2001).

8. For example, in May, 2000 Tim Lloyd, a former network administrator for Omega Engineering Corporation, was convicted of computer sabotage. *See, e.g.,* TANGLED WEB 184–187. Lloyd had planted, and then activated, a "timebomb" in the company's computer system; after being terminated as an employee, the activated the timebomb and it deleted more than a thousand programs that were essential to the company's operations. *Id. See also* U.S. Department of Justice, *News Release: Former Computer Network*

widely-publicized denial of service attacks against Yahoo!, eBay and CNN in February of 2000.[9] One might argue that these are not new crimes, since hacking can be analogized to trespassing and cracking can be analogized to burglary, but the analogies founder on the critical differences between the "real world" and the "virtual world."[10] The crimes that fall into this category are, therefore, really "new" crimes, i.e., crimes that cannot easily be prosecuted under existing law and so require the adoption of statutes that specifically outlaw these activities.[11]

Instead of being the victim of a cybercrime, a computer or computer system can be an instrument the use of which is integral to the commission of a cybercrime.[12] Here, the computer's role is analogous to the role telephones play in telephone fraud:[13] Fraud can be committed face-to-face or by using a telephone.[14] In the latter alternative, the telephone is simply a tool the perpetrator uses to commit fraud; the use of the telephone in no way substantively alters the nature of the offense.[15] Cybercrimes in which a

---

Administrator Guilty of Unleashing $10 Million Programming "Timebomb," http://www.usdoj.gov/criminal/cybercrime/njtime.htm (visited Jan. 14, 2001).

9. On February 7, 2000, the Yahoo! site was the victim of a distributed denial of service attack that shut it down for at least three hours; on February 8, eBay was the victim of a similar attack that incapacitated it for hours, and CNN was the victim of an attack that shut down all but 5% of the traffic to its site. *See, e.g.,* TANGLED WEB 126. *See also* Ann Harrison, *The Denial-of-Service Aftermath,* CNN.COM (February 14, 2000), http://www.cnn.com/2000/TECH/computing/02/14/dos.aftermath.idg/. In a distributed denial of service attack, the perpetrator hacks into hundreds or even thousands of innocent computers and installs software on them that makes them "zombies," slave computers the perpetrator can use to attack a target computer. *See, e.g.,* Bennett Todd, *Distributed Denial of Service Attacks,* http://www.opensourcefirewall.com/ddos_white paper_copy.html (visited Jan. 14, 2001). When the perpetrator is ready to attack, he or she issues a command that instructs the zombies to attack the victim; as a result of the attack, the victim's system is effectively shut down, since it is overloaded with packets coming in from the zombies. *See id.*

10. *See, e.g.,* Susan W. Brenner, *Can There Be Truly Virtual Crimes?,* Part III, http://www.cybercrimes.net/Virtual/Brenner/part3.html (visited Jan. 14, 2001) [hereinafter Brenner, *Can There Be Truly Virtual Crimes?*].

11. *See, e.g., Id.*

12. Goodman, *Why the Police Don't Care* § I(C). *See also Federal Searching Guidelines* § I(C) ("[T]he computer system may be a tool of the offense. This occurs when the computer system is actively used by a defendant to commit the offense. For example, a counterfeiter might use his computer, scanner, and color printer to scan U.S. currency and then print money.").

13. *See, e.g.,* Brenner, *Can There Be Truly Virtual Crimes?,* Part III.

14. *See, e.g., Id.*

15. *See, e.g., Id.*

computer is the tool used to carry out criminal activity include online fraud (such as fraud in auctions like eBay)[16], theft of funds or information,[17] embezzlement,[18] stalking,[19] forgery[20] and the creation and/or dissemination of child pornography.[21] These are not "new" crimes, but it may be difficult to

---

16. U.S. Department of Justice, *Internet Fraud*, http://www.usdoj.gov/criminal/fraud/text/Internet.htm (visited Jan. 14, 2001):
   [T]he same types of fraud schemes that have victimized consumers and investors for many years before the creation of the Internet are now appearing online (sometimes with particular refinements that are unique to Internet technology). With the explosive growth of the Internet, and e-commerce in particular, online criminals try to present fraudulent schemes in ways that look, as much as possible, like the goods and services that the vast majority of legitimate e-commerce merchants offer.
The Department of Justice report notes that "fraudulent schemes appearing on online auction sites are the most frequently reported form of Internet fraud.... These schemes induce their victims to send money for the promised items, but then deliver nothing or only an item far less valuable than what was promised." *Id.* In 1999, online auction fraud accounted for 87% of the frauds reported to the Internet Fraud Watch. *National Consumers League Warns Consumers Millions Are Lost to Internet Fraud*, http://www.fraud.org/internet/intset.htm (visited Jan. 14, 2001)

17. In 1994, for example, a Russian hacker named Vladimir Levin broke into the computer system at Citibank and incrementally transferred funds variously estimated at $3.7 million and $10 million to accounts in other banks. *See, e.g., Vladimir Levin*, LIVINGINTERNET.COM, http://www.livinginternet.com/i/ia_hackers_levin.htm (visited Jan. 14, 2001); TANGLED WEB 92–96 ($10 million). And as noted earlier, the Phonemasters gang stole and sold information from telephone companies, credit-reporting services, Dun & Bradstreet and Lexis-Nexis. *See, e.g.,* TANGLED WEB 102–113. *See also* D. Ian Hopper & Richard Stenger, *Large-scale Phone Invasion Goes Unnoticed by All But FBI*, SIGNALTONOISE.NET LIBRARY, http://www.signaltonoise.net/library/phonemasters.htm (visited Jan. 14, 2001).

18. *See, e.g.,* 1999 Revision of Model State Computer Crimes Code, § 5.01.5 commentary, http://www.cybercrimes.net/99MSCCC/MSCCC/Article5/5.01.5.html (visited Jan. 14, 2001). *See also* Brenner, *Can There Be Truly Virtual Crimes?*, Part III.

19. *See, e.g.,* 1999 Revision of Model State Computer Crimes Code, §§ 2.02 & 2.03 and related Commentary, http://www.cybercrimes.net/99MSCCC/MSCCC/Article2/2.02.html &.../2.03.html (visited Jan. 14, 2001). *See also* Brenner, *Can There Be Truly Virtual Crimes?*, Part III.

20. *See, e.g.,* 1999 Revision of Model State Computer Crimes Code, § 6.01 and related Commentary, http://www.cybercrimes.net/99MSCCC/MSCCC/Article6/6.01.html (visited Jan. 14, 2001). *See also* Brenner, *Can There Be Truly Virtual Crimes?*, Part III.

21. Goodman, *Why the Police Don't Care* § I(C). *See also* 1999 Revision of Model State Computer Crimes Code, § 3.02 and related Commentary, http://www.cybercrimes.net/99MSCCC/MSCCC/Article3/3.02.html (visited Jan. 14, 2001); Brenner, *Can There Be Truly Virtual Crimes?*, Part III.

prosecute this type of activity under existing laws since, for example, a jurisdiction's theft statute may not encompass a "theft" of intangible property, especially when the theft is carried out by copying the property, rather than appropriating it entirely.[22] Jurisdictions may, therefore, also find it necessary to adopt new legislation to prosecute crimes that fall into this category.[23]

The last category consists of cybercrimes in which the use of a computer or computer system is quite incidental to the commission of the crime, e.g., instances in which a computer is simply one of several alternative means used to carry out a crime.[24] This would, for example, include cases in which someone uses a computer to write a threatening letter or cases in which a drug dealer stores the financial records of his transactions on a computer.[25] Here, the computer is a source of evidence, nothing more.[26] Since the computer plays a non-essential role in the commission of the offense, new legislation is not needed to prosecute the crimes that fall into this category.

The offenses falling into the first two categories—e.g., computer as target and computer as instrument—are sufficiently distinct to require the adoption of specialized legislation directed at these kinds of activities. Such legislation can either create new offenses or simply amend an existing statute—such as a theft statute—to broaden its scope so that it encompasses the use of a computer to commit an already-defined offense. The next two sections review the federal and state legislation that has been adopted to this end.

III. Federal Cybercrime Legislation

By one estimate, there are more than forty federal statutes that can be used to prosecute cybercrime.[27] Many of these statutes—such as the wire

---

22. *See, e.g.,* Brenner, *Can There Be Truly Virtual Crimes?*.
23. *See, e.g.,* Ga. Code Ann. § 16-9-93 (1991) & § 16-9-93.1 (1996); Nev. Rev. Stat. § 205.481 (1999); Va. Code Ann. § 18.2-152.14 (1985); W. Va. Code § 61-3C-15 (1989).
24. *See* Goodman, *Why the Police Don't Care* § I(C) ("A computer is incidental to the crime if the computer itself is not required for the crime, but is used in some way connected with the criminal activity").
25. *See Id. See also Federal Searching Guidelines* § I(C).
26. *See, e.g., Federal Searching Guidelines* § I(C) (computer may be "nothing more than an electronic filing cabinet").
27. *See, e.g.,* Nicholson, *Computer Crimes* at 220.

fraud statute discussed below—antedate the emergence of cybercrime and were therefore not designed to reach the issues cybercrime presents. But, as is explained below, other federal legislation has been adopted that specifically targets some of the most commonly-encountered cybercrimes—such as hacking, cracking, virus dissemination, using computers to commit fraud and using computer equipment to create and disseminate child pornography.[28] Unfortunately, federal law is still lacking in other areas—such as online stalking and harassment—and legislation that has been adopted to deal with certain issues has been struck down as overbroad.

---

28. At the federal level, the basic approach has been to adopt new, cybercrime-specific statutes instead of amending existing laws so they encompass cybercrimes. *See, e.g. Id.* at 212 (notes omitted):
> Rather than attempting to deal with computer crime by amending every traditional statute to encompass new technologies, Congress has treated computer-related crimes as distinct federal offenses since the passage of the Counterfeit Access Device and Computer Fraud and Abuse Law in 1984. The 1984 Act was intentionally narrowly tailored to protect classified United States' defense and foreign relations information, financial institution and consumer reporting agency files, and access to computers operated for the government. Subsequently, the volume of such legislation greatly expanded to address many other types of computer-related crimes. As new computer crime issues have arisen and more statistics have become available, the law has attempted to adapt. In the Computer Fraud and Abuse Act of 1986, Congress expanded the scope of the law and attempted to define its terms more clearly. Congress continued to expand the scope of the computer crime law in 1988, 1989, and 1990. In 1994, Congress rewrote part of the Act again, and then passed the National Information Infrastructure Protection Act of 1996 [NIIPA].

See also Counterfeit Access Device and Computer Fraud and Abuse Act, Pub. L. No. 98-473, Title II, Chapter XXI, § 2102(a), 98 Stat. 1837, 2190 (1984); Computer Fraud and Abuse Act, Pub. L. No. 99-474, § 2, 100 Stat. 1213 (1986); Pub. L. No. 100-690, Title VII, § 7065, 102 Stat. 4404 (1988); Pub. L. No. 101-73, Title IX, § 962(a)(5), 103 Stat. 502 (1989); Pub. L. No. 101-647, Title XII, § 1205(e), Title XXV, § 2597 (j), Title XXXV, § 3533, 104 Stat. 4831, 4910, 4925 (1990); Pub. L. No. 103-322, Title XXIX, § 290001 (b)-(f), 108 Stat. 2097-2099 (1994); Pub. L. No. 104-294, Title II, § 201, 110 Stat. 3488, 3491–94 (1996). The original act and the 1986–1996 amendments were all codified as 18 U.S.C. § 1030 (1994 & Supp. IV 1998), which is discussed in the text above.

A. Copyright Infringement[29]

Copyright infringement in the form of software piracy is a cybercrime,[30] a very expensive cybercrime.[31] Federal copyright law, which is codified in title 17 of the U.S. Code, protects "rights of authorship" in various kinds of intellectual property, including computer software.[32] To be protected under federal copyright law, intellectual property must be "original," must be "fixed in any tangible medium of expression" and must have been registered with the Register of Copyrights.[33] For a work to be "original," it must have "originated" with, e.g., been created by, the author claiming the copyright; originality does not require novelty, but to be original an item cannot simply be a copy of another, pre-existing item.[34] For a work to be "fixed" in a "tangible medium of expression," it must be embodied in a form

---

29. The protection of intellectual property under federal law encompasses four discrete areas: copyrights; trademarks; trade secrets and patents. *See, e.g.,* U.S. Department of Justice—Computer Crime and Intellectual Property Section, *Prosecuting Intellectual Property Crimes Manual* § I(B), http://www.usdoj.gov/criminal/cybercrime/ipmanual.htm (visited Jan. 14, 2001) [hereinafter *Prosecuting I.P. Crimes Manual*]. Patent infringement does not carry criminal penalties, and so is outside the scope of this chapter. *See id.* Federal law governing the imposition of criminal liability for theft of trade secrets and trademark violations is discussed later in this chapter.

30. Federal law creates criminal penalties—as well as civil remedies—for copyright infringement, along with trademark infringement and the theft of trade secrets. *See, e.g. Id.*

31. *See, e.g.,* Nicholson, *Computer Crimes,* at 220 (piracy of business applications cost software companies $3.2 billion in 1998).

32. *See, e.g., Prosecuting I.P. Crimes Manual* §§ I(B)(1) & II(A)(5). Computer software was explicitly granted copyright protection by the Computer Software Copyright Act of 1980, Pub. L. No. 96-517, § 10, 94 Stat. 3028 (1980) (codified at 17 U.S.C. §§ 101, 117 (1994)), but have been included within the scope of copyright since the 1976 Copyright Act was adopted. Tandy Corp. v. Personal Micro Computers, Inc., 524 F. Supp. 171, 173 (N.D. Cal. 1981).

33. *See* 17 U.S.C. §§ 101, 102(a) & 411(a) (1994 & Supp. IV 1998). *See also Prosecuting I.P. Crimes Manual* § II(A)(2).

34. *See* 17 U.S.C. § 101 (Supp. IV 1998). *See, e.g.,* Feist Publications, Inc. v. Rural Tel. Serv. Co., 499 U.S. 340, 345 (1991):

> The sine qua non of copyright is originality. To qualify for copyright protection, a work must be original to the author. Original, as the term is used in copyright, means only that the work was independently created by the author (as opposed to copied from other works), and that it possesses at least some minimal degree of creativity. Originality does not signify novelty; a work may be original even though it closely resembles other works so long as the similarity is fortuitous, not the result of copying.

which is "sufficiently permanent or stable to permit it to be perceived, reproduced, or otherwise communicated for a period of more than transitory duration."[35] Finally, while copyright technically attaches when a work is created, the author's registration of the copyright is a prerequisite for a civil or criminal action for copyright infringement.[36] The registration need not, however, have preceded the act of infringement—it is sufficient if the registration precedes the filing of the criminal action.[37]

The most stringent penalties for copyright infringement are contained in 17 U.S.C. §506(a), which encompasses software piracy.[38] Section 506(a) makes it a federal crime for someone willfully to infringe a copyright for purposes of commercial advantage or private financial gain[39] by reproducing or distributing, during any 180-day period, one or more copies or phono records of one or more copyrighted works having a total retail value in excess of $1,000.[40]

The Eighth Circuit parsed the elements of the 506(a) offense in *U.S. v. Manzer*.[41] Manzer was charged with infringing a copyright for the purpose of commercial advantage or private financial gain by copying the copyrighted software contained in a chip installed in a device used to descramble premium television channel broadcasts. He was convicted and appealed.[42] The Eighth Circuit upheld the conviction, finding that the

---

Accord Acuff-Rose Music, Inc. v. Jostens, Inc., 155 F.3d 140, 143 (2d Cir. 1998). *See also Prosecuting I.P. Crimes Manual* §II(A)(2).

35. *See* 17 U.S.C. §101 (Supp. IV 1994). *See, e.g.,* Kodadek v. MTV Networks, Inc., 1996 WL 807435 (C.D. Cal. 1996), *aff'd*, 152 F.3d 1209 (9th Cir. 1998).

36. *See* 17 U.S.C. §411(a) (1994 & Supp. IV 1998). *See, e.g.,* Leicester v. Warner Bros., 232 F.3d 1212 (9th Cir. 2000). *See also Prosecuting I.P. Crimes Manual* §II(A)(2).

37. *See* 17 U.S.C. §411(a) (1994 & Supp. IV 1998). *See, e g ,* Marshall & Swift v. BS & A Software, 871 F. Supp. 952, 957–958 (W.D. Mich. 1994). *See also Prosecuting I.P. Crimes Manual* §II(A)(2).

38. *See, e.g., Prosecuting I.P. Crimes Manual* §III.

39. The Commentary to the Sentencing Guideline for this offense defines "commercial advantage or private financial gain" as "the receipt, or expectation of receipt, of anything of value, including other protected works." *See U.S. Sentencing Guidelines Manual* §2B5.3, Commentary (1999) [hereinafter U.S.S.G.]. *See also Prosecuting I.P. Crimes Manual* §III(A)(1)(d).

40. *See also* 17 U.S.C. §501(a) (1994) (infringement of copyright consists of violating the exclusive rights of the copyright owner as provided by 17 U.S.C. §§106–118, e.g. reproducing the copyrighted work, preparing derivative works based upon it, distributing copies of it).

41. 69 F.3d 222 (8th Cir. 1995).

42. *See Id.* at 226.

government had adduced evidence sufficient to support a finding of guilt on all four elements of the offense:[43] (1) that the computer program in the satellite descrambler modules had a valid copyright; (2) that Manzer infringed on the copyright by preparing one or more derivative works or computer programs, or by reproducing or selling unauthorized copies of the computer program; (3) that he willfully infringed on the copyright; and (4) that the act of infringement was for commercial advantage or private financial gain.[44] The court rejected Manzer's claim that the evidence was insufficient to establish the second and third elements, e.g., that the computer programs he sold were derivative of the copyrighted software contained in the chip used in the descrambling device and that he willfully infringed on the copyrighted software.[45] With regard to the second element, the Eighth Circuit noted that Manzer's argument did not take into account an expert witness' testimony that the "computer files sold by Manzer were more than seventy-percent similar to the copyrighted software.[46] As such, the jury's determination that the computer programs sold by Manzer were derivative of copyrighted material is supported by sufficient evidence."[47] It also dismissed Manzer's claim that because he was "a businessman, not a technician, he had no notice that the contents of the...chip were copyrighted."[48] As the Eighth Circuit explained,

> [i]t was established at trial...that the sealed plastic module containing the copyrighted operating software utilized in the U-30 chip bore a legible copyright notice. In addition, the software program itself contained a copyright notice capable of being read through the use of either a common 'debug' program or 'DUMP' file. Were this a civil suit seeking actual or statutory damages for copyright infringement, either one of these methods would be sufficient to place Manzer on notice that the contents of the U-30 chip

---

43. *See, e.g., Prosecuting I.P. Crimes Manual* § III(A)(1) (to obtain a conviction under § 506(a), the government must prove "(1) that a valid copyright exists; (2) that it was infringed by the defendant; (3) willfully; and (4) for purposes of commercial advantage or private financial gain").
44. 69 F.3d at 227. *See also* U.S. v. Hux, 940 F.2d 314, 319 (8th Cir. 1991), *overruled in part on other grounds*, U.S. v. Davis, 978 F.2d 415, 416 (8th Cir. 1992) (en banc).
45. *See* 69 F.3d at 227.
46. *See Id.*
47. *See Id.*
48. *See Id.*

were copyrighted material for purposes of refuting a defense based on innocent infringement.....We believe that a reasonable jury could also find this type of notice sufficient to alert Manzer to the fact that the contents of the U-30 chip were copyrighted for purposes of proving willful infringement under 17 U.S.C. § 506(a).... The record also supports the reasonable inference that Manzer had actual notice that the software contained in the U-30 chip was copyrighted material. Specifically, it was established at trial that Manzer, under his alias 'V.C. Hacker' in a purported interview published in the Blank Box Newsletter, acknowledged the illegality of selling, leasing, or giving away a copy of copyrighted material such as that contained in the U-30 Chip. Consequently, we find the evidence of Manzer's willful infringement to be sufficient.[49]

With regard to punishment, § 506(a) incorporates the provisions of 18 U.S.C. § 2319.[50] Section 2319(a) of title 18 of the U.S. Code states that those who violate § 506(a) are to be punished in accordance with the provisions of 18 U.S.C. § 2319(b) and § 2319(c), these penalties to be "in addition to any other provisions of title 17 or any other law."

18 U.S.C. § 2319(b) specifies the punishment for felony violations of 17 U.S.C. § 506(a)(1): For a first offense involving the reproduction or distribution, within a 180-day period, of at least ten copies or phono records of one ore more copyrighted works having a total retail value of more than $2,500, the penalties are imprisonment not to exceed five years, a fine or both.[51] The period of imprisonment rises to a maximum of ten years for a second or other subsequent offense involving these same elements.[52]

---

49. *Id.* at 227–228 (citations and footnote omitted). *See also* U.S. v. Cross, 816 F.2d 297, 303 (7th Cir.1987) ("In order to understand the meaning of criminal copyright infringement it is necessary to resort to the civil law of copyright.").

50. *See* 17 U.S.C. § 506(a) (Supp. IV 1998) ("Any person who infringes a copyright willfully...shall be punished as provided under section 2319 of title 18, United States Code"). *See also Prosecuting I.P. Crimes Manual* § III(A).

51. *See* 18 U.S.C. § 2319(b) (1994 & Supp. IV 1998). *See also Prosecuting I.P. Crimes Manual* § III(A). In calculating fines, it is necessary to consider both 18 U.S.C. § 2319 (1994 & Supp. IV 1998) and 18 U.S.C. § 3571 (1994), because the latter statute increases the penalties that can be imposed on certain classes of offender. *See Id.*

"The ten copies can represent an infringement of one copyrighted work, or an aggregation of different works of authorship." Nicholson, *Computer Crimes*, at 223 n.105, citing H.R. REP. No. 102-997, at 4 (1992), *reprinted in* 1992 U.S.C.C.A.N. 3569, 3572.

52. *See* 18 U.S.C. § 2319(b)(2) (1994).

18 U.S.C. § 2319(c) specifies the punishment for felony violations of 17 U.S.C. § 506(a)(2): For a first offense involving the reproduction or distribution of at least ten copies or phono records of one or more copyrighted works having a total retail value of more than $2,500, the penalties are imprisonment not to exceed three years, a fine or both.[53] The period of imprisonment rises to a maximum of six years for a second or other subsequent offense involving these same elements.[54]

In calculating an offender's sentence, the court will base its calculations on the legitimate retail value of the infringed items, not on the lesser, "street" value of the copies.[55] This standard is incorporated into the Sentencing Guideline for this offense.[56]

---

53. *See Id.* § 2319(c) (Supp. IV 1998). As noted above, in calculating fines, it is necessary to consider both 18 U.S.C. § 2319 (1994 & Supp. IV 1998) and 18 U.S.C. § 3571 (1994), because the latter statute increases the penalties that can be imposed on certain classes of offender. *See Prosecuting I.P. Crimes Manual* § III(A).

And as was also noted above, the copies can represent the infringement of a single work or the aggregate infringement of multiple works. *See* Nicholson, *Computer Crimes*, at 223 n.105, *citing* H.R. REP. No. 102-997, at 4 (1992), *reprinted in* 1992 U.S.C.C.A.N. 3569, 3572.

54. *See* 18 U.S.C. § 2319(c)(2) (Supp. IV 1998).

55. *See, e.g.,* U.S. v. Hicks, 46 F.3d 1128 (4th Cir. 1995) (table). Between 1987 and 1991, Hicks illegally modified approximately 100 descrambling devices known as VideoCipher II. Hicks charged between $200 and $250 for each modification, which let satellite dish owners receive up to fifteen channels without paying any additional monthly service charge. Hicks usually modified boards brought to him by dealers, who then sold the boards to their customers. Hicks pled guilty to one count of violating 17 U.S.C. § 506(a) and was sentenced to three years' probation, a fine of $40,000 and ordered to make restitution in the amount of $20,000. He appealed, arguing that the district court overestimated the total retail value of the infringing items. The Fourth Circuit upheld the district court's determination that the retail value of the infringing items was $500–$650, the price a customer would pay for a modified board, not the $200–$250 Hicks charged for one. *See also* U.S. v. Larracuente, 952 F.2d 672, 674 (2d Cir. 1991) (sentencing court correctly used normal retail price of movie videos, rather than the lower "bootleg" price paid by those who purchase them); U.S. v. Levy, http://www.usdoj.gov/criminal/cybercrime/levy2rls.htm (D. Or. 1999) (sentence following plea modest given difficulty of establishing value of copyrighted software unlawfully distributed over Internet). *But see* U.S. v. Kim, 963 F.2d 65, 67–69 (5th Cir. 1992) (court held that, under the trademark counterfeiting act, 18 U.S.C. § 2320, the value to be used is the value of the infringing items, not of their legitimate counterparts).

56. *See* U.S.S.G. § 2B5.3, Commentary — Application Notes § 2(A)(v) ("The retail value of the infringed item provides a more accurate assessment of the pecuniary harm to the copyright or trademark owner than does the retail value of the infringing item").

Misdemeanor violations are punishable by imprisonment for up to one year, a fine of up to $100,000 or both.[57] Misdemeanors occur when the defendant "violated rights other than those of reproduction or distribution; if he made or distributed fewer than the requisite number of copies; or if the copies did not meet the statutory minimum value; so long as the other elements of 17 U.S.C. § 506(a) are satisfied."[58]

There are two basic defenses to a charge of criminal copyright infringement: (1) the "first sale" doctrine;[59] and (2) the claim that the defendant did not act "willfully."[60] The first sale doctrine lets someone who legally buys a copyrighted work freely distribute the copy she bought.[61] But the first sale doctrine only lets a purchaser distribute the copy she actually bought; it does not let her make copies of the purchased item and distribute those copies.[62] Since most computer software is distributed through licensing agreements, the first sale doctrine typically does not apply when someone is charged with software piracy.[63] As to willfulness, courts disagree as to

---

57. *See* 18 U.S.C. §§ 2319(b)(3) & 3571(b)(5) (1994).

58. *Prosecuting I.P. Crimes Manual* § III(A)(5). *See, e.g.,* U.S. v. Thornton, http://www.usdoj.gov/criminal/cybercrime/thornton.htm (D.D.C. 1999) (plea agreement in misdemeanor case involving the reproduction or distribution of copyrighted software over the Internet).

59. *See, e.g.,* U.S. v. Bernstene, 1982 WL 1284 *4–5 (C.D. Cal. 1982), *aff'd*, 715 F.2d 459 (9th Cir. 1983), *cert. denied*, 465 U.S. 1022 (1984).

60. *See, e.g.,* Nicholson, *Computer Crimes*, at 222–223.

61. *See* 17 U.S.C. § 109(a) (1994). *See, e.g.,* U.S. v. Cohen, 946 F.2d 430, 434–435 (6th Cir. 1991). *See also Prosecuting I.P. Crimes Manual* § III(A)(1)(e).

62. *See* 17 U.S.C. § 109(a) (1994). *See, e.g.,* U.S. v. Moore, 604 F.2d 1228, 1232 (9th Cir. 1979). *See also Prosecuting I.P. Crimes Manual* § III(A)(1)(e).

63. *See Prosecuting I.P. Crimes Manual* § III(A)(1)(e):
Under this distribution system, the copyright holder remains the 'owner' of all distributed copies. For this reason, alleged infringers should not be able to establish that any copies of these works have been the subject of a first sale. Thus, if A, the copyright owner, simply loans a copy of his work to B, B obtains no ownership interest in the work and is unable to assert first sale as a defense to an infringement action. This is an important limitation, as the distribution systems for some artistic works, most notably motion pictures and computer software, rely on licensing agreements, leases or other devices to transfer possession of copies of a copyrighted work. Under these distribution systems, the copyright holder remains the 'owner' of all distributed copies.
Some argue that the "first sale" doctrine should not apply to Internet transactions. *See, e.g.,,* NATIONAL INFORMATION INFRASTRUCTURE TASK FORCE—WORKING GROUP ON INTELLECTUAL PROPERTY RIGHTS, INTELLECTUAL PROPERTY AND THE NATIONAL INFORMATION INFRASTRUCTURE 95 (1995).

whether the defendant must have willfully intended to copy the copyrighted material or willfully intended to infringe the owner's copyright in that material.[64] The Second and Ninth Circuits take the position that wilfulness is only needed as to the act of copying the material,[65] but most courts hold that the defendant must have wilfully intended to infringe the owner's copyright in it.[66]

In addition to 17 U.S.C. § 506(a), other sections of title 17 and title 18 of the U.S. Code can be used to prosecute criminal copyright infringement.[67] The title 17 offenses are defined by 17 U.S.C. §§ 506 (c) and 506(d) which address the protection of copyright notices,[68] and 17 U.S.C. § 506(e) which makes it an offense to include false representations in an application for copyright.[69] The title 18 offenses that can apply to copyright infringement include mail and wire fraud,[70] smuggling,[71] trafficking in counterfeit

---

64. *See, e.g., Prosecuting I.P. Crimes Manual* § III(A)(1)(c).
65. *See, e.g.,* U.S. v. Backer, 134 F.2d 533, 535 (2d Cir. 1943); U.S. v. Taxe, 380 F. Supp. 1010 (C.D. Cal. 1974), *aff'd in part and vacated in part*, 540 F.2d 961 (9th Cir. 1976), *cert. denied*, 429 U.S. 1040 (1977).
66. *See, e.g., Prosecuting I.P. Crimes Manual* § III(A)(1)(c).
67. *See Id.* § III(D).
68. 17 U.S.C. § 506(c) (1994) makes it an offense punishable by a fine of up to $2,500 for someone acting with "fraudulent intent" (1) to put "on any article a notice of copyright or words of the same purport that such person knows to be false" or (2) to publicly distribute or import for "any article bearing such notice or words that such person knows to be false." Section 506(d) (1994) makes it an offense punishable by a fine of up to $2,500 for someone acting with fraudulent intent to remove or alter "any notice of copyright appearing on a copy of a copyrighted work." *See, e.g., Prosecuting I.P. Crimes Manual* § III(C).
69. 17 U.S.C. § 506(e) (1994) makes it an offense punishable by a fine of up to $2,500 for someone to knowingly make "a false representation of a material fact" in an application for copyright registration or in "any written statement filed in connection with the application." *See, e.g., Prosecuting I.P. Crimes Manual* § III(C).
70. *See* 18 U.S.C. § 1341 (1994) (mail fraud) and *id.* § 1343 (wire fraud). The mail and wire fraud statutes are discussed in more detail later in this chapter.

Actually, there is some uncertainty as to whether mail fraud and wire fraud can be used to prosecute those who infringe copyrights. *See, e.g., Prosecuting I.P. Crimes Manual* § III(D). *See also* Dowling v. U.S., 473 U.S. 207, 210 (1985) (mail fraud charges included in prosecution of defendant who ran "bootleg record operation"). *Compare* U.S. v. Wang, 898 F. Supp. 758, 759 (D. Colo. 1995) (defendants unauthorized transmission by wire of copyrighted computer files containing confidential source code could be prosecuted under wire fraud statute) *with* U.S. v. LaMacchia, 871 F. Supp. 535, 545 (D. Mass. 1994) (copyright prosecutions should be limited to 17 U.S.C. § 506(a), and should not rely on mail fraud or wire fraud statutes).

71. Under 17 U.S.C. §§ 501(a) and 602, the "[c]ommercial importation of unauthorized copies of copyrighted works constitutes copyright infringement." *Prosecuting*

labels[72] and trafficking in sound recordings of live musical performances.[73] Years ago, prosecutors sometimes charged those who infringed copyrights with the interstate transportation of stolen property in violation of 18 U.S.C. § 2314, but the Supreme Court eliminated this alternative when it held, in *Dowling v. U.S.*,[74] that the stolen property statute does not apply to acts of copyright infringement.[75] The *Dowling* Court found that § 2314 cannot be used for this purpose because the statute punishes those who physically seize and transport property belonging to another, thereby depriving the owner of the possession and use of his or her property; as the Court explained, the infringer of a copyright neither assumes physical control over the copyright nor wholly deprives the owner of its use.[76]

Section 371 of title 18 of the U.S. Code, which is the basic federal conspiracy provision, is used to prosecute conspiracy to commit criminal copyright infringement.[77]

The Digital Millennium Copyright Act[78] added two new sections to title 17 of the U.S. Code: Section 1201 makes it unlawful to circumvent mea-

---

I.P. Crimes Manual § III(D)(4). The Department of Justice advises prosecutors to consider charging those who engage in such activity with smuggling under 18 U.S.C. § 545. *See Id.* Section 545 of title 18 makes it an offense, punishable by a fine, imprisonment of up to five years or both, to do the following: (1) knowingly and willfully, with the intent to defraud the United States, smuggle, clandestinely introduce, or attempt to smuggle or clandestinely introduce into the United States merchandise which should have been invoiced; or (2) fraudulently or knowingly import or bring into the United States any merchandise contrary to law. *See, e.g.,* U.S. v. Gallo, 599 F. Supp. 241, 245 (W.D.N.Y. 1984) (smuggling statute could be used against infringers of copyright).

72. *See* 18 U.S.C. § 2318(a) (Supp. IV 1998) ("Who ever...knowingly traffics in a counterfeit label affixed or designed to be affixed to...a copy of a computer program or documentation or packaging for a computer program...and whoever...knowingly traffics in counterfeit documentation or packaging for a computer program, shall be fined under this title or imprisoned for not more than five years, or both"). *See, e.g.,* U.S. v. Bao, 189 F.3d 860, 862 (9th Cir. 1999). *See also Prosecuting I.P. Crimes Manual* § III(D).

73. *See* 18 U.S.C. § 2319A (1994 & Supp. IV 1998). *See, e.g.,* U.S. v. Moghadam, 175 F.3d 1269, 1971 (11th Cir. 1999), *cert. denied*, 120 S. Ct. 1529 (2000). *See also Prosecuting I.P. Crimes Manual* § III(B).

74. 473 U.S. 207 (1985).

75. *See id.* at 216–229.

76. *See id.*

77. *See, e.g.,* U.S. v. Hernandez, 952 F.2d 1110 (9th Cir.), *cert. denied*, 506 U.S. 920 (1992); U.S. v. Minor, 846 F.2d 1184, 1185 (9th Cir. 1988). *See also* U.S. v. Rothberg, http://www.usdoj.gov/criminal/cybercrime/pirates.htm (N.D. Ill. May 4, 2000). *See generally Prosecuting I.P. Crimes Manual* § III(A)(1).

78. Pub. L. No. 105-304, 112 Stat. 2860 (1998).

sures used to protect copyrighted works,[79] while section 1202 makes it unlawful to tamper with copyright management information.[80] Another new

---

79. See 17 U.S.C. § 1201(a)(1)(A) (Supp. IV 1998) ("No person shall circumvent a technological measure that effectively controls access to a work protected under this title"); id. § 1201(b)(1)(A) ("No person shall manufacture, import, offer to the public, provide, or otherwise traffic in any technology, product, service, device, component, or part thereof, that...is primarily designed or produced for the purpose of circumventing protection afforded by a technological measure that effectively protects a right of a copyright owner under this title...in a work or a portion thereof"). Under § 1201(a)(1), to "circumvent a technological measure" means "to descramble a scrambled work, to decrypt an encrypted work, or otherwise to avoid, bypass, remove, deactivate, or impair a technological measure, without the authority of the copyright owner," and a technological measure "'effectively controls access to a work" if the measure, in the ordinary course of its operation, requires the application of information, or a process or a treatment, with the authority of the copyright owner, to gain access to the work." Id. § 1201(a)(3)(A)-(B). See, e.g., Universal City Studios, Inc. v. Reimerdes, 111 F. Supp. 2d 294, 319–320 (S.D.N.Y. 2000); RealNetworks, Inc. v. Streambox, Inc., 2000 WL 127311 (W.D. Wash. 2000). Under 17 U.S.C. § 1201(b)(1)(A), to "circumvent protection afforded by a technological measure" means "avoiding, bypassing, removing, deactivating, or otherwise impairing a technological measure," and a technological measure "'effectively protects a right of a copyright owner under this title' if the measure, in the ordinary course of its operation, prevents, restricts, or otherwise limits the exercise of a right of a copyright owner under this title." 17 U.S.C. § 1201(b)(2)(A)-(B) (Supp. IV 1998).

80. See 17 U.S.C. §§ 1202(a) (Supp. IV 1998) ("No person shall knowingly and with the intent to induce, enable, facilitate, or conceal infringement...provide copyright management information that is false, or...distribute or import for distribution copyright management information that is false" and 1202(b) (no one shall, "without the authority of the copyright owner or the law (1) intentionally remove or alter any copyright management information, (2) distribute or import for distribution copyright management information knowing the copyright management information has been removed or altered without authority of the copyright owner or the law, or (3) distribute, import for distribution, or publicly perform works, copies of works, or phonorecords, knowing that copyright management information has been removed or altered without authority of the copyright owner or the law, knowing...that it will induce, enable, facilitate, or conceal an infringement of any right under this title"). Section 1202(c) defines "copyright management information" as

> any of the following information conveyed in connection with copies or phonorecords of a work or performances or displays of a work, including in digital form, except that such term does not include any personally identifying information about a user of a work or of a copy, phonorecord, performance, or display of a work:
>
> (1) The title and other information identifying the work, including the information set forth on a notice of copyright.
>
> (2) The name of, and other identifying information about, the author of a work.

section added by the Digital Millennium Copyright Act, 17 U.S.C. § 1204, creates criminal penalties for violating either sections 1201 or 1202 of the DMCA.[81]

One source of copyright infringement in the computer context is "warez" sites, e.g., "anonymous, often short-lived file-transfer protocol ["FTP"] sites that exist solely to disseminate unlicenced copies of software and/or passwords for pirate software."[82] The existence of these sites generated discussion as to whether the Internet Service Providers ["ISPs"] used to access them should be held liable for acts of copyright infringement perpetrated via the sites.[83] In 1998, Congress adopted the Online Copyright Infringement Liability Limitation Act[84] which shields ISPs from liability for monetary, injunctive or equitable relief for copyright infringement as long as certain conditions are met. An ISP[85] is not liable for infringement re-

---

(3) The name of, and other identifying information about, the copyright owner of the work, including the information set forth in a notice of copyright.
(4) With the exception of public performances of works by radio and television broadcast stations, the name of, and other identifying information about, a performer whose performance is fixed in a work other than an audiovisual work.
(5) With the exception of public performances of works by radio and television broadcast stations, in the case of an audiovisual work, the name of, and other identifying information about, a writer, performer, or director who is credited in the audiovisual work.
(6) Terms and conditions for use of the work.
(7) Identifying numbers or symbols referring to such information or links to such information.
(8) Such other information as the Register of Copyrights may prescribe by regulation, except that the Register of Copyrights may not require the provision of any information concerning the user of a copyrighted work.
See, e.g., Kelly v. Arriba Soft Corp., 77 F. Supp. 2d 1116, 1121–1122 (C.D. Cal. 1999).
  81. See 17 U.S.C. § 1204(a) (Supp. IV 1998) ("Any person who violates section 1201 or 1202 willfully and for purposes of commercial advantage or private financial gain... shall be fined not more than $500,000 or imprisoned for not more than 5 years, or both, for the first offense; and... shall be fined not more than $1,000,000 or imprisoned for not more than 10 years, or both, for any subsequent offense").
  82. Ronnie Heather Brandes, Bonnie L. Kane & Kelly A. Librera, *Intellectual Property Crimes*, 37 AM. CRIM. L. REV. 657, 687 (2000) [hereinafter Brandes, *I.P. Crimes*].
  83. See, e.g., id. at 688.
  84. Pub. L. No. 105-304, 112 Stat. 2877 (1998) (Codified at 17 U.S.C. § 512).
  85. As used in the statute, "service provider" means "an entity offering the transmission, routing, or providing of connections for digital online communications, between or among points specified by a user, of material of the user's choosing, without

sulting from its "transmitting, routing, or providing connections for, material" through a system or network it controls or operates "or by reason of the intermediate and transient storage of that material in the course of such transmitting, routing, or providing connections" if:

> (1) the transmission of the material was initiated by or at the direction of a person other than the service provider;
> (2) the transmission, routing, provision of connections, or storage is carried out through an automatic technical process without selection of the material by the service provider;
> (3) the service provider does not select the recipients of the material except as an automatic response to the request of another person;
> (4) no copy of the material made by the service provider in the course of such intermediate or transient storage is maintained on the system or network in a manner ordinarily accessible to anyone other than anticipated recipients, and no such copy is maintained on the system or network in a manner ordinarily accessible to such anticipated recipients for a longer period than is reasonably necessary for the transmission, routing, or provision of connections; and
> (5) the material is transmitted through the system or network without modifica tion of its content.[86]

An ISP is not liable for copyright infringement by virtue of storing information on a system it controls or operates if it: (1) does not have actual knowledge that the stored material or an activity involving the stored material is infringing or, absent actual knowledge, is not aware of "facts or circumstances from which infringing activity is apparent" or "upon obtaining such knowledge or awareness, acts expeditiously to remove, or disable access to, the material"; (2) does not receive "a financial benefit directly attributable to the infringing activity" if the service provider has the right and ability to control such activity; and (3) upon being notified of possible infringement "responds expeditiously to remove, or disable access to, the material that is claimed to be infringing or to be the subject of infringing ac-

---

modification to the content of the material as sent or received." 17 U.S.C. §512(k)(1) (Supp. IV 1998).

86. *Id.* §512(a).

tivity."[87] While the Act does not immunize ISPs from liability for criminal copyright infringement, there have so far been no cases in which such liability has been imposed.[88]

B. Trademarks and Trade Secrets[89]

The primary protection for trademarks is provided by the Lanham Act.[90] The Act defines a "trademark" as including

> "any word, name, symbol, or device, or any combination thereof... used by a person, or... which a person has a bona fide intention to use in commerce and applies to register on the principal register established by this chapter, to identify and distinguish his or her goods, including a unique product, from those manufactured or sold by others and to indicate the source of the goods, even if that source is unknown."[91]

The Lanham Act, however, only allows the recovery of civil damages for acts of trademark infringement.[92] Criminal penalties for trademark violations are imposed by the Trademark Counterfeiting Act, 18 U.S.C. § 2320.[93] To

---

87. *Id.* § 512(c)(1). This limitation of liability applies only if the ISP has designated an agent to receive notice of claimed infringement. *See id.* § 512(c)(2).

88. *See, e.g.,* Brandes, *I.P. Crimes* at 686.

89. The protection of intellectual property under federal law encompasses four discrete areas: copyrights; trademarks; trade secrets and patents. *See, e.g., Prosecuting I.P. Crimes Manual* § I(B). Patent infringement does not carry criminal penalties, and so is outside the scope of this chapter. *See id.* Federal law governing the imposition of criminal penalties for copyright infringement is discussed earlier in this chapter.

90. Act of July 5, 1946, ch. 540, 60 Stat. 427 (codified at 15 U.S.C. §§ 1051 *et seq.*)

91. 15 U.S.C.A. § 1127 (Elec. Update 2000). The procedures and requirements for registering trademarks are set out in *id.* §§ 1051–1064.

92. *See id.* § 1114.

93. *See* 18 U.S.C. § 2320(a) (1994) ("Whoever intentionally traffics or attempts to traffic in goods or services and knowingly uses a counterfeit mark on or in connection with such goods or services shall, if an individual, be fined not more than $2,000,000 or imprisoned not more than 10 years, or both, and, if a person other than an individual, be fined not more than $5,000,000. In the case of an offense by a person under this section that occurs after that person is convicted of another offense under this section, the person convicted, if an individual, shall be fined not more than $5,000,000 or imprisoned not more than 20 years, or both, and if other than an individual, shall be fined not more than $15,000,000"). *See, e.g.,* U.S. v. Sultan, 115 F.3d 321, 325 (5th Cir. 1997).

prove a violation of 18 U.S.C. § 2320(a), the government must establish that: (1) the defendant trafficked or attempted to traffic in goods or services; (2) the trafficking or the attempt to traffic was intentional; (3) the defendant used a counterfeit mark on or in connection with such goods or services; and (4) the defendant knew that the mark so used was counterfeit.[94] "Traffic" means to "transport, transfer, or otherwise dispose of, to another, as consideration for anything of value, or make or obtain control of with intent so to transport, transfer or dispose of."[95] A "counterfeit mark" is either (1) "a spurious mark" that is "used in connection with trafficking in goods or services," "that is identical with, or substantially indistinguishable from, a mark registered for those goods or services on the principal register in the United States Patent and Trademark Office and in use, whether or not the defendant knew such mark was so registered" the use of which "is likely to cause confusion, to cause mistake, or to deceive; or (2) a spurious designation "that is identical with, or substantially indistinguishable from, a designation as to which the remedies of the Lanham Act" are available but "does not include any mark or designation used in connection with goods or services of which the manufacturer or producer was, at the time of the manufacture or production in question authorized to use the mark or designation for the type of goods or services so manufactured or produced, by the holder of the right to use such mark or designation."[96]

The Economic Espionage Act of 1996[97] made the theft of trade secrets a federal crime.[98] Actually, it created two crimes: "economic espionage,"[99]

---

94. *See, e.g.*, U.S. v. Sultan, 115 F.3d 321, 325 (5th Cir. 1997). *See also Prosecuting I.P. Crimes Manual* § IV.
95. *See* 18 U.S.C. § 2320(e)(2) (Supp. IV 1998).
96. *See id.* § 2320(e)(1). *See, e.g.*, U.S. v. Giles, 213 F.3d 1247, 1251–1252 (10th Cir. 2000).
97. Pub. L. No. 104-294, 110 Stat. 3488 (1996).
98. *See, e.g.*, Brandes, *I.P. Crimes* at 659. *See also Prosecuting I.P. Crimes Manual* § V.
99. *See* 18 U.S.C. § 1831(a) (Supp. IV 1998):
   Whoever, intending or knowing that the offense will benefit any foreign government, foreign instrumentality, or foreign agent, knowingly—
   (1) steals, or without authorization appropriates, takes, carries away, or conceals, or by fraud, artifice, or deception obtains a trade secret;
   (2) without authorization copies, duplicates, sketches, draws, photographs, downloads, uploads, alters, destroys, photocopies, replicates, transmits, delivers, sends, mails, communicates, or conveys a trade secret;
   (3) receives, buys, or possesses a trade secret, knowing the same to have been stolen or appropriated, obtained, or converted without authorization;

which requires that the theft benefit a foreign government, and a generic offense, "theft of trade secrets."[100] The Act defines "trade secret" as

> all forms and types of financial, business, scientific, technical, economic, or engineering information, including patterns, plans, com-

---

> (4) attempts to commit any offense described in any of paragraphs (1) through (3); or
> (5) conspires with one or more other persons to commit any offense described in any of paragraphs (1) through (3), and one or more of such persons do any act to effect the object of the conspiracy,
> shall, except as provided in subsection (b), be fined not more than $500,000 or imprisoned not more than 15 years, or both.

Subsection (b) provides that if an organization commits the offense defined by § 1831(a), it "shall be fined not more than $10,000,000." *Id.* § 1831(b). "Foreign instrumentality" is defined as "any agency, bureau, ministry, component, institution, association, or any legal, commercial, or business organization, corporation, firm, or entity that is substantially owned, controlled, sponsored, commanded, managed, or dominated by a foreign government", and "foreign agent" is defined as "any officer, employee, proxy, servant, delegate, or representative of a foreign government". *Id.* § 1839(1)-(2).

100. *See Id.* § 1832(a):
> Whoever, with intent to convert a trade secret, that is related to or included in a product that is produced for or placed in interstate or foreign commerce, to the economic benefit of anyone other than the owner thereof, and intending or knowing that the offense will, injure any owner of that trade secret, knowingly—
> (1) steals, or without authorization appropriates, takes, carries away, or conceals, or by fraud, artifice, or deception obtains such information;
> (2) without authorization copies, duplicates, sketches, draws, photographs, downloads, uploads, alters, destroys, photocopies, replicates, transmits, delivers, sends, mails, communicates, or conveys such information;
> (3) receives, buys, or possesses such information, knowing the same to have been stolen or appropriated, obtained, or converted without authorization;
> (4) attempts to commit any offense described in paragraphs (1) through (3); or
> (5) conspires with one or more other persons to commit any offense described in paragraphs (1) through (3), and one or more of such persons do any act to effect the object of the conspiracy,
> shall, except as provided in subsection (b), be fined under this title or imprisoned not more than 10 years, or both.

See, e.g., U.S. v. Martin, 228 F.3d 1, 10–11 (1st Cir. 2000). Subsection (b) provides that if an organization commits the offense defined by § 1832(a), it "shall be fined not more than $5,000,000." 18 U.S.C. § 1832(b) (Supp. IV 1998).

pilations, program devices, formulas, designs, prototypes, methods, techniques, processes, procedures, programs, or codes, whether tangible or intangible, and whether or how stored, compiled, or memorialized physically, electronically, graphically, photographically, or in writing if—

> (A) the owner thereof has taken reasonable measures to keep such information secret; and
>
> (B) the information derives independent economic value, actual or potential, from not being generally known to, and not being readily ascertainable through proper means by, the public.... 101

The Economic Espionage Act gives the federal government the authority to prosecute based on conduct occurring outside the United States if (1) the offender is a "natural person who is a citizen or permanent resident alien of the United States" or an organization "organized under the laws of the United States" or a political subdivision thereof, or (2) "an act in furtherance of the offense was committed in the United States."[102] The Act has been used to prosecute thefts of software, among other things.[103]

C. Hacking, Cracking, Fraud, Virus Dissemination and Extortion

Section 1030 of Title 18 of the U.S. Code is the basic federal cybercrime provision.[104] As such, it defines a number of computer-related offenses, e.g.,

---

101. 18 U.S.C. § 1839(3) (Supp. IV 1998). "Owner" is defined as "the person or entity in whom or in which rightful legal or equitable title to, or license in, the trade secret is reposed." *Id.* § 1839(4).

102. 18 U.S.C. § 1837 (Supp. IV 1998). *See Prosecuting I.P. Crimes Manual* § V.

103. *See, e.g.,* U.S. v. Morch, http://www.usaondca.com/press/html/2000_11_22_morch.html (N.D. Cal. 2000); Brandes, *I.P. Crimes* at 664 n.40. For a listing of cases that have been prosecuted under the Economic Espionage Act, *see* U.S. Department of Justice, *Economic Espionage Act Case Summaries*, http://www.usdoj.gov/criminal/cybercrime/eeapub.htm (visited Jan. 3, 2001).

104. This statute is the general federal cybercrimes statute:

> ...Congress has treated computer-related crimes as distinct federal offenses since the passage of the Counterfeit Access Device and Computer Fraud and Abuse Law in 1984. The 1984 Act was intentionally narrowly tailored to protect classified United States' defense and foreign relations information, financial institution and consumer reporting agency files, and access to computers operated for the government.... As new computer crime issues have arisen and more statistics have become available, the law has attempted to adapt. In

hacking, cracking, virus dissemination, fraud, password trafficking, and extortion.[105]

---

the Computer Fraud and Abuse Act of 1986, Congress expanded the scope of the law and attempted to define its terms more clearly. Congress continued to expand the scope of the computer crime law in 1988, 1989, and 1990. In 1994, Congress rewrote part of the Act again, and then passed the National Information Infrastructure Protection Act of 1996 [NIIPA].

Nicholson, *Computer Crimes* at 212 (notes omitted). *See* Counterfeit Access Device and Computer Fraud and Abuse Act, Pub. L. No. 98-473, Title II, Chapter XXI, § 2102(a), 98 Stat. 1837, 2190 (1984); Computer Fraud and Abuse Act, Pub. L. No. 99-474, § 2, 100 Stat. 1213 (1986); Pub. L. No. 100-690, Title VII, § 7065, 102 Stat. 4404 (1988); Pub. L. No. 101-73, Title IX, § 962(a)(5), 103 Stat. 502 (1989); Pub. L. No. 101-647, Title XII, § 1205(e), Title XXV, § 2597 (j), Title XXXV, § 3533, 104 Stat. 4831, 4910, 4925 (1990); Pub. L. No. 103-322, Title XXIX, § 290001 (b)-(f), 108 Stat. 2097-2099 (1994); Pub. L. No. 104-294, Title II, § 201, 110 Stat. 3488, 3491-94 (1996). The original act and the 1986–96 amendments were all codified as 18 U.S.C. § 1030 (1994 & Supp. IV 1998).

105. *See* 18 U.S.C. § 1030(a) (Supp. IV 1998):

Whoever—

(1) having knowingly accessed a computer without authorization or exceeding authorized access, and by means of such conduct having obtained information that has been determined by the United States Government pursuant to an Executive order or statute to require protection against unauthorized disclosure for reasons of national defense or foreign relations, or any restricted data, as defined in paragraph y of section 11 of the Atomic Energy Act of 1954, with reason to believe that such information so obtained could be used to the injury of the United States, or to the advantage of any foreign nation willfully communicates, delivers, transmits, or causes to be communicated, delivered, or transmitted, or attempts to communicate, deliver, transmit or cause to be communicated, delivered, or transmitted the same to any person not entitled to receive it, or willfully retains the same and fails to deliver it to the officer or employee of the United States entitled to receive it;

(2) intentionally accesses a computer without authorization or exceeds authorized access, and thereby obtains—

(A) information contained in a financial record of a financial institution, or of a card issuer as defined in section 1602(n) of title 15, or contained in a file of a consumer reporting agency on a consumer, as such terms are defined in the Fair Credit Reporting Act 15 U.S.C. 1681 et seq.);

(B) information from any department or agency of the United States; or

(C) information from any protected computer if the conduct involved an interstate or foreign communication;

(3) intentionally, without authorization to access any nonpublic computer of a department or agency of the United States, accesses such a computer

Section 1030 reaches conduct directed at a "protected computer."[106] A "protected computer" is one that falls into either of two categories: (1) a computer that is used exclusively by a financial institution or the federal government or that is used, albeit nonexclusively, by a financial institution or the federal government but the conduct constituting the offense affects that use; or (2) a computer that is used in interstate or foreign commerce or communication.[107] The concept of basing liability on conduct targeting "protected computers" was introduced by an amendment enacted in 1996;

---

of that department or agency that is exclusively for the use of the Government of the United States or, in the case of a computer not exclusively for such use, is used by or for the Government of the United States and such conduct affects that use by or for the Government of the United States;

(4) knowingly and with intent to defraud, accesses a protected computer without authorization, or exceeds authorized access, and by means of such conduct furthers the intended fraud and obtains anything of value, unless the object of the fraud and the thing obtained consists only of the use of the computer and the value of such use is not more than $5,000 in any 1-year period;

(5) (A) knowingly causes the transmission of a program, information, code, or command, and as a result of such conduct, intentionally causes damage without authorization, to a protected computer;
(B) intentionally accesses a protected computer without authorization, and as a result of such conduct, recklessly causes damage; or
(C) intentionally accesses a protected computer without authorization, and as a result of such conduct, causes damage;

(6) knowingly and with intent to defraud traffics (as defined in section 1029) in any password or similar information through which a computer may be accessed without authorization, if—
(A) such trafficking affects interstate or foreign commerce; or
(B) such computer is used by or for the Government of the United States;

(7) with intent to extort from any person, firm, association, educational institution, financial institution, government entity, or other legal entity, any money or other thing of value, transmits in interstate or foreign commerce any communication containing any threat to cause damage to a protected computer;

shall be punished as provided in subsection (c) of this section.
Punishment for violating 18 U.S.C. § 1030(a) is discussed in the text, above.
106. *See id.*
107. *See id.* § 1030(e)(2) ("the term 'protected computer' means a computer—(A) exclusively for the use of a financial institution or the United States Government, or, in the case of a computer not exclusively for such use, used by or for a financial institution or the United States Government and the conduct constituting the offense affects

until then, § 1030 only reached conduct targeting "federal interest computers," e.g., computers used by the federal government or computers located in more than one state.[108] As a result of the 1996 amendment, the statute now reaches conduct directed at any computer connected to the Internet, regardless of whether the computers involved are located in the same state.[109]

Section 1030(a) makes it a federal crime to do any of the following:

(1) To (a) knowingly access a computer without authorization or by exceeding authorized access and thereby obtain information that is protected against disclosure which the perpetrator has reason to believe could be used to the disadvantage of the U.S. or to the advantage of any foreign nation and (b) willfully either deliver that information to a person not entitled to receive it or retain the information and refuse to deliver it to the federal agent entitled to receive it;[110]

(2) To intentionally access a computer without authorization or by exceeding authorized access and thereby obtain (a) information contained in a financial record of a financial institution, or of a card issuer or contained in a file of a consumer reporting agency on a consumer,[111] (b) information from any federal department or agency,[112] or (c) information from any protected computer if the conduct involved an interstate or foreign communication;[113]

(3) To intentionally and without authorization access (a) a computer used exclusively by a federal department or agency or (b) a com-

---

that use by or for the financial institution or the Government; or (B) which is used in interstate or foreign commerce or communication").

108. *See, e.g.,* Nicholson, *Computer Crimes* at 213, *citing* 18 U.S.C. § 1030(e)(2) (1994 & Supp. IV 1998).

109. *See, e.g., id.* at 213–214.

110. 18 U.S.C. § 1030(a)(1) (Supp. IV 1998).

111. *See, e.g.,* U.S. v. Tanimowo, 199 F.3d 1324 (2d Cir. 1999) (table) (defendant pled guilty to one count of accessing computer without authorization for the purpose of obtaining confidential consumer credit information in violation of 18 U.S.C. § 1030(a)(2)(A)).

112. *See, e.g.,* U.S. v. Gray, 78 F. Supp. 2d 524 (E.D. Va. 1999) (defendant charged with unlawfully accessing a government computer in violation of 18 U.S.C. § 1030(a)(2) and with unlawfully accessing a government computer and causing damage to it in violation of 18 U.S.C. § 1030(a)(5)).

113. 18 U.S.C. § 1030(a)(2) (Supp. IV 1998).

puter not used exclusively by a federal department or agency when the conduct affects the computer's use by or for the federal government;[114]

(4) To knowingly and with the intent to defraud access a protected computer without authorization or by exceeding authorized access and thereby further the intended fraud and obtain anything of value unless the object of the fraud and the thing obtained consist only of the use of the computer and the value of that use does not exceed $5,000 in any one-year period;[115]

(5) To (a) knowingly cause the transmission or a program, information, code or command and thereby intentionally cause damage to a protected computer;[116] (b) intentionally access a protected com-

---

114. *Id.* § 1030(a)(3).
115. *Id.* § 1030(a)(4). *See, e.g.,* U.S. v. Sadolsky, 234 F.3d 938 (6th Cir. 2000) (defendant pled guilty to seven counts of using a computer to facilitate the commission of fraud in violation of 18 U.S.C. § 1030(a)(4)); U.S. v. Magnuson, 120 F.3d 263 (4th Cir. 1997) (table) (defendant pled guilty to one count of using a computer to facilitate the commission of fraud in violation of 18 U.S.C. § 1030(a)(4)); U.S. v. Petersen, 98 F.3d 502, 505 (9th Cir. 1996) (same). *But see* U.S. v. Czubinski, 106 F.3d 1069, 1078–79 (1st Cir. 1997) (defendant could not be convicted of computer fraud under 18 U.S.C. § 1030(a)(4) based on unauthorized accessing of taxpayer records because he did not obtain "anything of value" by doing so and therefore did not further a fraudulent scheme).
   Kevin Mitnick, probably the most notorious "hacker" to be prosecuted in any U.S. jurisdiction, was charged under § 1030. *See, e.g.,* Chris Gulker, *The Kevin Mitnick/Tsutomu Shimomura Affair,* RANDOM ACCESS (January 21, 2000), http://www.gulker.com/ra/hack/ [hereinafter Gulker, *Mitnick/Shimomura Affair*]; *Free Kevin Mitnick,* http://www.kevinmitnick.com/ (visited Jan. 3, 2001). One of the charges against Mitnick was that he used a computer to commit fraud in violation of § 1030(a)(4). *See* Indictment, U.S. v. Mitnick, http://www.kevinmitnick.com/indictment.html (C.D. Cal. 1996). The fraud count alleged that Mitnick, knowingly and without obtaining authorization from software manufacturer Motorola, Inc., used "computers in one state to access computers in another state belonging to Motorola," duplicated proprietary software belonging to Motorola and then "electronically transferred the proprietary software stolen from Motorola in Illinois, across state lines to computers located in Denver, Colorado, and then to computers located at USC, in Los Angeles, California." *See id.,* Count Fifteen.
116. *See, e.g.,* U.S. v. Middleton, 35 F. Supp. 2d 1189 (N.D. Cal. 1999), *aff'd* 231 F.3d 1207 (9th Cir. 2000) (defendant charged with one count of knowingly causing the transmission of a code or program and thereby intentionally causing damage to a protected computer in violation of 18 U.S.C. § 1030(a)(5)). Among other things, Middleton deleted "the entire billing system" and "two internal databases" from the computer system of his former employer, an Internet service provider. *See* U.S. v. Middleton, 231 F.3d

puter without authorization and thereby recklessly cause damage; or (c) intentionally access a protected computer without authorization and thereby cause damage;[117]

(6) To knowingly and with intent to defraud traffic in any password or other information used to access a computer if (a) the trafficking

---

1207, 1208–09 (9th Cir. 2000). After being charged with violating 18 U.S.C. § 1030(a)(5), Middleton moved to dismiss the charges on the grounds that the company was not an "individual" under 18 U.S.C. § 1030(e)(8)(A). *Id.* at 1209–10. Middleton conceded that the computer he broke into was a "protected computer" under § 1030(e)(2)(B), but he claimed that his conduct did not fall within the scope of 18 U.S.C. § 1030(e)(8)(A), which defines "damage" as "any impairment to the integrity or availability of data... that causes losses aggregating at least $5,000 in value during any one year period to one or more individuals." Middleton argued that Congress did not intend to include corporations in its definition of "individuals." *See id.* at 1210. The Ninth Circuit disagreed, noting that

[a] large number of the computers that are used in interstate or foreign commerce or communication are owned by corporations.... It is highly unlikely, in view of Congress' purpose to stop damage to computers used in interstate and foreign commerce and communication, that Congress intended to criminalize damage to such computers only if the damage is to a natural person. Defendant's interpretation would thwart Congress' intent.

Id. at 1211. The Ninth Circuit also reviewed the statute's legislative history and concluded that "18 U.S.C. § 1030(a)(5) criminalizes computer crime that damages natural persons and corporations alike." *Id.* at 1212–13.

117. 18 U.S.C. § 1030(a)(5) (Supp. IV 1998). *See, e.g.*, U.S. v. Sablan, 92 F.3d 865 (9th Cir. 1996) (former bank employee who used old password to break into computer where she altered and deleted files charged with computer damage); U.S. v. Gray, 78 F. Supp. 2d 524 (E.D. Va. 1999) (defendant charged with unlawfully accessing a government computer in violation of 18 U.S.C. § 1030(a)(2) and with unlawfully accessing a government computer and causing damage to it in violation of 18 U.S.C. § 1030(a)(5)); U.S. v. Khanna, 1998 WL 67678 (S.D.N.Y. 1998) (former consultant to bank charged with gaining unauthorized access to bank's computers where he deleted files and databases). *See also* U.S. v. Morris, 928 F.2d 504 (2d Cir. 1991), *cert. denied*, 502 U.S. 817 (1992) (defendant's releasing computer "worm" punishable under prior version of statute).

Kevin Mitnick who, as noted above, is probably the most notorious "hacker" to be prosecuted in any U.S. jurisdiction, was charged under § 1030. *See, e.g.*, Gulker, *Mitnick/Shimomura Affair; Free Kevin Mitnick*, http://www.kevinmitnick.com/ (visited Jan. 3, 2001). One of the charges against Mitnick was that he damaged a protected computer in violation of § 1030(a)(5). *See* Indictment, U.S. v. Mitnick, http://www.kevinmitnick.com/indictment.html (C.D. Cal. 1996). The damaging count alleged that Mitnick, "using computers located outside California, knowingly, and without authorization, altered, damaged and destroyed information contained in, and prevented authorized use of the computers of USC, located in Los Angeles, California." *See id.*, Count Sixteen.

affects interstate or foreign commerce or (b) the computer to which access can be gained is by or for the federal government;[118] or

(7) To transmit in interstate or foreign commerce any threat to cause damage to a protected computer with the intent to extort money or any thing of value from any person, firm, association, educational institution, financial institution, government or other legal entity.[119]

Section 1030(b) makes it a federal crime to attempt to commit any of the above offenses, and section 371 of Title 18 of the U.S. Code can be used to charge conspiracy to violate 18 U.S.C. § 1030.[120]

Section 1030(c) sets out the punishment for these offenses. The penalties for obtaining confidential government information and disseminating it or refusing to surrender it to federal authorities in violation of 18 U.S.C. § 1030(a)(1) are: (1) a fine, imprisonment for up to ten years or both if the offender has not previously been convicted of an offense or an attempt to commit an offense under § 1030 or (2) a fine, imprisonment for up to twenty years or both if the offender has previously been convicted of such an offense or an attempt to commit such an offense.[121]

The basic penalties for breaking into a computer and obtaining information, breaking into a computer, intentionally breaking into a computer and causing damage and for trafficking in passwords in violation of 18 U.S.C. §§ 1030(a)(2), (a)(3), (a)(5)(C) or (a)(6) are a fine, imprisonment for not more than one year or both if the offender had not been previously convicted of an offense under § 1030 or an attempt to commit such an offense. If the offender was previously convicted of an offense under § 1030 or an attempt to commit such an offense, the maximum period of imprisonment for breaking into a computer and obtaining information, breaking into a computer and for trafficking in passwords rises to not more than ten years. The period of imprisonment imposed for breaking into a computer

---

118. 18 U.S.C. § 1030(a)(6) (1994).
119. *Id.* § 1030(a)(7) (Supp. IV 1998).
120. Section 371 makes it an offense for "two or more persons" to conspire either to commit an offense against the United States or to defraud the United States "or any agency thereof in any manner or for any purpose." 18 U.S.C. § 371 (1994). *See, e.g.,* U.S. v. Petersen, 98 F.3d 502, 503 (9th Cir. 1996) (defendant charged with conspiring to violate 18 U.S.C. § 1030(a)(4)); U.S. v. Fernandez, 1993 WL 88197 (S.D.N.Y. 1993) (defendant charged with conspiring to violate 18 U.S.C. § 1030(a)(5)).
121. 18 U.S.C. § 1030(c)(1) (Supp. IV 1998).

and obtaining information is increased to up to five years if the offense was committed for commercial advantage or financial gain, if it was committed to further a criminal or tortuous act or if the value of the information obtained exceeds $5,000.[122]

The penalties for using a computer to perpetrate fraud, for disseminating a virus or other harmful program, for intentionally accessing a computer and recklessly causing damage and for using a computer to commit extortion in violation of 18 U.S.C. §§ 1030(a)(4), (a)(5)(A), (a)(5)(B), (a)(5)(C) or (a)(7) are a fine, imprisonment for not more than five years or both if the offender was not previously convicted of an offense under § 1030 or an attempt to commit such an offense. If the offender has been convicted of such an offense, the maximum period of imprisonment rises to not more than ten years.[123]

D. Mail Fraud and Wire Fraud

Although they are not cybercrime-specific statutes, both mail fraud and wire fraud have been and can be used to prosecute those who use computers and the Internet to commit fraud.[124] Indeed, the wire fraud statute was used in one prosecution of the notorious hacker Kevin Mitnick, in conjunction with charges brought under 18 U.S.C. § 1030,[125] which is discussed in Section II(C) of this chapter.

The mail fraud and wire fraud statutes differ only in terms of the predicate that confers federal jurisdiction to prosecute what is, in effect, a simple fraud offense: Section 1341 of Title 18 of the U.S. Code makes it an offense for anyone who, "having devised or intending to devise any scheme or artifice to defraud, or for obtaining money or property by means of false or fraudulent pretenses" to use the U.S. mails or "any private or commercial interstate carrier" (such as Federal Express) " for the purpose of executing such scheme or artifice or attempting so to do." Section 1343 of Title 18 of the U.S. Code makes it an offense for anyone who,

---

122. *Id.* § 1030(c)(2).
123. *Id.* § 1030(c)(3).
124. As the previous section of this chapter explains, computer-assisted fraud can also be prosecuted under 18 U.S.C. § 1030 (1994 & Supp. IV 1998).
125. *See, e.g.,* Gulker, *Mitnick/Shimomura Affair, Free Kevin Mitnick,* http://www.kevinmitnick.com/ (visited Jan. 3, 2001). *See also* Indictment, U.S. v. Mitnick, http://www.kevinmitnick.com/indictment.html (visited Jan. 3, 2001).

"having devised or intending to devise any scheme or artifice to defraud, or for obtaining money or property by means of false or fraudulent pretenses, representations, or promises, transmits or causes to be transmitted by means of wire, radio, or television communication in interstate or foreign commerce, any writings, signs, signals, pictures, or sounds for the purpose of executing such scheme or artifice [to defraud]."[126]

Because of the similarity of the language employed in the two statutes, courts have held that they are "*in pari materia* and are, therefore" to be construed in a similar fashion.[127]

Both offenses consist of two elements. The elements of mail fraud are: (1) that the defendant devised or intended to devise a scheme to defraud; and (2) that the mails were used for the purpose of executing the scheme to defraud.[128] The elements of wire fraud are: (1) that the defendant intentionally participated in a scheme to defraud or for obtaining money or property by means of false or fraudulent pretenses; and (2) that wire transmissions were used for the purpose of executing the scheme to defraud.[129]

Wire fraud may seem the more obvious choice for prosecuting cybercrimes and, indeed, has been successfully used for this purpose.[130] In *U.S. v. Schreier*,[131] for example, the Tenth Circuit upheld the defendants' convictions for wire fraud because it found they had acquired property be-

---

126. 18 U.S.C. § 1343 (1994).
127. *See, e.g.,* U.S. v. Tarnopol, 561 F.2d 466, 475 (3d Cir. 1977).
128. *See, e.g.,* Carter v. U.S., 530 U.S. 255, 120 S. Ct. 2159, 2164–65 (2000).
129. *See, e.g.,* U.S. v. Autuori, 212 F.3d 105, 115 (2d Cir. 2000); U.S. v. deVegter, 198 F.3d 1324, 1328 n.4 (11th Cir. 1999), *cert. denied*, 120 S. Ct. 2723 (2000).
130. *But see* U.S. v. Czubinski, 106 F.3d 1069, 1072–74 (1st Cir. 1997) (court reversed defendant's wire fraud conviction because it found that his unauthorized browsing of confidential taxpayer information did not defraud Internal Revenue Service of its property within the meaning of the wire fraud statute; the court found that the government failed to prove beyond a reasonable doubt that the defendant intended to carry out a scheme to defraud the Internal Revenue Service by depriving it of its property interest in intangible information); U.S. v. LaMacchia, 871 F. Supp. 535, 541–43 (D. Mass. 1994) (court held that defendant's operating computer bulletin boards which let visitors download copies of copyrighted software did not violate the wire fraud statute; it rejected the government's argument that the defendant's nondisclosure of his activities to the copyright holders served as the basis of a scheme to defraud because the court found that nondisclosure can form the basis of a scheme to defraud only when the defendant had an independent duty to disclose and failed to do so, and the defendant had no fiduciary or statutory duty to disclose his activities to the copyright holders).
131. 908 F.2d 645, 646 (10th Cir. 1990), *cert. denied*, 498 U.S. 1069 (1991).

longing to American Airlines by accessing the airline's computer reservation system and manipulating its frequent flyer program, replacing names of actual passengers who made particular flights with that of a fictitious person whom they enrolled as a member of the frequent flyer program.[132] The defendants thereby caused American Airlines to issue coupons that could be used to obtain tickets for American Airlines flights and, as the court noted, "created liability for the airline and obtained property for themselves."[133]

Wire fraud and mail fraud charges can, however, work in tandem in the cybercrime context. Assume, for example, that a perpetrator is using an online auction to commit fraud by selling products he falsely represents as being antiques. The offender has clearly devised a scheme to defraud those to whom he sells his false antiques. The remaining element to charge mail fraud or wire fraud is, as noted earlier, the execution or attempted execution of the scheme to defraud by using the mails or the wires. This hypothetical perpetrator can be charged with wire fraud based on his use of the Internet to execute the fraud, e.g., to access the online auction site where he advertises his merchandise and arranges sales with the victims of his fraud. And since he is unlikely to be in a position to accept payment by credit card, the perpetrator will no doubt have the victims send him payment by check, cash or money order; since these payments will travel either via the U.S. mails or a private commercial carrier like Federal Express, and since the sending of payment is an essential part of executing the scheme to defraud, the perpetrator can also be charged with mail fraud.[134]

The general federal conspiracy provision, 18 U.S.C. § 371, can be used to charge conspiracy to commit mail fraud or wire fraud.[135]

---

132. *See id.* at 646–47.
133. *See id.* at 647–48. The court found it irrelevant that the scheme involved defrauding the airline out of intangible property: "We need not pursue a metaphysical argument regarding whether the 'property' existed as such in the possession of American to conclude that the creation of a liability on the part of a corporation is no less the misappropriation of its property than would be the theft of an asset worth an equal amount". *Id.* at 647, *citing* Carpenter v. U.S., 484 U.S. 19, 25 (1989).
134. *See, e.g., Internet Auction Fraud Defendant Pleads Guilty,* http://www.usdoj.gov/usao/cas/cas00306.1.htm (Mar. 6, 2000); *Online Auctioneer Pleads Guilty,* WIRED NEWS (July 15, 1999), http://www.wirednews.com/news/topstories/0,1287, 20766,00.html.
135. Section 371 makes it an offense for "two or more persons" to conspire either to commit an offense against the United States or to defraud the United States "or any agency thereof in any manner or for any purpose." 18 U.S.C. § 371 (1994). *See, e.g.,*

As to punishment, 18 U.S.C. § 1341 provides that a basic violation of its provisions is punishable by a fine, imprisonment for not more than five years or both. If the violation affects a financial institution, the offender can be fined "not more than $1,000,000," imprisoned for not more than thirty years or both.[136] The punishment for wire fraud under 18 U.S. Code is identical, i.e., a fine, imprisonment for not more than five years or both for basic violations and a fine of up to $1,000,000, imprisonment for not more than thirty years or both if the violation affected a financial institution.[137]

E. Sexual Exploitation of Children

In 1996 Congress, concerned about the increased proliferation of child pornography, adopted the Child Pornography Protection Act ["CPPA"], which was codified as 18 U.S.C. §§ 2251–2260. As one source explained, much of the impetus for the CPPA came from the use of computer technology:

> Advances in computer and computer imaging technology have only exacerbated the problem. With these technological advances, child pornographers can now create child pornography without using 'real' children. The computer-generated images pornographers can create are virtually indistinguishable from child pornography using real children. In addition to revolutionizing the production of child pornography, technological changes facilitated its distribution. As of December 1995, nearly one million sexually explicit pictures of children were on the Internet at any given time. Of these pictures, over eight hundred were graphic depictions of 'adults or teenagers engaged in sexual activity with children between eight and ten years of age.'[138]

Pereira v. U.S. 347 U.S. 1, 12 (1954) (conspiracy to commit mail fraud); U.S. v. Petersen, 98 F.3d 502, 503 (9th Cir. 1996) (conspiracy to commit wire fraud).
  136. *See* 18 U.S.C. § 1341 (1994). *See also* U.S.S.G. §§ 2C1.7 & 2F1.1.
  137. *See* 18 U.S.C. § 1343 (1994). *See also* U.S.S.G. §§ 2C1.7 & 2F1.1.
  138. Michael J. Eng, Note, *Free Speech Coalition v. Reno: Has the Ninth Circuit Given Child Pornographers a New Tool To Exploit Children?*, 35 U.S.F. L. Rev. 109, 109-10 (2000) (notes omitted) (*quoting* Jennifer Stewart, Comment, *If This Is The Global Community, We Must Be on the Bad Side of Town: International Policing of Child Pornography on the Internet*, 20 Hous. J. Int'l L. 205, 207 (1997)) [hereinafter Eng, *Free Speech Coalition v. Reno*].

Congress first outlawed child pornography, which has been held to be outside the protections of the First Amendment,[139] in 1977.[140] The 1977 enactment focused on the use of children—"real" minors—in the production of child pornography.[141] The development of computer technology allowed the creation of "virtual" child pornography, something the drafters of the 1977 legislation had not taken into consideration:

> [C]hild pornographers can now create.... [c]omputer-generated child pornography [which] is divided into two categories—virtual and computer-altered child pornography. Virtual child pornography does not depict a real or identifiable child. Through a technique called 'morphing,' the image of a Playboy Bunny or Penthouse Pet can be scanned into a computer and transformed through animation techniques into a sexually explicit image of a child. Although the morphed image is 'virtual,' it is practically indistinguishable from an 'unretouched' photographic image of a real child in a sexually explicit pose. By contrast, computer-altered child pornography depicts the image of a real or identifiable child. A photograph of an innocent child can be scanned into the computer, and with the 'cut and paste' feature, the child's head can be superimposed onto the body of someone who is engaged in sexually explicit activity. Furthermore, with image-altering software and computer hardware, that same photograph of the innocent child can be altered in such a manner as to remove the child's clothing and to arrange the child into 'sexual positions involving children, adults and even animals.'[142]

---

139. *See* Osborne v. Ohio, 495 U.S. 103 (1990); New York v. Ferber, 458 U.S. 747 (1982). In *Ferber*, the Supreme Court concluded that child pornography can be outlawed because of the compelling interest in protecting children, who are used in its production, and because child pornography is "intrinsically related" to the sexual abuse of children. *See id.* at 758–59. In *Osborne*, it seemed to go further, holding that child pornography can be outlawed, among other things, because it represents a permanent record of a child's sexual abuse and because pedophiles can use it in an attempt to lure other children into sexual activity. *See* 495 U.S. at 111.

140. *See* The Protection of Children Against Sexual Exploitation Act of 1977, Pub. L. 95-225, §2(a), 92 Stat. 7 (codified as amended at 18 U.S.C. §§2251–53 (Supp. IV 1998)).

141. *See, e.g.,* Eng, *Free Speech Coalition v. Reno* at 111–12.

142. *Id.* (notes omitted).

The CPPA was adopted to bring federal legislation outlawing child pornography up to date, to allow it to deal with the enforcement problems that had arisen due to the emergence of computer-generated child pornography.[143] To this end, it introduced a new definition of child pornography:[144] Section 2256(8) of Title 18 now defines "child pornography" as "any visual depiction, including any photograph, film, video, picture, or computer or computer-generated image or picture...of sexually explicit conduct" in which: (1) the production of the visual depiction involved the use of a minor engaging in sexually explicit conduct; (2) the visual depiction is or appears to be of a minor engaging in sexually explicit conduct; (3) the visual depiction was created, adapted or modified to appear that an identifiable minor is engaging in sexually explicit conduct; or (4) the visual depiction is advertised, promoted, presented, described or distributed in a way that gives the impression it contains a visual depiction of a minor engaging in sexually explicit conduct.[145]

The CPPA also created a number of offenses, the first of which was codified as 18 U.S.C. § 2251. Section 2251 prohibits: (1) the persuasion, enticement, inducement, or transportation of minors with the intent that the minor engage in sexually explicit conduct for the purpose of producing any visual depiction of such conduct if such materials will be transported in interstate or foreign commerce; (2) a parent or anyone in control of a minor from permitting a minor to engage in sexually explicit conduct, for the purpose of producing any visual depiction of such conduct if the parent knows that such materials will be transported in interstate or foreign commerce; and (3) printing or publishing advertisements for the sexual exploitation of children. The statute makes an offense to conspire and/or to attempt to commit any of these crimes.[146] Substantive violations of the statute, along with conspiring and/or attempting to commit a substantive violation, are punishable by a fine, imprisonment for not less than ten or more than twenty years or both a fine and imprisonment.[147] If the offender has a prior

---

143. *See, e.g., id.* at 112. Since computer-generated child pornography need not involve the participation of "real" children, it fell outside the compass of the 1977 legislation which, as noted in the text above, made the use of actual minors a requisite for imposing criminal liability. *See id.*
144. *See* 18 U.S.C. § 2256 (1994 & Supp. IV 1998).
145. *See id.* § 2256(8) (Supp. IV 1998).
146. *See id.* § 2251(d) (Supp. IV 1998).
147. *See id. See also* U.S.S.G. §§ 2G2.1 & 2G2.2.

conviction, under either state or federal law, for sexually exploiting children, the allowable period of imprisonment rises to not less than fifteen or more than thirty years; if the offender has two or more prior convictions, again under state or federal law, the allowable period of imprisonment rises to not less than thirty years or more than life.[148] If someone causes the death of another person while engaging in conduct that constitutes an offense under the statute, he or she is to be punished by death or imprisonment for any term of years or life.[149]

Another section of the CPPA—codified at 18 U.S.C. § 2252—prohibits: (1) knowingly transporting in interstate commerce, by any means, including by computer or mail, visual depictions of minors engaged in sexually explicit conduct;[150] (2) knowingly receiving or distributing visual depictions of minors engaged in sexually explicit conduct that have been mailed or shipped in interstate commerce; (3) selling or possessing such depictions with intent to sell them; and (4) possessing books, magazines, periodicals, films and other matter which contain such depictions.[151] The statute makes an offense to conspire or attempt to violate any of these prohibitions.[152] Conspiring to commit, attempting to commit or committing the first three substantive offenses is punishable by a fine, imprisonment for not more than fifteen years or both, unless the person has a prior conviction, under state or federal law, for the sexual exploitation or abuse of children; if the person has such a conviction, the period of allowable imprisonment rises to not less than five years nor more than thirty years.[153] Conspiring to commit, attempting to commit or committing the fourth offense is pun-

---

148. See 18 U.S.C. § 2251(d) (Supp. IV 1998).
149. See id.
150. See U.S. v. X-Citement Video, Inc., 513 U.S. 64, 68–78 (1994) (Section 2252(a)(1)'s use of "knowingly" applies not only to act of transporting material but also to elements such as minority of performers and sexually explicit nature of performance). See, e.g., U.S. v. Campos, 221 F.3d 1143, 1151 (10th Cir. 2000) (evidence was sufficient to support defendant's conviction for transporting child pornography in interstate commerce via computer); U.S. v. Johnson, 221 F.3d 83 (2d Cir. 2000) (defendant charged with violating § 2252(a)(1) by using laptop computer to send graphic image of minor engaged in sexual activity across state lines); U.S. v. McIntosh, 216 F.3d 1251, 1252–53 (11th Cir. 2000) (defendant pled guilty to nine counts of violating § 2252(a)(1) by sending images of minors engaged in sexually explicit conduct via computer).
151. See U.S. v. Dauray, 215 F.3d 257, 261–65 (2d Cir. 2000) (parsing the meaning of "other matter" as used in prior version of §2252(a)(4)).
152. See 18 U.S.C. § 2252(b) (Supp. IV 1998).
153. See id. See also U.S.S.G. § 2G2.2.

ishable by a fine, imprisonment for not more than five years or both, unless the person has a prior conviction, under state or federal law, for the sexual exploitation or abuse of children; if the person has such a conviction, the period of allowable imprisonment rises to not less than two years nor more than ten years.[154]

Section 2252 creates an affirmative defense for the fourth offense—possessing visual depictions of minors engaged in sexually explicit conduct.[155] To establish this defense, an accused must show that he or she possessed less than three matters containing depictions prohibited by the statute and either took reasonable steps to destroy those depictions or reported the matter to a law enforcement agency and gave the agency access to the depictions.[156] One circuit has held that the First Amendment does not provide a journalist with a defense to sending or receiving material in violation of the statute.[157]

Another provision of the CPPA, codified at 18 U.S.C. § 2252A, makes it an offense to do any of the following: (1) knowingly mail, transport or ship child pornography in interstate or foreign commerce by any means, including by computer; (2) knowingly receive or distribute child pornography or any material that contains child pornography and that has been mailed, transported or shipped in interstate or foreign commerce by any means, including by computer; (3) knowingly reproduce child pornography for distribution through the mails or in interstate or foreign commerce by any means, including by computer; (4) knowingly sell or possess with the intent to sell child pornography; and (5) knowingly possess "any book, magazine, periodical, film, videotape, computer disk, or any other material that contains an image of child pornography."[158] The statute also makes

---

154. *See* 18 U.S.C. § 2252(b) (Supp. IV 1998). *See also* U.S.S.G. § 2G2.4.
155. *See* 18 U.S.C. § 2252(c) (Supp. IV 1998).
156. *See id.*
157. *See* U.S. v. Matthews, 209 F.3d 338, 342–50 (4th Cir.), *cert. denied*, 121 S. Ct. 260 (2000).
158. 18 U.S.C. § 2252A(a) (Supp. IV 1998). *See, e.g.*, U.S. v. Mento, 231 F.3d 912 (4th Cir. 2000) (conviction for possession of child pornography upheld); U.S. v. Burnette, 234 F.3d 1270 (6th Cir. 2000) (table) (defendant pled guilty to receiving and distributing child pornography via computer); U.S. v. Jones, 210 F.3d 356 (2d Cir. 2000) (table) (defendant pled guilty to possessing child pornography). The prohibitions on selling, on possessing with the intent to sell and on possessing child pornography require that the violation have occurred within the jurisdiction of the United States or that the item(s) sold or possessed were, in whole or in part, mailed, transported or shipped in interstate or foreign commerce by any means, including by a computer. *See* 18 U.S.C. § 2252A(a)(4)-(5) (Supp. IV 1998). *See also* U.S. v. Kallestad, 2000 U.S. App. LEXIS

it a crime either to conspire or to attempt to commit any of these offenses.[159]

Section 2252A also creates an affirmative defense to each of the violations it defines.[160] The defense to a charge of committing any of the first four offenses defined by the statute requires a defendant to establish (1) that each of the "actual" person or persons featured in the alleged child pornography was an adult at the time the material was produced and (2) that he or she "did not advertise, promote, present, describe, or distribute the material in such a manner as to convey the impression" that it depicted a minor engaging in sexually explicit conduct.[161] The statute also creates an affirmative defense to a charge of committing the fifth offense it defines, e.g., knowingly possessing child pornography.[162] To qualify for this defense, a defendant must establish that he or she (1) possessed less than three images of child pornography and (2) "promptly and in good faith, and without retaining or allowing any person, other than a law enforcement agency, to access" any of those items "took reasonable steps to destroy each such image" or "reported the matter to a law enforcement agency and afforded that agency access to each such image."[163]

One who commits, conspires to commit or attempts to commit any of the first four offenses defined by 18 U.S.C. § 2252A(a) is to be fined or imprisoned for not more than fifteen years or both, but, if the offender has a prior conviction for child pornography or other offenses involving the abuse of children, he or she is to be fined and "imprisoned for not less than 5 years nor more than 30 years."[164] One who commits, conspires to commit or attempts to commit the remaining offense defined by 18 U.S.C.

33128, 2000 WL 1855084 (5th Cir. 2000) (rejecting challenge to the constitutionality of the possession offense on the grounds that the statute exceeds the scope of Congress' authority under the commerce clause).

Section 2260 makes it an offense for someone outside the United States to knowingly receive, transport, ship, distribute, sell, or possess with intent to transport, ship, sell, or distribute "any visual depiction of a minor engaging in sexually explicit conduct (if the production of the visual depiction involved the use of a minor engaging in sexually explicit conduct), intending that the visual depiction will be imported into the United States or into waters within a distance of 12 miles of the coast of the United States". 18 U.S.C. § 2260(b) (Supp. IV 1998).

159. *See* 18 U.S.C. § 2252A(b) (Supp. IV 1998).
160. *Id.* § 2252A(c)-(d).
161. *Id.* § 2252A(c).
162. *Id.* § 2252A(d).
163. *Id.*
164. *See id.* § 2252A(b)(1).

§ 2252A(a), e.g., possessing child pornography, is to be fined and imprisoned for not more than five years or both, but if the offender has a prior conviction for child pornography or other offenses involving the abuse of children, he or she is to be fined and "imprisoned for not less than 2 years nor more than 10 years."[165]

In addition to the penalties described above, the child pornography statutes also provide for the criminal and civil forfeiture of (1) depictions produced, transported, mailed or received in violation of its prohibitions; (2) property used to commit an offense involving the sexual exploitation of children; and (3) the proceeds of such an offense.[166]

In *Free Speech Coalition v. Reno*,[167] a trade association involved in the production and distribution of "adult-oriented materials" challenged the statute's prohibiting "as child pornography computer images that do not involve the use of real children in their production or dissemination."[168] The district court rejected their contention, but the Ninth Circuit held that "the First Amendment prohibits Congress from enacting a statute that makes criminal the generation of images of fictitious children engaged in imaginary but explicit sexual conduct."[169] The court explained that there are three "compelling interests" cited for outlawing child pornography which uses images of "actual children." The first is that children must participate "in sexually explicit situations to create the images," the second "stems from the belief that dissemination of such pornographic images may encourage more sexual abuse of children because it whets the appetite of pedophiles," and the third is "that such images are morally and aesthetically repugnant. "[170] Noting that the Supreme Court has "implicitly rejected the regulation of pornography that does not involve children," the Ninth Circuit found that none of these rationales warrants the prohibition of child pornography involving fictive images of children.[171] Other courts have disagreed, finding that there are "compelling interests" in banning even virtual child pornography.[172]

---

165. *See id.* § 2252A(b)(2).
166. *Id.* § 2253 (1994 & Supp. IV 1998) & 18 U.S.C.A. 2254 (2000).
167. 198 F.3d 1083 (9th Cir. 1999), *reh'g and suggestion for reh'g en banc denied*, 220 F.3d 1113 (9th Cir. 2000), *cert granted*, 2001 WL 46070 (U.S. 2001).
168. *Id.* at 1086.
169. *Id.*
170. *Id.* at 1091–92.
171. *Id.* at 1093.
172. *See, e.g.,* U.S. v. Mento, 231 F.3d 912 (4th Cir. 2000). *See also* U.S. v. Hilton, 167 F.3d 61 (1st Cir.), *cert. denied*, 528 U.S. 844 (1999); U.S. v. Acheson, 195 F.3d 645 (11th Cir. 1999).

F. Transporting Stolen Property

Section 2314 of Title 18 of the U.S. Code makes it an offense to transport stolen goods worth $5,000 or more in interstate or foreign commerce. As Section II(A) of this chapter explains, the Supreme Court has held that § 2314 cannot be used to prosecute those who infringe copyrights, on the theory that they are "transporting" stolen property in interstate or foreign commerce.[173] It can, thought, be used to prosecute anyone who physically transports stolen property—including stolen computer hardware—in interstate or foreign commerce, as long as the property is worth $5,000 or more and the other requirements are met.[174]

G. Unauthorized Access to Stored Electronic Communications

Section 2701(a) of Title 18 of the U.S. Code makes it an offense either to (1) intentionally access without authorization a facility through which an electronic communication is provided or (2) intentionally exceed an authorization to access such a facility and thereby obtain, alter or prevent authorized access to a wire or electronic communication while it is in electronic storage.[175] Section 2701(c) of Title 18 of the U.S. Code creates an exception to the liability established under § 2701(a) for access which is authorized by a user of an electronic service with respect to a communication

---

173. *See* Dowling v. U.S., 473 U.S. 207 (1985).
174. *See, e.g.,* U.S. v. Pollani, 146 F.3d 269, 270 (5th Cir. 1998) (defendant prosecuted under § 2314 for aiding and abetting the transportation of stolen computer parts). *But see* U.S. v. Tasy, 203 F.3d 1060, 1062 (8th Cir. 2000) (lack of evidence that defendants transported stolen computers in interstate commerce or were motivating factor in their movement interstate precluded prosecution under the statute). Courts have held that the statute cannot be used to prosecute the "transportation" of software because its intangible nature means it is not encompassed by the statute's prohibition on transporting "goods" or "wares." *See, e.g.,* U.S. v. Brown, 925 F.2d 1301, 1308 (10th Cir. 1991); U.S. v. Wang, 898 F. Supp. 758, 760 (D. Colo. 1995).
175. *See, e.g.,* Sherman & Co. v. Salton Maxim Housewares, Inc., 94 F. Supp. 2d 817, 821 (E.D. Mich. 2000) ("Because section 2701...prohibits only unauthorized access and not the misappropriation or disclosure of information, there is no violation of section 2701 for a person with authorized access to the database no matter how malicious or larcenous his intended use of that access. Section 2701 outlaws illegal entry, not larceny").

of or intended for that user.[176] The basic punishment for violating the statute is a fine, imprisonment for not more than six months, but the penalties increase if the offense was committed for purposes of commercial advantage, malicious destruction or damage or private commercial gain.[177] If the offense is committed for the purpose of commercial advantage, malicious destruction or damage or private commercial gain, the allowable period of imprisonment rises to not more than one year for a first offense and to not more than two years for a subsequent offense.[178]

H. Sending Obscene, Abusive or Harassing Communications

The Internet and other forms of online communication have been a boon to stalkers, as they make it easy for one bent on stalking someone to pursue his or her victim with a fair assurance of anonymity.[179] This anonymity can not only be unnerving to the victim, it also makes it difficult for law enforcement to identify and apprehend the perpetrator.[180] There is as yet no federal statute that is specifically directed at cyberstalkers,[181] but there are statutes that can be used to prosecute the sending of obscene, abusive or harassing communications.

Section 223(a) of Title 47 of the U.S. Code makes it an offense to use a telecommunications device in interstate or foreign communications to: (1) make, create solicit and initiate the transmission of "any comment, request, suggestion, proposal, image, or other communication which is obscene, lewd, lascivious, filthy, or indecent, with intent to annoy, abuse, threaten, or harass another person;" (2) make, create solicit and initiate the transmission of "any comment, request, suggestion, proposal, image, or other communication which is obscene or indecent, knowing that the recipient of the communication is under eighteen years of age, regardless of whether the maker of such communication placed the call or initiated the commu-

---

176. *See, e.g.*, Sega Enterprises v. MAPHIA, 948 F. Supp. 923, 930 (N.D. Cal. 1996) (employee's access was authorized directly or indirectly by user of online bulletin board service and so fell within the exception).
177. *See* 18 U.S.C. §2701(b) (1994 & Supp. IV 1998).
178. *See id.*
179. *See, e.g.*, U.S. Department of Justice, *1999 Report on Cyberstalking: A New Challenge for Law Enforcement and Industry*, http://www.usdoj.gov/criminal/cybercrime/cyberstalking.htm (visited Jan. 4, 2001) [hereinafter *1999 Report on Cyberstalking*].
180. *See, e.g., id.*
181. *See, e.g., id.* Online stalking is discussed in more detail later in this chapter.

nication;" (3) make a telephone call or "utilize a telecommunications device, whether or not conversation or communication ensues, without disclosing his identity and with intent to annoy, abuse, threaten, or harass any person at the called number or who receives the communications;" (4) make or cause "the telephone of another repeatedly or continuously to ring, with intent to harass any person at the called number;" (5) make repeated telephone calls or repeatedly initiate communication "with a telecommunications device, during which conversation or communication ensues, solely to harass any person at the called number or who receives the communication;" or (6) knowingly permit any telecommunications facility under his or her control to be used to commit any of the previously-listed activities. The penalties for these offenses include fines, imprisonment for up to two years, or both.[182]

Section 223(b) of Title 47 of the U.S. Code makes it a federal crime for any person (1) knowingly to use a telephone to make an obscene or indecent communication for commercial purposes or to allow a telephone facility under his or her control to be used for this purpose, or (2) knowingly to use a telephone to make an indecent communication for commercial purposes which is available to anyone under the age or eighteen or to allow a telephone facility under his or her control to be used for this purpose. The penalties for these offenses include fines, imprisonment or both.[183]

I. Sending Offensive Material to Minors

Two provisions of the Communications Decency Act of 1996[184] ["CDA"] attempt to protect minors from "indecent" material being transmitted online: Section 223(a)(1)(B)(ii) of Title 47 of the U.S. Code makes it an offense for someone "knowingly" to transmit "obscene or indecent" messages to minors.[185] Section 223(d) of Title 47 of the U.S. Code makes it an offense

---

182. *See* 47 U.S.C. § 223(a) (Supp. IV 1998).
183. *See id.* § 223(b) (1994). The basic penalty for using a telephone to make an obscene communication for commercial purposes is a fine and/or imprisonment for up to two years; the basic penalty for using a telephone to transmit an indecent communication to a minor is a fine and/or imprisonment for up to six months. *See id.* § 223(b)(1)-(2). The statute also permits the imposition of enhanced penalties for intentional violations. *See id.* § 223(b)(4)-(5).
184. *See* Reno v. ACLU, 521 U.S. 844, 858–59 (1997).
185. 47 U.S.C. § 223(a)(1)(B)(ii) (Supp. IV 1998):
    (a) Whoever—
        (1) in interstate or foreign communications...

to use interstate or foreign commerce to send or display offensive material to persons under 18.[186]

In *Reno v. ACLU*,[187] the Supreme Court invalidated portions of this statute relating to "indecent" communication by means of a telecommunication device and "patently offensive" communications through use of interactive computer service to persons under the age of 18 on First Amendment grounds. The Court held that these provisions were facially overbroad in violation of the First Amendment. Further, it held that, in trying to prevent minors from being exposed to potentially harmful speech, the provisions effectively suppressed speech adults have a constitutional right to receive from and communicate to each other. Finally, the Court determined that there had not been a showing that a less restrictive alternative would not be at least as effective in achieving the purposes of the statute.[188]

      (B) by means of a telecommunications device knowingly—
         (i) makes, creates, or solicits, and
         (ii) initiates the transmission of,
      any comment, request, suggestion, proposal, image, or other communication which is obscene or indecent, knowing that the recipient of the communication is under 18 years of age, regardless of whether the maker of such communication placed the call or initiated the communication...
shall be fined under title 18, United States Code, or imprisoned not more than two years, or both.

186. *Id.* §223(d):
   (d) Whoever—
      (1) in interstate or foreign communications knowingly—
         (A) uses an interactive computer service to send to a specific person or persons under 18 years of age, or
         (B) uses any interactive computer service to display in a manner available to a person under 18 years of age,
      any comment, request, suggestion, proposal, image, or other communication that, in context, depicts or describes, in terms patently offensive as measured by contemporary community standards, sexual or excretory activities or organs, regardless of whether the user of such service placed the call or initiated the communication; or
      (2) knowingly permits any telecommunications facility under such person's control to be used for an activity prohibited by paragraph (1) with the intent that it be used for such activity,
shall be fined under Title 18, or imprisoned not more than two years or both.

187. 521 U.S. 844 (1997).

188. *See id.* at 878–79:
      The breadth of the CDA's coverage is wholly unprecedented.... [T]he scope of the CDA is not limited to commercial speech or commercial entities. Its

J. Sending Commercial Communications Containing Material Harmful to Minors

The Child Online Protection Act added § 231 to Title 18 of the U.S. Code, the purpose being to protect children from harmful material posted on the Internet.[189] The section makes it an offense to "knowingly and with

---

> open-ended prohibitions embrace all nonprofit entities and individuals posting indecent messages or displaying them on their own computers in the presence of minors. The general, undefined terms 'indecent' and 'patently offensive' cover large amounts of nonpornographic material with serious educational or other value. Moreover, the "community standards" criterion as applied to the Internet means that any communication available to a nationwide audience will be judged by the standards of the community most likely to be offended by the message....
>
> For the purposes of our decision, we need neither accept nor reject the Government's submission that the First Amendment does not forbid a blanket prohibition on all 'indecent' and 'patently offensive' messages communicated to a 17-year old—no matter how much value the message may contain and regardless of parental approval. It is at least clear that the strength of the Government's interest in protecting minors is not equally strong throughout the coverage of this broad statute. Under the CDA, a parent allowing her 17-year-old to use the family computer to obtain information on the Internet that she, in her parental judgment, deems appropriate could face a lengthy prison term.... Similarly, a parent who sent his 17-year-old college freshman information on birth control via e-mail could be incarcerated even though neither he, his child, nor anyone in their home community, found the material 'indecent' or 'patently offensive,' if the college town's community thought otherwise.
>
> The breadth of this content-based restriction of speech imposes an especially heavy burden on the Government to explain why a less restrictive provision would not be as effective as the CDA. It has not done so. The arguments in this Court have referred to possible alternatives such as requiring that indecent material be 'tagged' in a way that facilitates parental control of material coming into their homes, making exceptions for messages with artistic or educational value, providing some tolerance for parental choice, and regulating some portions of the Internet—such as commercial web sites—differently than others, such as chat rooms. Particularly in the light of the absence of any detailed findings by the Congress, or even hearings addressing the special problems of the CDA, we are persuaded that the CDA is not narrowly tailored if that requirement has any meaning at all.

189. *See, e.g.,* ACLU v. Reno, 217 F.3d 162, 165 (3d Cir. 2000):
> COPA is Congress's second attempt to regulate the dissemination to minors of indecent material on the Web/Internet. The Supreme Court had ear-

knowledge of the character of the material, in interstate or foreign commerce by means of the World Wide Web, make[] any communication for commercial purposes that is available to any minor and that includes any material that is harmful to minors."[190] Offenders can be fined not more than $50,000, imprisoned for not more than six months or both.[191] If the violation is intentional, a fine of not more than $50,000 is imposed for each violation, and each day the violation occurs is considered to be a separate violation.[192] It is an affirmative defense that the defendant in good faith restricted minors' access to material that is harmful to them by requiring the use of a credit card or other method of indicating age or by employing "any other reasonable measures that are feasible under available technology."[193]

In *ACLU v. Reno*,[194] the Third Circuit upheld the issuance of an injunction barring enforcement of the statute because it believed the provision would "more likely than not" be found to be unconstitutional.[195] According to the Third Circuit,

> [b]ecause material posted on the Web is accessible by all Internet users worldwide, and because current technology does not permit a Web publisher to restrict access to its site based on the geographic locale of each particular Internet user, COPA essentially requires that every Web publisher subject to the statute abide by the most restrictive and conservative state's community standards in order to avoid criminal liability. Thus, because the standard by which COPA gauges whether material is 'harmful to minors' is based on identifying 'contemporary community standards' the inability of Web publishers to restrict access to their Web sites based on the geographic locale of the site visitor, in and of itself, imposes an im-

---

lier, on First Amendment grounds, struck down Congress's first endeavor, the Communications Decency Act, ["CDA"] which it passed as part of the Telecommunications Act of 1996. *See* ACLU v. Reno, 521 U.S. 844 (1997).... The CDA and the Supreme Court's decision in *ACLU v. Reno* are discussed above in this chapter.
190. 47 U.S.C. §231(a)(1) (Supp. IV 1998).
191. *See id.*
192. *See id.* §231(a)(2).
193. *Id.* §231(c)(1).
194. 217 F.3d 162 (3d Cir. 2000).
195. *See id.* at 178.

permissible burden on constitutionally protected First Amendment speech.[196]

K. Transmitting Information about a Minor

Section 2425 of Title 18 of the U.S. Code makes it an offense for someone "using the mail or any facility or means of interstate or foreign commerce, or within the special maritime and territorial jurisdiction of the United States" to "knowingly" initiate

> the transmission of the name, address, telephone number, social security number, or electronic mail address of another individual, knowing that such other individual has not attained the age of 16 years, with the intent to entice, encourage, offer, or solicit any person to engage in any sexual activity for which any person can be charged with a criminal offense....[197]

The statute also criminalizes attempts to violate its provisions.[198] A violation of 18 U.S.C. § 2425 is punishable by a fine, imprisonment for not more than five years or both.[199]

L. Online Stalking, Harassment and Threats

As section II(H) of this chapter noted, the Internet and other forms of online communication have been a boon to stalkers, as they can make it easy for someone bent on stalking another person to find the information (e.g., home address, telephone number, e-mail address, financial information, etc.) he or she may need to stalk the victim, as well as allowing a stalker to pursue the victim with a fair assurance of anonymity.[200] This anonymity can not only be unnerving to the victim, it also makes it difficult for law enforcement to identify and apprehend the perpetrator.[201] There is as yet no federal statute that is specifically directed at cyberstalkers,[202] and it can

---

196. *Id.* at 166.
197. 18 U.S.C. § 2425 (Supp. IV 1998).
198. *See id.* This is one of several federal statutes that can be used against cyberstalkers. *See, e.g., 1999 Report on Cyberstalking.*
199. *See* 18 U.S.C. § 2425 (Supp. IV 1998).
200. *See, e.g., 1999 Report on Cyberstalking.*
201. *See, e.g., id.*
202. *See, e.g., id.* Online stalking is discussed in more detail above.

be difficult to use statutes drafted for "real world" crimes against stalkers and others who exploit online communications for undesirable ends.

Section 875 of Title 18 of the U.S. Code makes it a federal crime to transmit any of the following in interstate or foreign commerce: (1) a communication containing a demand for a ransom for the release of any kidnaped person; (2) a communication with the intent to extort any money, (3) a communication threatening to injure a person; and (4) a communication that threatens damage to property.[203]

Section 875 has successfully been used to prosecute individuals who send threatening communications via the Internet. In *U.S. v. Kammersell*,[204] for example, the Tenth Circuit held that the defendant's sending a threatening communication from his computer to the recipient's computer could be prosecuted under the statute even though the defendant and the recipient were located in the same state. The court found that the jurisdictional element of the statute was satisfied because the message was transmitted over interstate telephone lines and traveled through a server located outside the state.[205] Unfortunately, the statute cannot be applied in the absence of a

---

203. 18 U.S.C. § 875 (1994):

(a) Whoever transmits in interstate or foreign commerce any communication containing any demand or request for a ransom or reward for the release of any kidnaped person, shall be fined under this title or imprisoned not more than twenty years, or both.

(b) Whoever, with intent to extort from any person, firm, association, or corporation, any money or other thing of value, transmits in interstate or foreign commerce any communication containing any threat to kidnap any person or any threat to injure the person of another, shall be fined under this title or imprisoned not more than twenty years, or both.

(c) Whoever transmits in interstate or foreign commerce any communication containing any threat to kidnap any person or any threat to injure the person of another, shall be fined under this title or imprisoned not more than five years, or both.

(d) Whoever, with intent to extort from any person, firm, association, or corporation, any money or other thing of value, transmits in interstate or foreign commerce any communication containing any threat to injure the property or reputation of the addressee or of another or the reputation of a deceased person or any threat to accuse the addressee or any other person of a crime, shall be fined under this title or imprisoned not more than two years, or both.

204. 196 F.3d 1137 (10th Cir. 1999), *cert. denied* 120 S. Ct. 2664 (2000).

205. *See id.* at 1138–39. *See generally* U.S. v. Johnson, 221 F.3d 83 (2d Cir. 2000) (defendant's conviction upheld because evidence established that he transmitted a "true threat" in interstate or foreign commerce).

"threat," which means it cannot be used against much of the conduct which falls into the category of stalking. The statute's limitations, especially with regard to online conduct, are illustrated by *U.S. v. Alkhabaz*.²⁰⁶ In *Alkhabaz*, the Sixth Circuit upheld the district court's dismissal of charges that the defendant violated 18 U.S.C. § 875(c) because it found that he did not transmit a "credible threat" to his alleged victim.²⁰⁷ The defendant, a student at the University of Michigan, had used e-mail to correspond with a friend, much of his part of the correspondence consisting of vivid descriptions of fantasized sexual violence against a woman whose name was the same as that of one of his classmates.²⁰⁸ When the correspondence came to light, he was prosecuted under § 875 for sending "threats" via interstate commerce.²⁰⁹ The district court dismissed the charge because it found that the e-mail correspondence did not constitute "true threats" and was, therefore, protected by the First Amendment.²¹⁰ The Sixth Circuit affirmed the dismissal because it agreed that the e-mail correspondence did not rise to the level of a "threat."²¹¹

---

206. 104 F.3d 1492 (6th Cir. 1997).
207. *See id.* at 1495–96.
208. *See id.* at 1498 (Krupansky, J., dissenting):
By November 1994, Baker's sadistic stories attracted the attention of an individual who called himself "Arthur Gonda," a Usenet service subscriber residing in Ontario, Canada, who apparently shared similarly misdirected proclivities. Baker and Gonda subsequently exchanged at least 41 private computerized electronic mail ["e-mail"] communications between November 29, 1994 and January 25, 1995. Concurrently, Baker continued to distribute violent sordid tales on the electronic bulletin board. On January 9, 1995, Baker brazenly disseminated publicly, via the electronic bulletin board, a depraved torture-and-snuff story in which the victim shared the name of a female classmate of Baker's referred to below as "Jane Doe"...This imprudent act triggered notification of the University of Michigan authorities by an alarmed citizen on January 18, 1995. On the following day, Baker admitted to a University of Michigan investigator that he had authored the story and published it on the Internet.
209. *See id.* at 1493.
210. *See id.*
211. *See id.* at 1497:
Accordingly, to achieve the intent of Congress, we hold that, to constitute "a communication containing a threat" under Section 875(c), a communication must be such that a reasonable person (1) would take the statement as a serious expression of an intention to inflict bodily harm (the *mens rea*), and (2) would perceive such expression as being communicated to effect some change or achieve some goal through intimidation (the *actus reus*)....
Applying our interpretation of the statute to the facts before us, we conclude

M. Fraud in Connection with Access Devices

Section 1029 of Title 18 of the U.S. Code makes it an offense to engage in certain activities involving "access devices,"[212] which are defined as "any

---

that the communications between Baker and Gonda do not constitute "communications containing a threat" under Section 875(c). Even if a reasonable person would take the communications between Baker and Gonda as serious expressions of an intention to inflict bodily harm, no reasonable person would perceive such communications as being conveyed to effect some change or achieve some goal through intimidation. Quite the opposite, Baker and Gonda apparently sent e-mail messages to each other in an attempt to foster a friendship based on shared sexual fantasies.

212. 18 U.S.C. § 1029(a) (1994 & Supp. IV 1998):
Whoever —

(1) knowingly and with intent to defraud produces, uses, or traffics in one or more counterfeit access devices;

(2) knowingly and with intent to defraud traffics in or uses one or more unauthorized access devices during any one-year period, and by such conduct obtains anything of value aggregating $1,000 or more during that period;

(3) knowingly and with intent to defraud possesses fifteen or more devices which are counterfeit or unauthorized access devices;

(4) knowingly, and with intent to defraud, produces, traffics in, has control or custody of, or possesses device-making equipment;

(5) knowingly and with intent to defraud effects transactions, with 1 or more access devices issued to another person or persons, to receive payment or any other thing of value during any 1-year period the aggregate value of which is equal to or greater than $1,000;

(6) without the authorization of the issuer of the access device, knowingly and with intent to defraud solicits a person for the purpose of—

(A) offering an access device; or

(B) selling information regarding or an application to obtain an access device;

(7) knowingly and with intent to defraud uses, produces, traffics in, has control or custody of, or possesses a telecommunications instrument that has been modified or altered to obtain unauthorized use of telecommunications services;

(8) knowingly and with intent to defraud uses, produces, traffics in, has control or custody of, or possesses a scanning receiver;

(9) knowingly uses, produces, traffics in, has control or custody of, or possesses hardware or software, knowing it has been configured to insert or modify telecommunication identifying information associated with or contained in a telecommunications instrument so that such instrument may be used to obtain telecommunications service without authorization; or

card, plate, code, account number, electronic serial number, mobile identification number, personal identification number, or other telecommunications service, equipment, or instrument identifier, or other means of account access that can be used...to obtain money, goods, services, or any other thing of value."[213] Section 1029 also prohibits activities involving counterfeit access devices, which it defines as "any access device that is counterfeit, fictitious, altered, or forged, or an identifiable component of an access device or a counterfeit access device."[214]

As to offenses, § 1029 makes it a federal crime to do any of the following:

(1) knowingly and with the intent to defraud produce, use or traffic in a counterfeit access device;[215]

---

(10) without the authorization of the credit card system member or its agent, knowingly and with intent to defraud causes or arranges for another person to present to the member or its agent, for payment, 1 or more evidences or records of transactions made by an access device;

shall, if the offense affects interstate or foreign commerce, be punished as provided in subsection (c) of this section.

Punishment is discussed in the text, *infra*.

See also U.S. Department of Justice, *Criminal Resource Manual* 1024 (1997), http://www.usdoj.gov/usao/eousa/foia_reading_room/usam/title9/crm01024.htm [hereinafter *Criminal Resource Manual*]:

The access device fraud provisions enacted under the Credit Card Fraud Act of 1984, part of the Comprehensive Crime Control Act of 1984, Pub. L. No. 98-473, 98 Stat. 2183–4 (1984), and codified at 18 U.S.C. § 1029 expand upon the older, limited provisions at 15 U.S.C. § 1644 (fraudulent use of credit cards) and 15 U.S.C. § 1693n (fraudulent use of debit instruments). Most significantly, the provisions at 18 U.S.C. § 1029, in comparison with those of Title 15, broaden the definitions of credit card and debit instrument to any "access device," including an account number; increase the maximum penalties of incarceration and fines; and provide a substantial repeat-offender penalty.

213. 18 U.S.C. § 1029(e)(1) (1994). See U.S. v. Brady, 820 F. Supp. 1346, 1356–57 (D. Utah), aff'd 13 F.3d 334 (10th Cir. 1993) (EPROM—erasable programmable read-only memory—not an access device under the statute).

214. *Id.* § 1029(e)(2). *See, e.g.*, U.S. v. Brannan, 898 F.2d 107 (9th Cir. 1990), *cert. denied*, 498 U.S. 833 (1991) (credit cards defendant acquired by submitting false information were counterfeit access devices); U.S. v. Brewer, 835 F.2d 550 (5th Cir. 1987) (long distance telephone service access codes fabricated by defendant were counterfeit access devices).

215. *See, e.g.*, U.S. v. Johnson, 132 F.3d 1279, 1282 (9th Cir. 1997). *See also Criminal Resource Manual* 1024.

(2) knowingly and with the intent to defraud traffic in or use one or more access devices during any one-year period and thereby obtain anything of a value aggregating $1,000 or more;[216]
(3) knowingly and with the intent to defraud possess fifteen or more devices which are counterfeit or unauthorized access devices;[217]
(4) knowingly and with the intent to defraud produce, traffic in, have custody or control of or possess access device-making equipment;[218]
(5) knowingly and with the intent to defraud effect transactions with one or more access devices issued to another person or other persons to receive anything of value during any one-year period of a value aggregating $1,000 or more;[219]
(6) without the authorization of the issuer of an access device, knowingly and with the intent to defraud solicit someone for the purpose, either, of offering an access device or selling information regarding or an application to obtain an access device;[220]
(7) knowingly and with intent to defraud use, produce, traffic in, have custody or control of, or possess a telecommunications instrument that has been modified or altered to obtain unauthorized use of telecommunications services;[221]
(8) knowingly and with intent to defraud use, produce, traffic in, have control or custody of, or possess a scanning receiver;
(9) knowingly and with the intent to defraud use, produce, traffic in, have custody or control of or possess hardware or software know-

---

216. *See, e.g.,* U.S. v. Swint, 223 F.3d 249 (3d Cir. 2000); U.S. v. Casey, 158 F.3d 993, 994 (8th Cir. 1998); U.S. v. Thomas, 159 F.3d 1349 (2d Cir. 1998) (table). *See also Criminal Resource Manual* 1024.

217. *See, e.g.,* U.S. v. Sepulveda, 115 F.3d 882, 885 (11th Cir. 1997); U.S. v. Petersen, 98 F.3d 502, 505 (9th Cir. 1996). In one prosecution, Kevin Mitnick, an infamous hacker, was charged with several offenses, including wire fraud, but pled guilty to possession of unauthorized access devices with the intent to defraud, in violation of 18 U.S.C. § 1029(a)(3) (1994). *See* U.S. v. Mitnick, 145 F.3d 1342 (9th Cir.), *cert. denied,* 525 U.S. 917 (1998). *See also Criminal Resource Manual* 1024.

218. *See, e.g.,* U.S. v. Liu, 180 F.3d 957, 959 (8th Cir. 1999); U.S. v. Cabrera, 172 F.3d 1287, 1289 (11th Cir. 1999). *See also Criminal Resource Manual* 1024.

219. *Cf.,* U.S. v. Darnell, 225 F.3d 664 (9th Cir. 2000) (table, restitution order); U.S. v. Spinner, 180 F.3d 514, 515 (3d Cir. 1999) (indictment dismissed for lack of jurisdiction), *cert. denied,* 120 S. Ct. 2232 (2000). *See also Criminal Resource Manual* 1025.

220. *See, e.g.,* U.S. v. O'Shield, 139 F.3d 902 (7th Cir. 1998) (table). *See also Criminal Resource Manual* 1025.

221. *See, e.g.,* U.S. v. Alvelo-Ramos, 957 F. Supp. 18, 18 (D.P.R. 1997). *See also Criminal Resource Manual* 1027.

ing it has been configured to insert or modify telecommunications identifying information associated with or contained in a telecommunications instrument so that the instrument can be used to obtain telecommunications service without authorization;[222] or

(10) without the authorization of a credit card owner or its agent, knowingly and with the intent to defraud cause or arrange for another person to present one or more records of transactions made by an access device to the owner or its agent for payment.[223]

The sanctions for the offenses set out in 18 U.S.C. § 1029(a) are divided into two categories: the basic penalty for the offenses listed in paragraphs (1), (2), (3), (6), (7) and (10), above, is a fine, imprisonment for not more than ten years or both, and for the offenses listed in paragraphs (4), (5), (8) and (9), above it is a fine, imprisonment for not more than fifteen years or both; if the offender has a prior conviction under § 1029, the penalty rises to a fine, imprisonment for not more than twenty years or both.[224] The

---

222. *See, e.g.,* U.S. v. Alvelo-Ramos, 957 F. Supp. 18, 18 (D.P.R. 1997). It is not a violation of this sub-section for "an officer, employee, or agent of, or a person engaged in business with, a facilities-based carrier, to engage in conduct (other than trafficking) otherwise prohibited...for the purpose of protecting the property or legal rights of that carrier, unless such conduct is for the purpose of obtaining telecommunications service provided by another facilities-based carrier without the authorization of such carrier." 18 U.S.C. § 1029(g)(1) (Supp. IV 1998). The statute creates an affirmative defense to a charge of violating this sub-section; to qualify for the defense, the person charged with the violation must establish, by a preponderance of the evidence, that "the conduct charged was engaged in for research or development in connection with a lawful purpose." *Id.* § 1029(g)(2).
223. 18 U.S.C. § 1029(a)(10) (Supp. IV 1998).
224. 18 U.S.C. § 1029(c) (Supp. IV 1998):
Penalties.—
   (1) Generally.—The punishment for an offense under subsection (a) of this section is—
      (A) in the case of an offense that does not occur after a conviction for another offense under this section—
         (i) if the offense is under paragraph (1), (2), (3), (6), (7), or (10) of subsection (a), a fine under this title or imprisonment for not more than 10 years, or both; and
         (ii) if the offense is under paragraph (4), (5), (8), or (9), of subsection (a), a fine under this title or imprisonment for not more than 15 years, or both;
      (B) in the case of an offense that occurs after a conviction for another offense under this section, a fine under this title or imprisonment for not more than 20 years, or both; and

statute also permits the forfeiture of any property "used or intended to be used to commit the offense."[225]

Section 1029 also makes it a crime for someone to attempt[226] or to conspire to violate its prohibitions.[227] The punishment for an attempt is the same as that for the offense attempted; the punishment for conspiracy is a fine not greater than that allowed for the offense which was the object of the conspiracy or imprisonment for a period that is not longer than one-half the period of imprisonment allowed for the substantive offense, or both a fine and imprisonment.[228]

IV. STATE CYBERCRIME LEGISLATION

State cybercrime legislation tends to be quite idiosyncratic. The greatest areas of consistency exist with regard to the computer "break-in" offenses (e.g., hacking and cracking) and with regard to using a computer to disseminate child pornography and/or to attempt to lure a minor into a sexual relationship. Beyond these areas of general agreement, there are gaps and areas of inconsistency in state laws targeting cybercrime.

A. Hacking/Cracking

Most states make it a crime to purposely access a computer, computer system or network without authorization.[229] Most make it a more serious crime to purposely access a computer without authorization and alter, dam-

---

(C) in either case, forfeiture to the United States of any personal property used or intended to be used to commit the offense.

225. *Id.* § 1029(c)(1)(C). *See also id.* § 1029(c)(2).
226. *Id.* § 1029(b)(1). *See, e.g.,* U.S. v. Casey, 158 F.3d 993, 994 (8th Cir. 1998).
227. 18 U.S.C. § 1029(b)(2) (1994) (penalty imposable upon anyone who "is a party to a conspiracy to commit an offense under subsection (a)...if any of the parties engages in conduct in furtherance of such offense"). *See, e.g.,* U.S. v. Sepulveda, 115 F.3d 882, 885 (11th Cir. 1997).
228. *See* 18 U.S.C. § 1029(b) (1994 & Supp. IV 1998).
229. *See, e.g.,* IND. CODE ANN. § 35-43-2-3 (1998). *See also* ALA. CODE § 13A-8-102 (1985); ALASKA STAT. § 11.46.484(a)(5) (1996); ARK. CODE ANN. § 5-41-104 (Michie 1987); CAL. PENAL CODE § 502 (West 2001); COL. REV. STAT. § 18-5.5-102 (2000); CONN. GEN. STAT. § 53a-251 (1999); DEL. CODE ANN. tit. 11, § 932 (1999); FLA. STAT. ch. 815.06 (2000); WASH. REV. CODE § 9A.52.120 (2000); W. VA. CODE § 61-3C-5 (1989); WIS. STAT. § 943.70 (1996); WYO. STAT. § 6-3-504 (1983).

age or disrupt the operation of the computer and/or the data it contains.[230] Some states have a "misuse of computer information" statute which prohibits copying, receiving or using information that was obtained by violating a hacking or cracking statute.[231] New York has what is in effect a cyber-burglary statute that makes it a crime to break into a computer or computer system "with an intent to commit or attempt to commit or further the commission of any felony."[232]

B. Disseminating Viruses and Other Harmful Programs

A surprisingly few states have outlawed outlaw the creation and transmission of virii and other harmful programs.[233] Legislation to this effect has been introduced in a few other states.[234]

C. Miscellaneous Computer-Related Offenses

A few states make it a crime to introduce false information into a computer system for the purpose of "damaging or enhancing" someone's credit rating.[235]

A surprising number of states have an "offense against computer equipment or supplies," which consists of modifying or destroying "equipment

---

230. *See, e.g.*, ARK. CODE ANN. § 5-41-104 (Michie 1987). *See also* ALA. CODE § 13A-8-102 (1985); ARIZ. REV. STAT. ANN. § 13-2316 (2000); CAL. PENAL CODE § 502 (West 2001); COL. REV. STAT. § 18-5.5-102 (2000); CONN. GEN. STAT. § 53a-251 (1999).

231. *See, e.g.*, ALA. CODE § 13A-8-102 (1985); CONN. GEN. STAT. § 53a-251 (1999); DEL. CODE ANN. tit. 11, § 935 (1999); FLA. STAT. ch. 815.04 (2000); KY. REV. STAT. ANN. § 434.855 (Baldwin 1984); N.H. REV. STAT. ANN. § 638:17 (1986). *See also* N.Y. PENAL LAW § 156.35 (McKinney 1998).

232. *See* N.Y. PENAL LAW § 156.10 (McKinney 1998).

233. *See, e.g.*, CAL. PENAL CODE § 502 (West 2001); ILL. ANN. STAT. ch. 720, para. 5/16D-3 (Smith-Hurd 1993 & Elec. Supp. 2000); Iowa Code § 716A.3 (2000); ME. REV. STAT. ANN. tit. 17-A, § 433 (West 2000); Mich. Comp. Laws § 752.795 (2000); MINN. STAT. ANN. § 609.87 (West 2000); MISS. CODE ANN. § 97-45-9 (1999); NEB. REV. STAT. § 28-1345 (1991); NEV. REV. STAT. § 205.4765 (1999); N.M. STAT. ANN. § 30-45-4 (Michie 1989); N.C. GEN. STAT. § 14-455 (2000); TENN. CODE ANN. § 39-14-602 (1993).

234. *See, e.g.*, 1999 California Assembly Bill No. 451, California 1999–00 Regular Session, 1999 CA A.B. 451 (SN) (Westlaw); 1999 Pennsylvania Senate Bill No. 1077, Pennsylvania 183d General Assembly, 1999 PA S.B. 1077 (SN) (Westlaw).

235. *See, e.g.*, ALASKA STAT. § 11.46.740 (2000); HAW. REV. STAT. § 708-891 (1992); NEV. REV. STAT. § 205.477 (1999); N.M. STAT. ANN. § 30-45-4 (Michie 1989).

or supplies that are used or intended to be used in a computer, computer system, or computer network."[236] Even more make it a crime to deny, disrupt, degrade, interrupt or cause the denial, disruption, degradation or interruption of computer services or of access to a computer.[237] A few make it a crime to destroy computer equipment.[238]

Several states outlaw "computer invasion of privacy," which consists of using a "computer or computer network with the intention of examining any employment, medical, salary, credit, or any other financial or personal data relating to any other person with knowledge that such examination is without authority."[239] Others make it a crime to disclose someone else's computer password.[240]

D. Offenses Involving Children

A number of states make it a crime to use a computer to solicit or lure a minor to engage in an "unlawful sex act."[241] Several make it a crime to use a computer to compile information about a child "for the purpose of facilitating, encouraging, offering or soliciting a prohibited sexual act" from

---

236. *See, e.g.,* ALA. CODE § 13A-8-103 (1985); CONN. GEN. STAT. § 53a-251 (1999); DEL. CODE ANN. tit. 11, § 936 (1999); FLA. STAT. ch. 815.05 (2000); IOWA CODE § 716A.3 (2000); LA. REV. STAT. ANN. § 14:73.3 (West 1997); W. VA. CODE § 61-3C-7 (2000); WYO. STAT. § 6-3-501 (1982).

237. *See, e.g.,* CONN. GEN. STAT. § 53a-251 (1999); DEL. CODE ANN. tit. 11, § 934 (1999); FLA. STAT. ch. 815.06 (2000); LA. REV. STAT. ANN. § 14:73.4 (West 1997); MISS. CODE ANN. § 97-45-5 (1999); WYO. STAT. § 6-3-504 (1983).

238. *See, e.g.,* CONN. GEN. STAT. § 53a-251 (1999); N.H. REV. STAT. ANN. § 638:17 (1986); N.J. STAT. ANN. § 2A:38A-3 (West 2000); W. VA. CODE § 61-3C-7 (2000).

239. *See* GA CODE ANN. § 16-9-93 (1991); ME. REV. STAT. ANN. tit. 17-A, § 432 (West 2000); VA. CODE ANN. § 18.2-152.5 (1985); W. VA. CODE § 61-3C-12 (1989). *See also* NEV. REV. STAT. § 205.477 (1999) (crime to obtain personal information about another).

240. *See, e.g.,* GA. CODE ANN. § 16-9-93 (1991); KAN. STAT. ANN. § 21-3755 (1999); MISS. CODE ANN. § 97-45-5 (1999); MO. ANN. STAT. § 569.095 (Vernon 1999); S.D. CODIFIED LAWS ANN. § 43-43B-1 (1984); W. VA. CODE § 61-3C-10 (1989).

241. *See, e.g.,* ALA. CODE § 13A-6-110 (1997); CAL. PENAL CODE § 288.2 (West 1999); FLA. STAT. ANN. ch. 847.0135 (West 2000); GA. CODE ANN. § 16-12-100.2 (1999); ILL. ANN. STAT. ch. 720, para. 5/11-6 (Smith-Hurd 1993); IND. CODE § 35-42-4-6 (1998); ME. REV. STAT. ANN. tit. 17-A, § 259 (West 2000); MICH. COMP. LAWS ANN. § 750.145d (West 2000); N.H. REV. STAT. ANN. § 649-B:4 (1998); N.M. STAT. ANN. § 30-37-3.2 (Michie 1998); N.C. GEN. STAT. § 14-202.3 (1996); TENN. CODE ANN. § 39-13-528 (2000); VA. CODE ANN. § 18.2-374.3 (Michie 1999). *See also* DEL. CODE ANN. tit. 11, § 1112A (1999).

that child.[242] These statutes are part of an effort to outlaw child pornography.[243] Many states prohibit using a computer to create, store and/or distribute child pornography,[244] and many also prohibit using a computer to send obscene material to a child.[245] Pennsylvania makes it an offense to use a computer to communicate with a child for the purpose of engaging in prostitution.[246]

E. Stalking and Harassment

Only about sixteen states outlaw online stalking or harassment, and several of them require that an offender transmit a "credible threat" to injure the victim, the victim's family or "any other person."[247] Other statutes are broader, making it a crime to use a computer to "engage in a course of conduct" that would cause a "reasonable person" to "suffer intimidation or serious inconvenience, annoyance or alarm," as well as fearing death or injury to themselves or to members of their family.[248]

Some states have expanded their "obscene phone call" statutes so they encompass using the telephone or an "electronic communication device"

---

242. *See, e.g.,* DEL. CODE ANN. tit. 11, § 1112A (1999); FLA. STAT. ANN. § 847.0135 (West 2000); 27 MD. ANN. CODE art. 27, § 419A (1996); N.H. REV. STAT. ANN. § 649-B:3 (1998); OKLA. STAT. ANN. tit. 21, § 1040.13a (West 2001); VA. CODE ANN. § 18.2-374.3 (Michie 1999).
243. *See, e.g.,* FLA. STAT. ANN. § 847.0135 (West 2000); GA. CODE ANN. § 16-12-100.2 (1999); MD. ANN. CODE art. 27, § 419A (1996); N.H. REV. STAT. ANN. § 649-B:3 (1998); OKLA. STAT. ANN. tit. 21, § 1040.13a (2001); VA. CODE ANN. § 18.2-374.3 (Michie 1999).
244. *See, e.g.,* CAL. PENAL CODE § 311.11 (West 1999); FLA. STAT. ANN. § 847.0135 (West 2000); GA. CODE ANN. § 16-12-100.2 (1999); ILL. ANN. STAT. ch. 720, para. 5/11-20.1 (Smith-Hurd 2000); IND. CODE ANN. § 35-42-4-4 (West 1998); MD. ANN. CODE art. 27, § 419A (1996); N.H. REV. STAT. ANN. § 649-B:3 (1998); N.J. STAT. ANN. § 2C:24-4 (West 2000); OKLA. STAT. ANN. tit. 21, § 1040.13a (West 2001); 18 Penn. Cons. Stat. Ann. § 6312 (2000); TEX. PENAL CODE ANN. § 43.26 (West 1994 & 2001 Elec. Update); VA. CODE ANN. § 18.2-374.3 (Michie 1999); WYO. STAT. § 6-4-303 (1999).
245. *See, e.g.,* ALA. CODE § 13A-6-111 (1997); GA. CODE ANN. § 16-12-100.1 (1993).
246. *See* 18 PENN. CONS. STAT. ANN. § 6318 (2000).
247. *See* ALA. CODE § 13A-11-8 (1997); WASH. REV. CODE ANN. § 9A.46.110 (West 2000); WISC. STAT. ANN. § 947.0125 (West 2000); WYO. STAT. § 6-2-506 (1993). *See also* CAL. PENAL CODE § 422 (West 1999) (offense to transmit "credible threat" even absent intent to carry out threat).
248. *See* ALA. CODE § 13A-11-8 (1997); ARIZ. REV. STAT. ANN. § 13-2921 (2000); WASH. REV. CODE ANN. § 9A.46.110 (West 2000); WISC. STAT. ANN. § 947.0125 (West 2000); WYO. STAT. § 6-2-506 (1993). *See also* MASS. GEN. L. ch. 265, § 43 (2000).

to contact someone and threaten to injure that person or his/her family, to use obscene language or to make repeated contacts in an effort to annoy the person.[249] A New York court has held that a similar provision encompasses harassing or threatening messages sent via the Internet.[250] Bills have been introduced to make online stalking and/or harassment an offense in states where it is not currently outlawed.[251]

F. Fraud and Theft

A substantial number of states outlaw using computers to commit fraud,[252] i.e., using a "computer, computer system, computer network, or any part thereof for the purpose of devising or executing any scheme or artifice to defraud" or for "obtaining money, property, or services by means of false or fraudulent pretenses, representations, or promises."[253] States tend to incorporate embezzlement crimes into their computer fraud statutes, rather than creating separate "computer embezzlement" provisions.[254]

A substantial number of states also outlaw "computer theft,"[255] which can encompass any of several discrete offenses: information theft,[256] software

---

249. *See* Ark. Code Ann. § 5-41-108 (Michie 1997); Cal. Penal Code § 653m (West 2001); Ind. Code Ann. § 35-45-2-2 (West 1998); Kan. Stat. Ann. § 21-4113 (1993); Md. Ann. Code art. 27, § 555A (1998); N.C. Gen. Stat. § 14-196 (2000); N.D. Cent. Code § 12.1-17-07 (1999).

250. *See* People v. Munn, 688 N.Y.S.2d 384, 385 (N.Y. City Crim. Ct. 1999).

251. *See, e.g.,* 1999 New Hampshire House Bill No. 345, 1999 NH H.B. 345 (SN) (Westlaw); 1998 New Jersey Assembly Bill No. 3506, New Jersey 208th Legislature.

252. *See, e.g.,* N.M. Stat. Ann. § 30-45-3 (West 1989); N.C. Gen. Stat. § 14-454 (2000); N.D. Cent. Code § 12.1-06.1-08 (1987); Okla. Stat. tit. 21, § 1953 (2001); Or. Rev. Stat. § 164.377 (1991); R.I. Gen. Laws §§ 11-52-2 & 11-52-7 (1994); S.C. Code Ann. § 16-16-20 (Law. Co-op. 1993); Tenn. Code Ann. § 39-14-602 (1993); Wis. Stat. § 943.70 (1996).

253. *See* Col. Rev. Stat. § 18-5.5-102 (2000).

254. *See, e.g.,* Haw. Rev. Stat. § 708-891(b) (1992); N.M. Stat. Ann. § 30-45-3 (Michie 1989).

255. *See, e.g.,* Col. Rev. Stat. § 18-5.5-102 (2000); Ga. Code Ann. § 16-9-93 (1991); Haw. Rev. Stat. § 708-891 (1992); Idaho Code § 18-2202 (1984); Iowa Code § 716A.9 (1993); Minn. Stat. Ann. § 609.89 (West 2000); N.J. rev. Stat. § 2C:20-25 (1995); R.I. Gen. Laws § 11-52-4 (1994); Vt. Stat. Ann. tit. 13, § 4105 (1999.

256. *See, e.g.,* Col. Rev. Stat. § 18-4-412 (2000); Iowa Code § 716A.9 (1993); Minn. Stat. Ann. § 609.89 (2000); N.J. Rev. Stat. § 2C:20-25 (1995); R.I. Gen. Laws § 11-52-4 (1994).

theft,[257] computer hardware theft,[258] and theft of computer services.[259] It can also encompass using a computer to commit a theft in a more traditional sense, e.g., to steal property other than data or computer hardware or software.[260] A few states prohibit the unlawful possession of computer data and/or computer software.[261] Some have "identity theft" statutes, which make it a crime to "knowingly and with intent to defraud for economic benefit" obtain, possess, transfer, use or attempt "to obtain, possess, transfer or use, one or more identification documents or personal identification number of another person other than that issued lawfully for the use of the possessor."[262]

G. Forgery

A few states outlaw computer forgery, which is defined as follows: "Any person who creates, alters, or deletes any data contained in any computer or computer network, who, if such person had created, altered, or deleted a tangible document or instrument would have committed forgery...shall be guilty of the crime of computer forgery."[263] At least one state makes it a crime to possess "forgery devices," which include computers, computer

---

257. *See, e.g.,* MINN. STAT. ANN. § 609.89 (West 2000); N.J. REV. STAT. §§ 2C:20-25 & 2C:20-33 (1995); R.I. GEN. LAWS § 11-52-4 (1989).

258. *See, e.g.,* N.J. REV. STAT. § 2C:20-25 (1995); R.I. GEN. LAWS § 11-52-4 (1989).

259. *See, e.g.,* CONN. GEN. STAT. § 53a-251 (1999); DEL. CODE ANN. tit. 11, § 933 (1999); IOWA CODE ANN. § 716A.9 (West 1993); MASS. GEN. LAWS ANN. ch. 266, § 33A (West 2000); N.H. REV. STAT. ANN. § 638:17 (1986); VA. CODE ANN. § 18.2-152.6 (Michie 1985).

260. *See, e.g.,* LA. REV. STAT. ANN. § 14:73.2 (West 1997); MICH. COMP. LAWS § 752.795 (2000); MINN. STAT. ANN. § 609.89 (West 2000); MISS. CODE ANN. §§ 97-45-5 & 97-45-9 (1999); MO. ANN. STAT. §§ 569.095 & 569.097 (Vernon 1999); MONT. CODE ANN. § 45-6-311 (1999); NEB. REV. STAT. § 28-1344 (1991); S.C. CODE ANN. § 16-16-20 (Law. Co-op. 1993); UTAH CODE ANN. § 76-6-703 (1997); VA. CODE ANN. §§ 18.2-152.3, 18.2-152.4 & 18.2-152.6 (Michie 1985).

261. *See, e.g.,* W. VA. CODE § 61-3C-6 (1989).

262. *See, e.g.,* ARK. CODE ANN. § 5-37-227 (Michie 1999); GA. CODE ANN. § 16-9-121 (1999); KAN. STAT. ANN. § 21-4018 (1998); MD. ANN. CODE art. 27, § 231 (1999); MASS. GEN. LAWS ANN. ch. 266, § 37E (West 2000); OKLA. STAT. ANN. tit. 21, § 1533.1 (West 2001); WASH. REV. CODE § 9.35.020 (2000).

263. GA. CODE ANN. § 16-9-121 (1999). *See also* NEV. REV. STAT. § 205.481 (1999); VA. CODE ANN. § 18.2-152.14 (Michie 1985); W. VA. CODE § 61-3C-15 (1989).

equipment and computer software "specifically designed or adapted to such use."[264]

H. Crimes Against Government

Only a few states have make it a crime to use computers to obstruct law enforcement or the provision of government services. Illinois forbids using a computer to cause a "disruption of or interference with vital services or operations of state or local government or a public utility."[265]

Several states make it a crime to use a computer to interrupt or impair the delivery of essential services (e.g., services of a public or private utility, medical services, communication services or government services) or to otherwise endanger public safety.[266]

Some states make it a crime to use a computer to obtain information "with the state or any political subdivision which is by statute required to be kept confidential."[267] West Virginia prohibits the unauthorized accessing of information stored in a computer owned by its state legislature.[268] Rhode Island makes it a crime to use a computer to destroy evidence for the purpose of obstructing an official investigation.[269] Utah makes it an offense to fail to report a computer crime.[270]

V. Conclusion

There are certain notable areas of consistency in substantive cybercrime legislation at both the state and federal levels: the federal system and most, if not all, of the states have adopted legislation specifically outlawing computer "break-ins," either simple unauthorized intrusion ["hacking"] or consequential intrusion ["cracking"]. The other area in which there is a fair degree of consensus is the use of computers to create and disseminate child pornography; the federal system and many states have adopted legislation outlawing this type of activity. It is also interesting to note that the federal

---

264. N.J. STAT. ANN. § 2C:21-1(c) (West 1995).
265. ILL. ANN. STAT. ch. 720, para. 5/16D-4 (Smith-Hurd 1993).
266. *See* NEV. REV. STAT. § 205.4765 (1999); W. VA. CODE § 61-3C-14 (1989); WYO. STAT. § 6-3-501 (1982).
267. NEB. REV. STAT. § 28-1346 (1991); W. VA. CODE § 61-3C-11 (1989).
268. *See* W. VA. CODE § 61-3C- 4 (1989).
269. *See* R.I. GEN. LAWS § 11-52-8 (1994).
270. *See* UTAH CODE ANN. § 76-6-705 (1993).

system and many of the states have taken steps explicitly to outlaw the use of computers to commit fraud; this no doubt reflects the frequency with which instances of online fraud are reported to various agencies.

It is interesting to note the gaps that exist in state and federal cybercrime legislation. The most glaring problem is the lack of laws adequate to address cyberstalking: as was explained earlier, in sections III and IV, laws at the federal level and in many states tend to equate stalking with the making of a threat—a "credible threat" or a "true threat." Unfortunately, cyberstalking can manifest itself in behaviors that do not involve the transmission of a direct threat but that still inflict fear and trauma on its victims. This is an area in which legislative solutions need to be adopted, at both the state and federal levels.

The other omission one immediately notices—especially given all the discussion the phenomenon has received in the media—is the almost total lack of any cyber-terrorism statutes. As section IV notes, only a few states have statutes which make it a crime to use a computer to shut down or impair the delivery of essential public services. At the federal level, there are statutes—such as 18 U.S.C. § 1030, which is discussed in section III—that could be used to prosecute someone who uses a computer to cause injury to citizens and damage to property, but it is interesting to note that computers have yet to be included in the category of "weapons of mass destruction."[271] Hopefully, such legislation will not be needed.

---

271. *See, e.g.,* 18 U.S.C. § 2332a(c)(2) (Supp. IV 1998) (defining "weapon of mass destruction" as including explosive devices, radiation-releasing devices, chemical weapons and biological weapons).

CHAPTER THREE

THE INVESTIGATION AND PROSECUTION OF A CYBERCRIME

IVAN ORTON[*]

I. INTRODUCTION

The deputy prosecutor was in a quandary.[1] The police had executed a search warrant at the home of a plastic surgeon, accused of molesting his female patients while under anesthesia. They were looking for pictures he was alleged to have taken of his victims.

They found a computer at the doctor's home. Although the computer was not specifically listed in the warrant, the items they were searching for could be in the computer (they found a digital camera near the computer). So they searched the computer.

In their search they came across pictures of children in sexually explicit poses. They stopped the search and reported their findings to the deputy prosecutor. "What do we do?" they asked. "Should we get a new

---

[*] Sr. Deputy Prosecuting Attorney, Fraud Division, King County (Seattle), Washington. Member of the bar of Washington.

1. This hypothetical is based loosely on the facts of Washington v. Gregory Johnson, No. 97-1-01564-9 SEA (Wash. Super. Ct., Nov. 3, 1997).

warrant to search for the child pornography? Do we explain what we found on the computer already as part of our probable cause to search the computer?"

The prosecutor was concerned that, notwithstanding the plain view doctrine (which allows items in plain view to be seized if the incriminating nature of the item is immediately apparent and the officer is lawfully located in a position from which he or she can plainly see the item), a warrant based on the child pornography already viewed would be overturned on appeal. "Do you have other evidence of child pornography besides that found in the computer that would justify searching the computer?" he asked.

"Yes," he was told. There were computer printouts of child pornography found at the scene strongly suggesting those images were stored on a computer. "Prepare an affidavit based solely on the information found outside the computer," he instructed, figuring this was the safest course. While he believed the encounter with the computerized child pornography fell within the plain view exception, he felt the safest course would be to present the warrant judge with only the information found outside the computer and justify the search based on that information.

With the new warrant in hand, the police searched the computer for child pornography and found numerous digital images. And so, in addition to the assault charges relating to the actions with the patients, charges of sexual exploitation of a minor were made.

The defense moved to suppress the child pornography evidence from both searches. The trial judge upon learning that the warrant judge had not been advised of the examination of the computer prior to the issuance of the second warrant, suppressed the evidence and the sexual exploitation charges were dismissed. The judge made this decision notwithstanding that the initial discovery of the child pornography was done in the legitimate execution of a valid warrant and that the second warrant was based on facts independent of the child pornography found in the computer.

This case illustrates the difficulties faced by law enforcement in the investigation and prosecution of cybercrimes and crimes where crucial evidence is computerized. Do the laws of real world searches apply to searches of the electronic and virtual world? This chapter explores this issue and related questions that arise during the prosecution of a cybercrime.

II. Acquisition of Evidence

A. What Crimes?

While this book's focus is on cybercrime, the issues raised in this chapter apply to any case where the evidence is contained within a computer. These cases run the gamut from thefts to drugs, from child pornography to homicide.

B. What Computers?

One of the first questions that must be asked is whose computer are we talking about. These fall into three categories:

- The Victim's Computer
- The Suspect's Computer
- The Computers of Third Parties.

It is important to distinguish between computers in this manner because the law distinguishes among them. For example:

- In most circumstances a suspect has no expectation of privacy in evidence found in the victim's computer.[2]
- The Privacy Protection Act,[3] which sets significant limits on searches of publishers (including computer based publishers), does not usually apply when the alleged publisher is a target.
- The Electronic Communications Privacy Act[4] also sets limits on the access to stored electronic communication, but the limits only apply to records stored on third party service providers, not to records on the suspect's computer.
- Searches of the suspect's computer will always be subject to the full scrutiny of the Fourth Amendment and other constitutional protections.

---

2. *See* Washington v. Townsend, No. 99-1-01239-0 (Wash. Super. Ct., Dec. 24, 1999) (Defendant had no privacy right in e-mail and chat messages sent to undercover detective).
3. 42 U.S.C. § 2000aa(a)(1) (1994).
4. 18 U.S.C. § 2701-11 (1994 & Supp. IV 1998).

C. Legal Limits on Searches

Legal limits on searches flow from three sources:

- Constitutional Limits (Federal and State)
- Statutory Limits
- Limits Imposed by Court Rule

The restrictions on searches have different impacts. Searches that violate constitutional protection are likely to be suppressed. Searches that violate court rules may be suppressed or some lesser sanction may be applied. Searches that violate statutory restrictions may be subject to suppression, but more typically, while providing a civil remedy to the aggrieved party, do not provide suppression as a remedy. Each of these limitations will be examined in turn.

1. Constitutional Limits

The Fourth Amendment guarantees protection against unreasonable searches and seizures.[5] The questions to be asked in the Fourth Amendment context are three:

- Does the Fourth Amendment apply to the situation?
- Is there a legal warrant?
- If there is not a legal warrant does the search fall within the exceptions to the warrant requirement?

a. Does the Fourth Amendment Apply to the Situation?

This involves two separate considerations:

- Is there a reasonable expectation of privacy?
- Is government action involved?

(1) Is There a Reasonable Expectation of Privacy?

In determining whether there is a reasonable expectation of privacy in a place searched, courts look at two factors—the subjective expectation of the person asserting a privacy interest and whether society accepts that as

---

5. "The right of the people to be secure in their persons, houses, papers, and effects, against unreasonable searches and seizures, shall not be violated, and no Warrants shall issue, but upon probable cause, supported by Oath or affirmation, and particularly describing the place to be searched, and the persons or things to be seized."

objectively reasonable.⁶ Our courts have consistently ruled that the highest privacy interest is attached to private dwellings.⁷ A computer inside a private dwelling will likely be accorded a similar privacy status.

Expectation of privacy in the contents of a computer is less clear when the computer is not in the home and when the contents of the computer are routinely shared with members of the public.

Is there a diminished expectation of privacy in a laptop computer outside the home? Laptop computers are like automobiles by virtue of their mobility. Should they have the same diminished expectation of privacy as automobiles? Probably not. Laptops are similar to automobiles in their mobility, but dissimilar in the other two ways that courts have used to justify a lower standard for automobiles — subject to government regulation, and the public nature of automobile travel.⁸

Is there a reasonable expectation of privacy by an employee in data stored on a work computer? The answer to that question is fact specific. This topic is discussed in more detail later in this chapter in the section dealing with consent by third parties.

What about situations where the suspect's computer is used as a public bulletin board, or an FTP site that allows public access? Is there a reasonable expectation of privacy in the areas that are open to the public. This is highly unlikely as there would seem not to be a legitimate expectation of privacy on a computer available to the public.⁹

(2) Is Government Action Involved?

The exclusionary rule was not intended and does not apply to the actions of private citizens or foreign law enforcement.¹⁰ Nor, under the "silver platter" doctrine, does it apply to the actions of non forum-state law enforcement officers.

(a) Searches by Non-forum, State Law Enforcement

The silver platter doctrine arose in the early 1900's when federal search and seizure law was more restrictive than state search and

---

6. California v. Greenwood, 486 U.S. 35, 39 (1988).
7. Welsh v. Wisconsin, 466 U.S. 740, 748 (1984).
8. South Dakota v. Opperman, 428 U.S. 364, 367–68 (1976).
9. *Cf.* Maryland v. Macon, 472 U.S. 463, 469 (1985) (discussing the absence of a legitimate expectation of privacy in the books displayed to the public in a bookstore).
10. Burdeau v. McDowell, 256 U.S. 465, 475 (1921); Weeks v. U.S., 232 U.S. 383, 398 (1914).

seizure law, and suppression was a remedy for violation of the federal law. When state law enforcement officers conducted a search legal under state law but illegal under federal law, could the fruits of the search be used in federal courts? The answer was yes, if the federal authorities received the fruits on a silver platter, i.e., they were not so involved in the illegal search as to require suppression.

...

The essential principle underlying the development of this "silver platter" doctrine is that protections afforded by the constitution of a sovereign entity control the actions only of the agents of that sovereign entity.[11]

---

11. New Jersey v. Mollica, 554 A.2d 1315 (N.J. 1989). *Mollica* contains the New Jersey Supreme Court's superb discussion of the history of the silver platter doctrine. *Mollica* involved an FBI investigation of illegal bookmaking being conducted from rooms at Caesar's Palace in Atlantic City, New Jersey. Acting without a warrant the FBI obtained from Caesar's the telephone toll records for the suspect's room for the duration of his stay. The FBI subsequently turned this information over to the New Jersey State Police who used the information to obtain a warrant. Evidence used at trial was discovered during the search. The crucial issues before the New Jersey Supreme Court were whether the seizure of telephone records by the FBI without a warrant was illegal under state law, and if so, whether the products of the state search under a warrant based upon the telephone records should be suppressed.

After concluding that state law prohibited the seizure of toll records without a warrant, the court addressed the second issue. After discussing the history and rationale of the doctrine, court focused on the crucial issue of agency:

> As with the earlier manifestations of the silver platter doctrine, and as seen in the numerous post-*Mapp* [*Mapp v. Ohio*, 367 U.S. 643] examples of interstate transfers of evidence, the salient factor continues to be agency *vel non* between the officers of the respective jurisdictions. The nature of the relationship between the officers participating in the search or seizure and the officers seeking to make use of such evidence is critical.
>
> ...
>
> This case thus requires us to consider the implications of the silver platter doctrine and its key element: intergovernmental agency. An important aspect of this determination is whether for constitutional purposes the federal agents can be said to be acting under the "color of state law." The assessment of the agency issue necessarily requires an examination of the entire relationship between the two sets of government actors no matter how obvious or obscure, plain or subtle, brief or prolonged their interactions may be. The reasons and the motives for making any search must be examined as well as the actions taken by the respective officers and the process used to find, select, and seize the evidence.

Mollica, at 1328–29.

There is no reason why the same principal should not apply to computer searches.[12]

(b) Searches by Private Citizens

The *Mollica* court viewed a transfer from a federal official to a state official as analogous to a transfer from a private citizen to a state official.[13] Searches by private citizens, not acting as the agent of law enforcement, are not entitled to constitutional protection. This view is consistent with numerous federal and state cases.[14] The results of searches of computers by private citizens (not acting as agents of law enforcement) should be admissible.

b. Is There a Legal Warrant?

(1) The Application for the Warrant Must Demonstrate Probable Cause to Believe That Evidence of a Crime Will Be Found in the Place to Be Searched

(a) Evidence of a Crime

The application for the warrant and the warrant itself must state specifically the statute believed to have been violated. This requirement serves as a limit on the search. Courts have held that the failure to state the crime specifically in the warrant itself is fatal, even if the officer executing the warrant knew what crime was being investigated.[15]

---

12. In Washington v. Paris, 76 Wash. App. 1056 (1994) (Unreported decision), a local detective accompanied the U.S. Marshal in the execution of a writ of seizure under the federal Copyright Act. The detective observed, but did not participate in the search. The appellate court reversed the trial court's determination that the detective's mere presence at the search scene made the Marshal his agent, and allowed the evidence under the silver platter doctrine.

13. Mollica, 554 A.2d at 1325, 1328.

14. U.S. v. Gomez, 614 F.2d 643 (9th Cir. 1979); U.S. v. Jennings, 653 F.2d 107 (4th Cir. 1981); U.S. v. Entringer, 532 F.2d 634 (8th Cir.), *cert. denied*, 429 U.S. 820 (1976); U.S. v. Sullivan, 544 F. Supp. 701 (D. Maine 1982), *aff'd*, 711 F.2d 1 (1st Cir. 1983); Oregon v. Blackshear, 511 P.2d 1272 (Or. App. 1973); New Mexico v. Cox, 674 P.2d 1127 (N.M. App. 1983); Wisconsin v. Bembenek, 331 N.W.2d 616 (Wis. App. 1983); New York v. Goodman, 380 N.Y.S.2d 768 (App. Div. 1976); Washington v. Smith, 756 P.2d 722 (Wash. 1988), *cert. denied*, 488 U.S. 1042 (1989).

15. Washington v. Riley, 846 P.2d 1365 (Wash. 1993).

(b) Will Be Found in the Place to Be Searched

The most commonly overlooked element in search warrants that have been presented to me for review is this one. What is the probable cause for believing that evidence of the crime you are investigating will be found in the location you wish to search. This requires articulable facts pointing to the location, not some generic "where else would it be" explanation.

A unique issue arises in the context of computer searches. Assume that you have traced an offending e-mail or computer attack back to a particular Internet Protocol ["IP"] address and through that to a specific Internet Service Provider ["ISP"]. From the service provider you obtain account information about who that IP address was assigned to at the time of the incident in question. The account identifies an individual, a physical address, a telephone number, and other information.

Clearly you have probable cause to believe that evidence of a crime will be found in the computer used to send the offending e-mail or other message. But do you have probable cause to believe that evidence will be found in the suspect's house?

If the account with the ISP is a dial-up account, the account holder can access the Internet via that account from any number of locations. If you are extremely lucky, and the ISP in question uses caller ID, and the caller ID information for the call in which you are interested in is still on the ISP's system, then you may have sufficient information to search the address associated with the phone number identified by the caller ID system.[16] If, on the other hand, the caller is using a wireless connection to the Internet your chances of getting a valid warrant to search the address associated with the ISP, without significant additional information, are slim. Where the IP address is associated with a physical address—a networked computer or a DSL or cable modem connection, for example—the physical relationship between the IP address and the physical location to be searched is more reliable.[17]

---

16. In U.S. v. Grant, 218 F.3d 72 (1st Cir.), *cert. denied*, 121 S. Ct. 596 (2000), the court upheld a search of the defendant's house based on an IP address that was assigned to the defendant's account, but without specific proof that the account was being used from the address that was searched. The court upheld the search even in the face of evidence showing that one of the accesses to the Internet was to a phone number in Virginia, while the defendant lived in Maine.

17. *See* U.S. v. Hay, 231 F.3d 630 (9th Cir. 2000), where the IP address in question was associated with the University of Washington. The University's records showed the IP address was associated with a network port wired to a specific apartment.

In one case with which I was involved, we had traced a suspect to a local ISP. We wanted a warrant to search the suspect's house. But with only the account information from the ISP (a dial-up account), we did not have probable cause to search the suspect's house. The suspect had left copies of sent and read e-mail on the server. We obtained copies of this e-mail. In one message the suspect stated it was after 9:30 (in the morning) and he had to go to class. The police staked out the suspect's house and on several occasions saw him leave his house between 9:30 and 9:45 and drive to a local community college where he was a student.

When the e-mail was coupled with the surveillance results I was satisfied that we now had probable cause to search the suspect's house. We had evidence that the suspect used the e-mail account in question from his home. This was sufficient to make this a valid search.[18]

(2) Signed by a Neutral and Detached Magistrate

The warrant must be signed by a magistrate who has authority to issue the warrant. Obviously the judge must occupy a position that has been property created and has authority to issue warrants.[19] In addition, and more important for Internet crimes and investigations, the judge must have authority to authorize a search of the location covered by the warrant. In some states, local or district court judges only have authority to authorize searches within their district or county. In all states, a judge's authority to authorize searches is limited to the boundaries of that state. A warrant issued by a judge from one state, to search an ISP in another state is beyond that judge's authority. If the defendant had a recognizable privacy interest in the evidence provided under the warrant, the evidence is subject to suppression.[20]

---

18. *See* U.S. v. Kennedy, 81 F. Supp. 2d 1103 (D. Kan. 2000). After identifying the account associated with a particular IP address, the FBI agent called the suspect and asked him if he was satisfied with his Internet service. The suspect confirmed that he accessed the Internet at his home. Although this was a cable modem service with a physical relationship between the IP address and the physical address, this same technique could be used in a dial-up account case.

19. In Washington, a district court commissioner was found to lack the authority to issue search warrants when the office of district court commissioner was not properly created. Washington v. Moore, 871 P.2d 1086 (Wash. App. 1994).

20. California has a statute which requires ISPs located in California to accept subpoenas and warrants from out of state as if they were issued in California. CAL. PENAL CODE § 1524.2 (West 2000). While this requires the California ISP to respond to a non-

(3) Reasonably Precise in Describing the Place to Be Searched and the Items to Be Seized

The first thing to understand under this topic is that a reviewing court will look at the four squares of the warrant itself and will not consider information provided in the affidavit in support of the warrant unless the affidavit is incorporated by reference in the warrant.[21]

Does your warrant need to specifically allow the search of a computer before you can search a computer at the search location? If officers are executing a warrant which does not specifically reference computers, may they search a computer if it could contain the item they are authorized to seize, without an additional warrant? Under existing law the answer is clear that they may search the computer without an additional warrant.[22] Despite this, if you anticipate searching a computer, the better practice is to mention that a computer will be searched in your affidavit. After all, the more general your description of the search is and the broader your intrusion into the suspect's private affairs becomes, the more likely it is that your evidence ultimately will be suppressed. Thus, you should articulate with some detail for what you are looking.[23]

California warrant, it does not make the warrant valid in the issuing state if the warrant is outside the issuing judge's authority.

21. Whether this means you should also leave a copy of the affidavit at the search site along with a copy of the warrant is an open question. U.S. v. Towne, 997 F.2d 537 (9th Cir. 1993), notes the different positions courts have taken on this issue, including: (1) incorporation by reference is by itself sufficient; (2) incorporation is unnecessary if the affidavit was available for the officers executing the warrant to refer to; (3) incorporation is necessary and the incorporated affidavit must accompany the warrant during execution; and (4) the affidavit must be incorporated in and physically attached to the warrant. U.S. v. Hayes, 794 F.2d 1348, 1355 (9th Cir. 1986), *cert. denied*, 479 U.S. 1086 (1987), states the purpose of the accompanying affidavit as both to "limit the officer's discretion and to inform the person subject to the search what items the officers executing the warrant can seize." *See also* Washington v. Riley, 846 P.2d 1365 (Wash. 1993).

22. *See* U.S. v. Ross, 456 U.S. 798 (1982) ("A lawful search of fixed premises generally extends to the entire area in which the object of the search may be found and is not limited by the possibility that separate acts of entry or opening may be required to complete the search..."); U.S. v. Hunter, 13 F. Supp. 2d 574 (D. Vt. 1998) (Upholding a search of computers even though the warrant did not specify computers because the items covered by the warrant could be found in the computer. "A finding of probable cause is not predicated on the government's knowing precisely how certain records are stored.").

23. For example here is an excerpt from a warrant I was involved with:
The computers and magnetic media seized may be searched for: Files spe-

If you know computers will be present, you should include them as items to be searched. But what if you don't know if computers will be present? As discussed, computers do not have to be specifically listed for you to be able to search them provided the items you are authorized to seize could be found in the computer. Despite this, should you, as a routine matter, request permission to search any computers that may be at the search site?

There are two views on this. Including this language over time may create a *de facto* requirement that computers have to be listed or they cannot be searched. In an odd way, requesting permission to search computers on the site when you do not have probable cause to believe that computers are there, may cause the search to be invalidated.[24] On the other hand, failure to include the language may lead to suppression, particularly at the trial court level.[25]

My suggestion is to include language like "including any computers and computer media located therein" in your warrant language describing where you are authorized to search. You still run the risk that judges will come to expect this, but by including a reference to computers and media in general rather than a reference to a specific computer you will diminish the likelihood of a *Nafzger* result.[26]

(4) Knock and Announce

In executing a warrant police are required to knock and announce their purpose. This is both a Fourth Amendment requirement[27] and a statutory

---

cific to the King County Library System, such as references to Dynix, the specific operating system used by the library, files containing library records, etc; Files similar or identical to those stored by Phree on the library computer; Messages and other substantive files referencing Phree, KoBK, the library, the method of access, etc; Files showing Higgins dominion and control over the computer(s) being seized; Files relating to Internet usage and familiarity; Files relating to UNIX familiarity.

24. Examine U.S. v. Nafzger, 965 F.2d 213 (7th Cir. 1992), where the warrant authorized the search of a specific stolen truck. The truck in question was in a tool shed. The police entered the shed and found the truck. The evidence was suppressed because there was "a total failure to show probable cause that the truck described could be found" at the location searched. Requesting a search of a computer when you don't show probable cause to believe a computer will be found at the search site may be subject to the same remedy.

25. See the hypothetical that opens this chapter.
26. *See* U.S. v. Nafzger, 965 F.2d 213 (7th Cir. 1992).
27. Wilson v. Arkansas, 514 U.S. 927 (1995).

requirement in many jurisdictions.[28] The purpose of such a requirement is to reduce the potential for violence to all parties from unannounced entry, prevent unnecessary property damage, and protect the privacy rights of occupants.[29]

The knock and announce requirement can cause difficulty as computer data can be destroyed (or at least made more difficult to recover) in a short period of time. If your jurisdiction allows, you may want to request authorization to execute the warrant without knocking and announcing. You must, of course, justify such a request by the facts of your particular case.

c. Take Items in Plain View

The plain view doctrine has two components. As an exception to the warrant requirement, contraband and instrumentalities may be seized without a warrant if they are in plain view and the incriminating nature of the item is immediately apparent. Related is the principle that while you are executing a warrant for one item you can seize other items in plain view.

This is discussed in more detail below in the discussion of the plain view exception to warrant requirements below.

d. Good Faith

The exclusionary rule does not apply in federal court when evidence is seized in reasonable, good faith, reliance on a search warrant that is later found to be unsupported by probable cause. The rationale behind this is that the deterrent function of the exclusionary rule is not furthered by penalizing an officer who has complied, in good faith with the warrant requirement. The exclusionary rule is, after all, intended to deter police misconduct, not to cure violations of rights.

The test is whether the officers acted in objectively reasonable reliance on what turned out to be an invalid warrant.[30]

The good faith rule has been adopted by some , but not all state courts. It has also been applied in non criminal contexts.[31]

---

28. *See, e.g.*, WASH. REV. CODE § 10.31.040 (1990).
29. Note, *Announcement in Police Entries*, 80 YALE L.J. 139, 140–42 (1970).
30. U.S. v. Leon, 468 U.S. 897 (1984).
31. See the discussion of the Privacy Protection Act and the Electronic Communications Privacy Act below.

e. Take Computers off Premises to Search

Often (and in these days of multi-gigabyte drives, usually) you will need to take a computer off-site to complete the search. So long as this has been justified and requested in the application and approved by the warrant judge, this is generally an accepted practice. As noted by District Court Judge Sessions in *U.S. v. Hunter*, "until technology and law enforcement expertise render on-site computer records searching both possible and practical, wholesale seizures, if adequately safeguarded, must occur."[32]

The more difficult issue is what time limits are there to the off-site search and forensic analysis. These issues are discussed later in this chapter.

f. Prompt Execution

Finally, a warrant, to be valid, must be executed promptly. What is prompt execution? There are two components. First the warrant must be executed while there is still probable cause to believe that evidence of a crime will be found at the place to be searched—before the information provided in support of the warrant becomes stale. This is a constitutional issue.[33]

A related but separate issue is when laws or court rules require a warrant to be executed within a certain amount of time, setting the outer limits on the time a magistrate may set for the execution of the warrant. This is discussed below in the section dealing with court rules and magistrate imposed restrictions.

2. *If There Is Not a Legal Warrant Does the Search Fall Within the Exceptions to the Warrant Requirement?*

There are exceptions to the rule that evidence obtained without a warrant is inadmissible. These are, of course, the "few, specific, established, and well-delineated exceptions" developed under the Fourth Amendment.[34]

A few of these exceptions, like consent, may justify the search of a computer without a warrant, but most do not. The more pertinent exceptions are discussed below.

---

32. 13 F. Supp. 2d 574, 583 (D. Vt. 1998).
33. *See* WAYNE R. LaFAVE, SEARCH AND SEIZURE, § 4.7 at 584–88 (3d. Ed. 1996).
34. Schneckloth v. Bustamonte, 412 U.S. 218, 219 (1973), *citing* Katz v. U.S., 389 U.S. 347, 357 (1967).

a. Consent

If the suspect or other person with authority over the property consents to a search, then a warrant is not required. The key questions are:
- Who has the authority to consent?
- Is the consent given voluntarily and intelligently?
- Is the consent limited?

(1) Who May Consent?

Obviously the suspect may consent to a search of his own premises and effects, subject to such a consent being given voluntarily and intelligently. As for third party consent, the general rule is that one "who possesses common authority over or other sufficient relationship to the premises to effects sought to be inspected" has the authority to consent to a search.[35]

In *United States v. Rith*,[36] the Tenth Circuit stated the *Matlock* test in the disjunctive: A person may give effective consent if they have mutual use of the property by virtue of joint access *or* if they have control of the property for most purposes of it.

The crucial analytical test is whether the defendant has a reasonable expectation of privacy in the premises or effects to which another has consented to be searched. In most instances of shared premises and effects the courts have ruled there is a reduced expectation of privacy in the premises or things shared with another.[37] As the Ninth Circuit stated: "Although there is always the fond hope that a co-occupant will follow one's known wishes, the risks remain. A defendant cannot expect sole exclusionary authority unless he lives alone, or at least has a special and private space within the joint residence."[38] The consent given by a third party may not be valid if the area involved has been set aside, or rented, for the exclusive use of the defendant.[39]

In the computer search context the issue of consent most commonly arises in searches where an employer, a parent, a spouse, or a co-user has

---

35. U.S. v. Matlock, 415 U.S. 164, 171 (1974).
36. 164 F.3d 1323 (10th Cir.), *cert. denied*, 528 U.S. 827 (1999).
37. *E.g.*, U.S. v. Ladell, 127 F.3d 622, 624 (7th Cir. 1997).
38. U.S. v. Morning, 64 F.3d 531, 536 (9th Cir. 1995), *cert. denied*, 516 U.S. 1152 (1996).
39. Washington v. Mathe, 688 P.2d 859 (Wash. 1984).

consented to the search of a computer containing evidence against the suspect. In analyzing consent in the computer context it is important to distinguish valid consent to search a room from valid consent to search a container in that room, such as a computer. The *Matlock* factors must apply to the computer itself, not merely the room containing the computer before consent is effective.[40]

(a) Employer

In *O'Connor v. Ortega*,[41] the Supreme Court held that a government employer may search the files and offices of an employee without consent or a warrant for work-related reasons (to locate a particular document, for example), or to investigate suspected employee wrongdoing.[42] It logically follows that such an employer could also consent to such a search.

But may a non-government employer consent to a search that exceeds these restrictions (searching for work related reasons or to investigate employee malfeasance)? In non-computer cases involving private employers, the courts have consistently held that the employer has the authority to consent to a search of those areas not set aside for exclusive use by a particular employee.[43] If the computer in question belongs to the employer and is provided to the employee for his/her use in work related activities, the employee's reasonable expectation of privacy is significantly reduced. This is particularly true if the employer has announced a policy that the employer may access such computers at any time.

On the other hand, if the employer explicitly allows (or tolerates) use of such a computer for private purposes and the employee sets aside a separate area of the computer for her/his private files, the question is much closer. If the employee encrypts those files or otherwise restricts access to

---

40. "While authority to consent to search of a general area must obviously extend to most objects in plain view within the area, it cannot be thought automatically to extend to the interiors of every discrete enclosed space capable of search within the area." U.S. v. Block, 590 F.2d 535, 541 (4th Cir. 1978) (While search of the room by consent was okay, search of a footlocker was not.).
41. 480 U.S. 709 (1987).
42. For a computer specific case, where a supervisor's seizure of a computer disk containing work related and personal files was upheld, *see* Williams v. Philadelphia Housing Authority, 826 F. Supp. 952 (E.D. Pa. 1993), *aff'd mem.*, 27 F.3d 560 (3d Cir. 1994).
43. U.S. v. Gargiso, 456 F.2d 584 (2d Cir. 1972).

them, the expectation of privacy is higher still. But the rules are still unclear in this developing area of law.[44]

(b) Parent

Courts generally find third-party consents easier to sustain "if the relationship between the parties—parent to child here, spouse to spouse in other cases—is especially close."[45]

In the computer context, the more the computer is a shared item, both in terms of use and location, the more likely it is that a parent can give a valid consent. Even when the computer belongs to the child or is used by them exclusively and is located in their room or private space, parents can generally consent to a search of such a computer so long as the child is "essentially dependent" on the parent. If the child pays rent or in other ways is independent of the parent, the parent may lack the authority to give valid consent to a search of the child's effects or private space.[46]

(c) Spouse

Spouses are generally considered to have joint control and equal right to occupancy of the premises and access to computers on the premises, and so may give a valid consent.

If the computer is used exclusively by the non-consenting spouse and is kept in a separate room (especially if locked), the other spouse may not be able to give valid consent.

(d) Co-user

A co-user of a computer is much like a co-tenant and should be analyzed the same way. Generally, allowing co-use results in a greatly reduced expectation of privacy. Whether password restricted or encrypted areas are the equivalent of locked bedrooms and thus not subject to a consent search by a co-user is an as yet undecided issue. Until you learn otherwise, however, I would assume that a co-user can *not* give consent to search such objectively private areas of a computer.

---

44. *See generally* WAYNE R. LAFAVE, SEARCH AND SEIZURE, § 8.6(f) (3d. Ed. 1996).
45. U.S. v. Ladell, 127 F.3d 622, 624 (7th Cir. 1997).
46. U.S. v. Rith, 164 F.3d 1323 (10th Cir.), *cert. denied*, 528 U.S. 827 (1999).

(2) Must the Consentor Be Advised of His/Her Right to Withhold Consent

The general rule is that the voluntariness of a consent to search is measured by the "totality of the circumstances."[47] In the Federal system, the burden is on the government to prove voluntariness of consent by "preponderance of the evidence."[48] In other jurisdictions, like Washington state, a higher standard is required. Consent must be proved by "clear and convincing evidence" from the totality of the circumstances.[49]

Factors to be considered in determining the voluntariness of consent include:

- The age of the suspect
- The level of intelligence of the suspect
- Whether the suspect was advised of her/his constitutional rights
- Whether the suspect was in custody, or detention, and the length
- Whether physical punishment was inflicted, including denying sleep or food.

None of these factors by themselves are dispositive, but some may be more important than others. "Although the Constitution does not require proof of knowledge of a right to refuse as the *sine qua non* of an effective consent to a search, such knowledge was highly relevant to the determination that there had been consent."[50]

Sometimes an officer will tell a defendant that she/he will ask for a search warrant if consent is not given. Most courts consider that such a scenario does not constitute coercion and consent in such circumstances is valid.[51]

In some jurisdictions there are additional limitations on consent searches when the police have gone to the to-be-searched house on a "knock and talk" mission.[52] In Washington, to be effective, consent obtained as a result

---

47. Schneckloth v. Bustamonte, 412 U.S. 218 (1968).
48. U.S. v. Matlock, 415 U.S. 164 (1974); U.S. v. Mendenhall, 446 U.S. 544 (1980).
49. Washington v. Werth, 571 P.2d 941 (Wash. App. 1977), *review denied*, 90 Wash. 2d 1010 (1978).
50. U.S. v. Mendenhall, 446 U.S. 544, 558–59 (1980).
51. Washington v. Smith, 801 P.2d 975 (Wash. 1990).
52. "Knock and talk" is generally understood to mean situations where the police go to a suspect's house without a warrant in an attempt to get the suspect to voluntarily talk to the police and/or consent to a search.

of a knock and talk must be preceded by advising the consentor that they need not consent to the entry/search.[53]

(3) Consent May Be Limited and May Be Withdrawn

Consent may be limited and may be withdrawn. A search of areas for which consent was not given or after consent is withdrawn is invalid.[54]

Some court have held searches invalid when the officers, acting under general consent, broke open locked or sealed containers.[55] Is a search of hidden, password protected or encrypted files under a general consent to search a computer open to the same attack? To the extent that analogy to the physical world is applicable, the answer is probably no. The line of cases represented by *Wells*, focus on the destruction of property necessary to open the sealed or locked container. Since there is no comparable destruction in accessing hidden, password protected or encrypted files, the search may be upheld.

One factor that influences courts in determining the scope of a consent is whether the person who gave the consent was told of the focus of the search. If so, then containers that could contain the focus can be searched under consent.[56] If consent is given when no focus is delineated, courts interpret the consent more generally.[57]

b. Search Incident to Arrest

"When an arrest is made, officers are allowed to search the person arrested for any weapons or for any evidence on the arrestee's person in order to prevent its concealment or destruction. The officer may also search areas within the arrestee's immediate control for the same purpose."[58] This doctrine would allow an officer to look for computers or computer evidence within the arrestee's immediate control but would not allow them to further search the computers without other legal justification.

---

53. Washington v. Ferrier, 960 P.2d 927 (Wash. 1998). *See also* New Jersey v. Johnson, 346 A.2d 66, 68 (N.J. 1975).

54. *See* Model Code of Pre-Arraignment Procedure § SS 240.3 (1975) (a consent search "shall not exceed, in duration or physical scope, the limits of the consent given"); Mason v. Pulliam, 557 F.2d 426 (5th Cir. 1977).

55. Florida v. Wells, 539 So.2d 464 (Fla. 1989), *aff'd*, 495 U.S. 1 (1990).

56. Florida v. Jimeno, 500 U.S. 248 (1991).

57. U.S. v. Snow, 44 F.3d 133 (2d Cir. 1995).

58. Chimel v. California, 395 U.S. 752, 762–63 (1969).

c. Exigent Circumstances

The exigent circumstances exception allows a warrantless search of premises where the officer has probable cause and exigent circumstances exist. The determination of whether exigent circumstances exist includes an examination of many factors.[59]

Analysis of exigent circumstances in computer based evidence cases will likely follow how such circumstances are analyzed in narcotics cases where there is a belief that contraband is being destroyed.

> We have long recognized that the imminent destruction of evidence may constitute an exigency excusing the failure to procure a warrant. This risk is particularly weighty where narcotics are involved, for it is commonly known that narcotics can be easily and quickly destroyed.... We held that a police officer can show an objectively reasonable belief that contraband is being, or will be, destroyed within a home if he can show 1) a reasonable belief that third persons are inside a private dwelling, and 2) a reasonable belief that these third persons are aware of an investigatory stop or arrest of a confederate outside the premises, so that they might see a need to destroy evidence.[60]

---

59. *See* U.S. v. Brown, 52 F.3d 415, 421 (2d Cir. 1995), *cert. denied*, 516 U.S. 1068 (1996) ("Our court has looked to six touchstones for determining the existence of exigent circumstances. Those are: '(1) the gravity or violent nature of the offense with which the suspect is to be charged; (2) whether the suspect is reasonably believed to be armed; (3) a clear showing of probable cause...to believe that the suspect committed the crime; (4) strong reason to believe that the suspect is in the premises being entered; (5) a likelihood that the suspect will escape if not swiftly apprehended; and (6) the peaceful circumstances of the entry.' Those factors are 'merely illustrative, not exhaustive, and the presence or absence of any one factor is not conclusive.'" (citations omitted)).

U.S. v. Rico, 51 F.3d 495, 501 (5th Cir.), *cert. denied*, 516 U.S. 883 (1995) ("In evaluating whether exigent circumstances existed, we have found relevant the following factors: (1) the degree of urgency involved and amount of time necessary to obtain a warrant; (2) [the] reasonable belief that contraband is about to be removed; (3) the possibility of danger to the police officers guarding the site of contraband while a search warrant is sought; (4) information indicating the possessors of the contraband are aware that the police are on their trail; and (5) the ready destructibility of the contraband and the knowledge 'that efforts to dispose of narcotics and to escape are characteristic behavior of persons engaged in the narcotics traffic.'" (citations omitted)) .

60. U.S. v. Dawkins, 17 F.3d 399, 405 (D.C. Cir. 1994).

In the context of computer searches, the important thing to understand about this exception is, like a search incident to arrest, it does not justify a search of computer. It might allow for a search for and seizure of a computer to preserve evidence under the right facts, but a separate legal justification to search the computer must be provided.

d. Inventory

While inventory searches are generally thought of as searches of vehicles, one type of an inventory search that might apply to computers is a booking search.[61]

While such a search, like a search incident to arrest or an exigent circumstances search, is probably limited to removing a computer (such as a laptop or other portable computing device) from a suspect's person as opposed to searching the computer itself, in some circumstances a search of the computer to ascertain or verify a defendant's identity may be appropriate.[62]

e. Stop and Frisk

"[A] law enforcement officer, for his own protection and safety, may conduct a pat-down to find weapons that he reasonably believes or suspects are then in the possession of the person he has accosted."[63] While any computing device found during such a frisk which is contraband may be seized, this exception to the warrant requirement is generally not applicable to computer based evidence search cases.

f. Mobility

An officer with probable cause to search a vehicle he/she has lawfully stopped, may conduct such a search without a warrant because the automobile's ready mobility constitutes an exigency sufficient to excuse failure to obtain a search warrant.[64] There may be a case where probable cause exists to search a vehicle for an item which could be found in a computer, thus allowing a warrantless search of a computer under this doctrine but

---

61. *See generally* Illinois v. Lafayette, 462 U.S. 640, 648 (1983); U.S. v. Thomas, 11 F.3d 620, 628 (6th Cir. 1993), *cert. denied*, 511 U.S. 1043 (1994).
62. *See* Illinois v. Lafayette, 462 U.S. at 646 (Discussion of inventory searches in general).
63. Ybarra v. Illinois, 444 U.S. 85, 93 (1979).
64. LaBron v. Kilgore, 518 U.S. 938, 940 (1996).

there are no reported decisions involving such a case. As stated earlier, there is little likelihood that a laptop computer could be searched without a warrant under this justification.

g. Plain View

> The rationale of the plain view doctrine is that if contraband is left in open view and is observed by a police officer from a lawful vantage point, there has been no invasion of a legitimate expectation of privacy and thus no search within the meaning of the Fourth Amendment—or at least no search independent of the initial intrusion that gave the officers their vantage point.[65]

This exception has three rules when applied in the computer evidence search context:

- The incriminating nature of the item in plain view must be immediately apparent
- The officer must be lawfully located in a position from which he or she can plainly see the item
- The officer must not change the focus of her/his search as a result of discovering the plain view item.

The first two of these rules come from the development of the plain view doctrine in the non-computer context.[66] The third comes from the unique aspects of a search for computerized evidence.

For example, if a search protocol calls for examining all files sequentially on a computer, then every file may be examined.[67] If incriminating evidence outside the scope of the warrant is observed in one file (such as child pornography) and then, still following the search protocol, other files are examined which also contain incriminating evidence outside the scope of the warrant, all qualify as plain view evidence.

On the other hand, however, if the search is for records of business transactions and the search protocol calls for a key word search and an examination of the directory and file structure, but not the examination of each

---

65. Minnesota v. Dickerson, 508 U.S. 355, 375 (1993).
66. U.S. v. Bradshaw, 102 F.3d 204, 211 (6th Cir. 1996), *cert. denied*, 520 U.S. 1178 (1997).
67. This and subsequent examples assume the officer has a valid warrant allowing her/him to be at the location, with the object they are authorized to seize being such that it could be found in a computer.

individual file, then the discovery of a possibly incriminating file name ("babyfuk.jpg," for example) does not justify the opening of that file. Furthermore the discovery of child pornography, in plain view and outside the scope of the warrant, does not justify a change in the search protocol or search focus.[68]

With a solid search protocol, the police can follow that protocol, even if they discover incriminating evidence outside the scope of the warrant, and be confident that the evidence will be admissible. Without such a protocol, or if the new evidence creates the need to go outside the protocol, the best practice when outside-the-scope-of-the-warrant evidence is discovered is to stop the search and get a new warrant based on the plain view evidence discovered.

3. State Constitutional Considerations

Some states' constitutions are more restrictive or have been interpreted in a more restrictive manner than the federal constitution. Many states do not allow a good faith exception to the requirements of a valid warrant. Some states provide more protection to occupants of vehicles and the vehicles themselves than do the federal courts. Obviously any consideration of whether a search of a computer is allowed must take the constitutional requirements of the forum state into account.

D. Statutes

1. Privacy Protection Act

The Privacy Protection Act[69] ["PPA"], was passed in response to *Zurcher v. Stanford Daily*.[70] In that case officers executed a search warrant at the of-

---

68. U.S. v. Carey, 172 F.3d 1268 (10th Cir. 1999). The defendant, who was under investigation for narcotics violations, consented to a search of his apartment. Two computers were seized and a warrant was issued allowing the computers to be searched for information relating to the sale and distribution of controlled substances. In conducting this search of the computer the police discovered child pornography. The officer testified that while he did not originally believe the jpg files he examined contained child pornography, after he saw the first one he had probable cause to believe the others contained child pornography. He continued to examine the jpg files, finding more child pornography. He did this examination on another computer because the files could not be viewed on the suspect's computer. The court interpreted this continued examination of the jpg files as an expansion of the scope of the search to include items outside the warrant's parameters.
69. 42 U.S.C. §2000aa (1994).
70. 436 U.S. 547 (1978).

fices of the Stanford Daily, a student newspaper, to search for pictures of a demonstration. The newspaper and some of its staff brought a 42 U.S.C. § 1983 action against the officer who conducted the search and others. The Supreme Court, in *Zurcher*, held that other than applying warrant requirements with particular exactitude, there were no limitations on warranted searches where First Amendment interests are involved.

The PPA, imposed limitations based on First Amendment concerns. It prohibits searches and seizures of material that an individual intends to publish or broadcast and "documentary material" possessed by a person in connection with a purpose to publish or broadcast the material. Such material must be obtained by subpoena.

There are exceptions:

- The law does not apply to material that constitutes contraband, fruits of a crime, or property designed or used to commit a crime
- It does not apply to searches and seizures needed to prevent imminent death or injury
- It does not apply when the material is possessed by the target of the investigation[71]
- It does not apply to child pornography.

In addition, for "documentary material," the law does not apply if there is a reason to believe that the possessor of the material would destroy, alter or conceal the evidence if a subpoena was issued, or if there is a finding that the materials have not been produced as directed under a subpoena and further delays would threaten the interests of justice. Further, the act only applies when there is a reasonable belief of the subject's intent to publish the material.

Most law enforcement professionals who did computer searches were unaware of this act until the Steve Jackson Games case. In March, 1990, Secret Service agents executed a search warrant at the offices of Steve Jackson Games, Inc. ["SJG"], searching for a computerized text file containing information about Bell South's emergency call system. SJG published books, magazines, role-playing games and other related products. SJG also hosted an electronic bulletin board system which, among other things, allowed customers to send and receive private e-mail. Among the items seized in the

---

71. In an exception to the exception, this exception does not apply when the alleged crime is the receipt, communication, or withholding of such evidence unless the material relates to national defense/is classified.

search was the computer which operated the Bulletin Board System. There were 162 items of unread, private e-mail on this system.

In 1991 SJG filed suit[72] against the Secret Service claiming violations of the Privacy Protection Act and the Electronic Communications Privacy Act (discussed in the following section.) The trial court held that the Secret Service violated the PPA and awarded damages of $51,040. The court also found a violation of the ECPA and awarded statutory damages of $1,000 to each individual plaintiff. It also awarded SJG over $250,000 in attorney fees and costs.

The court found that although the Secret Service may not have known that SJG was a publisher at the time of execution of the warrant, they were aware of this by the day after the execution of the warrant. Although SJG asked for the prompt return of the material seized, and, the court found, the material could have been copied and returned "within a period of hours and not more than eight days," the material was not returned for several months. It was the failure to return the seized property that exposed the Secret Service to liability.

The decision makes several things clear. First, a computer "publisher" is protected under the PPA. Second, even if there is no knowledge of publisher status at the time a search is executed, if the seized material shows publisher status, the seizing agents may be liable for their actions following their presumed acquisition of knowledge of publisher status. Finally, SJG was not itself a target in the investigation. Had the company been the target, the results might have been different.

The decision also makes it clear that a lack of familiarity with the Privacy Protection Act can be costly.

The most important point about the PPA that can be made in a summary discussion such as this one is that the Act applies almost exclusively to third party search situations. When you seek to search your target's computer you are usually (but not always) outside the parameters of the PPA.

a. Suppression

A violation of the Privacy Protection Act is not a basis for suppressing the evidence obtained. "[E]vidence otherwise admissible in a proceeding shall not be excluded on the basis of a violation of this chapter."[73]

---

72. Steve Jackson Games, Inc. v. U.S. Secret Service, 816 F. Supp. 432 (W.D. Tex. 1993), aff'd, 36 F.3d 457 (5th Cir. 1994).

73. 42 U.S.C. § 2000aa-6 (1994). In *Oklahoma ex rel. Macy v. One Pioneer CD-Rom Changer*, 891 P.2d 600 (Okla. Ct. App. 1994) (*cert. denied*, Feb. 15, 1995), the state sought

b. Civil liability

Civil liability can result from a violation of the Privacy Protection Act. The PPA states that an aggrieved person has a cause of action:

(1) against the United States, against a State which has waived its sovereign immunity under the Constitution to a claim for damages resulting from a violation of this chapter, or against any other governmental unit, all of which shall be liable for violations of this chapter by their officers or employees while acting within the scope or under color of their office or employment; and

(2) against an officer or employee of a State who has violated this chapter while acting within the scope of or under color of his office or employment, if such State has not waived its sovereign immunity as provided in paragraph (1).[74]

It was this provision that provided the legal basis for the liability found in the *Steve Jackson Games* case discussed above.[75]

c. Good Faith

Good faith reliance on an otherwise valid search warrant is a defense against civil liability under the PPA. In *Davis v. Gracey*,[76] the plaintiff sued law enforcement officers and entities involved in a search and seizure of a computer system involved in the distribution of pornography. The plaintiff contended the police seized materials which the defendant intended to publish on a CD, thus violating the PPA. The district court granted summary judgment to the defendants, holding that the defendants were entitled to the good faith defense of 42 U.S.C. § 2000aa-b(b) because the police had acted in reliance on a valid warrant.[77]

---

to forfeit computer equipment used in the distribution of pornography. The system owner claimed a violation of the PPA because the material seized contained non-offending material that was intended for publication on CDs. The court rejected this defense, noting that even if the PPA had been violated, this did not preclude a forfeiture so long as the equipment was seized pursuant to an otherwise lawful search and seizure.

74. 42 U.S.C. § 2000aa-6(a) (1994).
75. Liability was also found under the ECPA, discussed below.
76. 111 F.3d 1472 (10th Cir. 1997).
77. On appeal, the Tenth Circuit dismissed the suit because of an absence of subject matter jurisdiction. All of the entities had been previously dismissed leaving only the individual officers. The Court held that the PPA only allowed actions against governmental entities unless the state had not waived sovereign immunity. Since Oklahoma

2. Electronic Communications Privacy Act

The Electronic Communications Privacy Act ["ECPA"] updated the wiretap statute[78] and added the Stored Electronic Communications Act ["SECA"].[79] Although it is common to reference ECPA in discussing limitations on computer searches, most often it is the specific provisions of SECA that are in play.[80]

a. What Does the ECPA Cover?

The act covers the contents of electronic communications while in electronic storage by an "electronic communications service." An electronic communications service is "any service which provides to the users thereof the ability to send or receive wire or electronic communications."[81] The act also covers the contents of electronic communications in a "remote computing service." A remote computing service is on that provides "to the public...computer storage or processing service by means of an electronic communications system."[82]

b. What Does the ECPA Prohibit?

The act prohibits providers of electronic communication service or remote computing service from disclosing contents of electronic communications or customer records and transactional data to the government, except as provided.

c. When Is a Disclosure to the Government Allowed?

(1) Subscriber or Customer Records

Subscriber or customer records (name, address, telephone toll billing records, telephone number or other subscriber number or identity, and length and type of service for a subscriber or customer) may be obtained by subpoena, warrant or court order. Other subscriber/customer records,

---

had waived immunity, only the government, not the individual officers could be sued. *Id.*

78. 18 U.S.C. §§ 2510–22, (1994 & Supp. IV 1998).
79. *Id.* §§ 2701–11.
80. Keystroke monitoring/real-time monitoring of electronic communications is covered by the wiretap statute, *Id.* § 2511(1).
81. *Id.* § 2510(15) (1994).
82. *Id.* § 2711(2).

such as transaction history, IP logs, etc., may be obtained only by warrant or court order.

(2) Contents of Electronic Communications

In general, the contents of an electronic communication may be disclosed with the consent of any party to the communication. The consent of all of the parties to the communication is not needed — only one party need consent.

A government entity can compel the production of the contents of stored electronic communications by warrant. For communications in storage for more than 180 days these can be obtained by subpoena.[83]

d. What Is the Remedy for Violation of this Act?

(1) Criminal Liability

The ECPA provides for criminal liability for one who "(1) intentionally accesses without authorization a facility through which an electronic communication service is provided; or (2) intentionally exceeds an authorization to access that facility; and thereby obtains, alters, or prevents authorized access to a wire or electronic communication while it is in electronic storage in such system."[84] Punishment can be up to two years imprisonment.

(2) Civil Liability

The act creates a civil cause of action for violations, including damages and attorney's fees with punitive damages if the violation was willful. Although one decision held that only the service provider, not the government, was civilly liable for violations[85] a later decision found liability in the government official who obtained the information.[86] The different outcomes in these two cases may be explained by the different sections of the ECPA under which the plaintiffs sued. In *Tucker*, where the plaintiff sued under 18 U.S.C. § 2703(c) (which imposes limits on service providers), the court found no liability on the behalf of the government. In *McVeigh*, where

---

83. There are some differences between a provider of electronic communications services and a provider of remote computing service.
84. 18 U.S.C. §§ 2701(a)(1) & (2) (1994).
85. Tucker v. Waddell, 83 F.3d 688 (4th Cir. 1996).
86. McVeigh v. Cohen, 983 F. Supp. 215 (D.D.C. 1998).

the plaintiff also sued under 18 U.S.C. § 2703(a) and (b) (which impose limits on the government), the court found government liability.

(3) Suppression

Suppression is not a remedy for non-constitutional violations of ECPA.[87]

(4) Good Faith

§ 2707(e) of the ECPA states that "reliance on...a court warrant or order, a grand jury subpoena, a legislative authorization, or a statutory authorization...is a complete defense to any civil or criminal action brought under this chapter."

This provision was used by the Tenth Circuit in *Davis v. Gracey*,[88] to reject the defendants' civil claim under ECPA. The court noted that because the officers relied on a warrant supported by probable cause they were entitled to a "good faith" defense.[89]

E. Court Rules and Magistrate Imposed Restrictions

1. Court Rules—Time Within Which Search Must Be Completed

Some jurisdictions have statutes or court rules that require a search warrant to be executed within a specified period of time after it was issued. Some courts hold a violation of such statutes or court rules to require suppression.[90] Other courts have held that absent a Fourth Amendment violation (i.e., probable cause still existed when the warrant was executed) suppression is not appropriate even when the statute or court rule time limit was exceeded.[91]

In the context of computer searches the more problematic issue relates to the off-site search of a computer following the execution of the warrant. It is important to understand that even if your application justifies, and the warrant approves, an off-site search of a computer, the off-site search of the

---

87. 18 U.S.C. § 2708 (1994).
88. 111 F.3d 1472 (10th Cir. 1997).
89. *Id.* at 1484.
90. Sgro v. U.S., 287 U.S. 206 (1932) (holding a warrant void under the federal National Prohibition Act, 27 U.S.C. § 39 (repealed)).
91. U.S. v. Gerber, 994 F.2d 1556 (11th Cir. 1993).

computer must be done within the same time limits set for the search of the premises where the computer was located.

If a computer is contraband or an instrumentality, it may be seized. If it is a container of evidence it may be "seized" solely for the purpose of searching it off-site. There is no other legal basis for retaining the computer. Thus, if the warrant sets a three day deadline on the execution of the warrant, and the computer is not searched within that three day period, arguably there is no longer any justification for police to hold the computer and there is no authority for a search outside that three day period.

Even if the issuing judge is willing to allow additional time to search a computer off-site, the court rules discussed earlier may be an absolute limit on the judge's authority to extend that time.

Some argue that the justification for magistrate imposed and statute/rule imposed deadlines is to insure that a warrant will be executed before the information on which it is based becomes stale. Since the computer was seized during the required time, and since the information in that computer will not change between that seizure and the ultimate search of the computer, there is no staleness issue. This is a fine argument in principle and may be successful in many cases. If, however, you have a court that considers the magistrate/statute/rule deadline to be absolute, then this argument may not be successful.

What I advise the police to do is to make some search of the computer within the prescribed time sufficient to identify some contraband on the computer. Once that is done you are no longer holding the computer solely as a container which might contain evidence and which you will search in the future. You are now holding the computer as a container of actual, identified contraband. Any subsequent review of the computer will be separating the wheat from the chaff—separating the contraband from non-contraband. If you do not find contraband within that time period your choices are to request an extension (which may not be effective if your statute or court rule sets a maximum limit) or, if you continue to have probable cause, request a new warrant.

Both of these arguments are stopgap measures until some change is made that recognizes the reality of the length of time it takes to search multi-gigabyte drives.

2. *Magistrate Imposed Restrictions*

The magistrate issuing the warrant may impose deadlines for the search of computers seized during the execution of the warrant that are different from the date by which the warrant itself must be executed. If those deadlines are not complied, with the evidence may be suppressed. In *United States v. Brunnette*,[92] the warrant was approved on February 4 and executed on February 9, within the time set by the warrant. The government requested 30 days to examine the computer seized in the warrant, and subsequently requested a 30 day extension. The magistrate granted both requests. Notwithstanding this deadline of April 8 to examine the computer, the search of the computer was not started until April 10. Finding no good reason for this delay, the court suppressed the evidence from the search of the computer.

III. Analysis of Evidence

A. At the Search Location

It is beyond the scope of this chapter to discuss all of the details of what should be done at the search location. Other sources should be referenced for this information.[93] I will touch on a few legal issues, however.

1. Who Should Accompany the Officers Executing the Search?
a. Should an Expert Accompany the Officers?

At the federal level 18 U.S.C. § 3105 precludes anyone other than the officer being present at the search except for a person "in aid of the officer." The statute has been interpreted to allow experts, specifically provided for in the warrant, to accompany and participate in the search.[94] Many states have similar provisions.

This suggests that any time the presence of an expert will be useful (and an expert is available, of course), you should justify and request that the expert be allowed to accompany the officers and participate in the search.

---

92. 76 F. Supp. 2d 30 (D. Me. 1999).

93. *E.g.*, Kenneth Rosenblatt, High-Technology Crime, Investigating Cases Involving Computers (KSK Publications 1995); Franklin Clark & Kin Diliberto, Investigating Computer Crime (CRC Press 1996), http://www.ustreas.gov/usss/index.htm?electronic_evidence.htm&1.

94. U.S. v. Schwimmer, 692 F. Supp. 119 (E.D.N.Y. 1988).

b. Should a Representative of the Victim Accompany the Officers? But What If the Only Expert Is a Representative of the Victim?

Justifying the presence of an independent expert is merely a matter of explaining why an expert's assistance is needed. Justifying the presence of a representative of the victim is a more difficult task, and, even if approved in the warrant, the presence of a victim representative always creates a credibility issue.

The strongest argument in favor of having a victim representative present is that they can quickly identify specific items covered by the warrant and thus minimize the intrusion and inconvenience to the suspect. (Of course, the victim representative's unique familiarity and ability to recognize offending material is also the reason why their presence is particularly invasive.)

If you do request the presence of a victim representative, you must explain why only that person or other victim representative can do the identification necessary. You should stress that the person's ability to recognize offending evidence on sight will likely reduce the extent and time of the search.

The officers should be advised that notwithstanding this permission, they are the ones conducting the search, not the victim. To the extent possible the role of the victim representative should be clearly delineated in the application.

The problems associated with allowing a victim to accompany warrant executing officers is illustrated by a recent case in King County Washington, *In re U.S. Computer Corporation*.[95] In that case the trial judge discussed some of these problems:

> With the determinative issues before the court now fully resolved, any further discussion of the issues raised is certainly *dicta*. Fully aware of the shortcomings and limited value of *dicta*, this court would nonetheless feel remiss in its duties if it did not take this opportunity to give voice to its strong misgivings about the execution of the search warrant it signed on August 6, 1998.
>
> That warrant was a court order directed to "any peace officer in the state of Washington." A "peace officer" is "a duly appointed city, county or state law enforcement officer." RCW 9A.04.110(15).

---

95. No. 98-118 (Jun. 23, 2000).

The notion of peace officers as public servants has been with us for some time and deliberately so. In Great Britain, the harsh lessons learned from a system of private law enforcement are said to have led to Sir Robert Peel's creation of the first salaried, full-time police force in 1829.

In this country as well, frontier justice, vigilantism, and lynchings live in our history as sad reminders of the need for organized society to always provide adequate, public law enforcement. Accountable to the full citizenry from which its powers derive, a police agency knows it must scrupulously follow the procedural dictates of the law. Extensive training is now given to police officers (at the expense of the public they will serve) and a good officer who does not cut corners is said to do things "by the book."

Where private law enforcement is involved, there is no "book" but only loose pages. While many of these pages may spring to mind, one apt example is this verse from the Woody Guthrie song "Buffalo Skinners" describing the approach of some earlier westerners who felt cheated in their business dealings:

Well, those cowboys never had heard
Such a thing as a bankrupt law;
So we left that drover's bones to bleach
On the plains of the buffalo.

It is without question that private entities should be encouraged to support public law enforcement through a variety of means. The insurance industry does so in valuable ways and various reward programs have been quite successful. Private entities' financial support for a law enforcement effort is not, by itself, tantamount to private entities seeking to perform the law enforcement function.

What is called for, it would seem, is that this public/private relationship remain somewhat at arm's length. Some distance is essential both to the police agency's ability to maintain its loyalty solely to the broad public and also to that public's confidence that such is the case. Although it may sound Pollyannaish, the theory is that the police officer works at once for the suspect as well as the victim. A private security officer serves but one master.

If, for example, company "A" were to suspect itself to be being victimized by company "B" through illegal means, it would logically be motivated by a strong desire to gather confirmation. One approach would be to file a civil lawsuit and utilize the discovery process in hopes of gaining information. A second alternative would be for A's security personnel to travel to B's headquarters and announce "We'd like to come in and poke around a little bit and also ask your employees a few questions about your illegal activities."

The first alternative is slow and laborious and subject to obstructionism. The second is laughable in its chances of success; acting on their own, the security personnel would never get across the rival's threshold.

In this case, it was entirely appropriate for Hewlett-Packard security personnel to accompany law enforcement officials as they (the law enforcement officials) served this court's warrant to search USCC. A role for the "victim" in helping to identify stolen property for which there is probable cause to search, was contemplated by this court and is fully consistent with established law. *See, e.g., Wilson v. Layne*, 526 U.S. 603 (1999).

The role played by such a citizen participant in the service of a search warrant must be narrowly circumscribed. To the extent that his role is expressly or impliedly authorized in the warrant, he is acting under color of state law. Any actions beyond that, however, constitute "a frolic of his own" and cannot be countenanced.

In the service of this search warrant, the role for citizen participants that was impliedly authorized was to aid in identifying stolen memory modules bearing fictitious or no serial numbers. Actions beyond that were not authorized.

When private citizens necessarily accompany law enforcement personnel on the execution of a search warrant, it must be expected that the police officers—familiar with the requirements of the law—will ensure that the civilians do not engage in any unlawful conduct. It may very well be that the close relationship (financial and otherwise) between the entities involved in this search provides some explanation for the blurring of what should have been more clearly defined roles.[96]

2. *What Can Be Seized*[97]

So long as you have a valid basis for an off-site search, storage devices which could contain the evidence you are authorized to seize may them-

---

96. *Id.* at 8–11 (Search Warrant).
97. This discussion is limited to situations where you are seizing computers as containers of evidence.

selves be seized for searching off-site. But what about all the other computer "stuff" at the search location? Can you seize the CPU box (as opposed to removing the hard drives from the box)? The monitor? Printers? Cables and cords? Manuals?

The general rule is that you can request and seize those items necessary to achieve the core purpose of your search. If you seize floppies for searching offsite, then you may request permission to and seize floppy drives. The same rationale applies to other storage media that require particular devices to be useable — tape drives for tapes, DVD or CD players for DVD or CD media, etc.

A hard drive contains both the media and the device to read the information. May you nevertheless seize the CPU box and its contents — cards, memory, cables, etc? I am not aware of any decisions answering this question, but my answer is yes.

On one level you can seize the box and its contents to show that the defendant had an operating computer, a computer capable of connecting to the Internet, a computer capable of displaying a certain quality of video image, etc. On a more fundamental level, you do not search a hard drive by examining it with a magnifying glass. You search it by having it connected to an operating computer system, including a monitor. While you can search the drive by removing it from the suspect's system and inserting it into another system you are not required to do this. So long as you can justify why an object is necessary to achieve the core purpose of your search you can seize that object. Manuals and other instructional material, and cables and cords connected to the computer would also be covered by this rationale.

Can printers, scanners, digital cameras, and other peripheral devices be taken? The answer is less clear. If you have an incriminating printout that you want to tie to a particular printer, then you may have a basis to seize the printer. If you want to show the suspect had the capability to input images into a computer, you may have a basis for seizing a scanner or a digital camera.

3. *When to Get an Additional Warrant*

The simple answer is you get an additional warrant when you have probable cause to believe the evidence, not covered by your current warrant, may be found in a computer.

In fact, as discussed in the plain view section earlier, even if you develop probable cause to believe that evidence outside the scope of your warrant will be found in the computer you are searching, you need not get an additional warrant to take note of such additional evidence, so long as you follow your search protocol.

The safest course, however, is to request an additional warrant for the new information. You can do that by stopping your valid search to get the new warrant, or by completing the search authorized by the warrant, and then applying for a new warrant to complete the search with the new category of evidence as your focus.

B. Offsite/Detailed Analysis

Even more important than having an expert at the search scene is having an expert available to examine a seized computer. If there is a capable, trained and available police computer forensics expert, that is your first choice. Often there is no such person or that person is busy on other cases. The next best choice is an independent investigator, paid for by the police. Much further down the choice list is a representative of the victim or an expert provided or paid for by the victim. The last option is to examine the data without an expert. To do so, however, runs the risk of damaging or altering data, making evidence inadmissible and overlooking key evidence.

1. Accurate Pristine Mirror

In olden days, when I first started prosecuting computer crime, we actually worked with the original data. This was justifiable at first. The data was on floppy drives, the write protect tab could be set on the floppy so no alterations would be made. But even when the first hard drives started appearing in our cases, we worked with the original drives.

Then the conventional wisdom became to make a backup before working with the data. That way you could always compare the original, even if modified, to the backup. We slowly moved from just making a backup to actually installing the backup on a new hard drive and doing our analysis on that drive.

Why didn't we do that from the first? The primary reasons were time, the cost of a replacement drive (while much is made of the falling price of hard drives, what is often not understood is that prior to the early 1990s, nominal capacity hard drives cost $400–500 or more), and the lack of an expert who could make the backup and testify as to its accuracy. Often I was my only expert.

Making a backup, however, had a major weakness. Backups, as we think of them, back up files and directories, i.e., they recognize what the operating system recognizes as data. But there is much information on a drive that is not recognized by the file or operating systems. Deleted files are a common example. The operating system does not recognize deleted data, but if the area on the drive where the file existed has not been overwritten, the data still exists.

Even if the file has been overwritten, unless the new file takes up all of the cluster allocated to the old file, remnants of the old file will be found in the part of the cluster following the new file. Often the areas of a drive not recognized as data by the operating system—slack space, ambient space—contain the most incriminating information.

So always make a mirror image—a copy of all magnetic information on the drive. There are several programs that have established their validity in court for making accurate backups.[98]

My policy is to have one mirror image made, and that image restored to four hard drives. One for courtroom use, one for analysis, one for the defense and one for the prosecutor. In many cases only the courtroom and analysis copies are used. The prosecutor and defense attorney often don't want to see "how sausage is made."

2. Analysis Protocol

As seen earlier, it is important to have a protocol for analyzing the drive. A protocol is important to insure that you have exhaustively examined the drive. Further, a protocol helps establish the validity of your examination and the expert's report. Finally, a protocol allows you to demonstrate that your examination of the computer was as minimally invasive of the owner's privacy as possible.

While the general structure of the protocol will be the same in most cases, it will almost always vary in detail from case to case. The protocol will often be a dynamic process, changing as you examine the computer and gather information.

Think of a protocol as a crime scene investigation technique. Modern law enforcement officers know not to disturb the crime scene. Modern detectives and medical examiners follow certain sets of procedures in examining a dead body. You should have similar protocols for investigating computer scenes and computers.

---

98. *E.g.*, SafeBack by Sydex, http://www.sydex.com (visited Jan. 26, 2001) and Encase by Guidance Software, Inc., http://www.guidancesoftware.com (visited Jan. 14, 2001). Useful tools to use in conjunction with these programs are available from New Technologies of Portland, Oregon, http://www.secure-data.com (visited Jan. 14, 2001).

Examination of the directory and file structure and initial examination of only those directories and files that appear relevant on their face is an appropriate first step. Subsequent action may be based on what your initial examination reveals. For example, examination of other directories and files may be justified if the names of the directories and files you do examine do not match their contents.

Most investigators I work with use key word searches of all of the drive's binary data (obtained from the mirror image) as an initial first step. This is a useful way to determine if evidence exists which allows you to retain the computer without concern that the time limits on the execution of your warrant will expire. This also helps you focus in on suspect directories and files. But framing the search terms requires the assistance of someone who is familiar with the information for which you are searching—often a representative of the victim.

3. What Must Be Returned and When

Occasionally this is dictated by the warrant itself. The magistrate may instruct you to complete the examination of the computer and return items not covered by the warrant within a certain amount of time. Other times the defendant or other owner of the computer may request (or demand) its return. In other situations you may want to return items not covered by the warrant on your own, particularly if this is a third party's equipment or data and you need their continued cooperation.

So, what do you do when the computer owner wants the original items returned?

There may be times when the prudent course is to return the original computer, or, more particularly, the original hard drive, to the owner. Courts may be more inclined to view your search more generously, and to give you more leeway as a defendant in a civil case, when you have made every effort to accommodate the reasonable requests of the original computer owner. If the computer is the center of an ongoing legitimate business, even the defendant's own legitimate business, you should make efforts to return enough of the data you seized to allow the business to continue. One could argue that the Secret Service was treated more harshly in the *Steve Jackson Games* case because they held on to the defendant's e-mail that was crucial to the operation of his business for several months, despite the owner's repeated requests for its return, and despite the e-mail's irrelevance to the case the Secret Service was investigating.

a. Stipulation

If you are returning original evidence, whether it be just the hard drive, or the complete computer system, you should be careful to get a stipulation from the defendant, eliminating any objections as to authenticity or foundation, before returning the evidence. If the defendant refuses to so stipulate, you have a valid reason for hanging on to the original evidence. Some suggested language would be:

> [suspect], in the interest of expediting the searching and seizing of records and other evidence as authorized by Search Warrant #_____, signed by _____, Judge, on _____, 2000, so as to minimize interruption of the normal computing activities of [suspect or suspect's company], stipulate to the following terms applicable to the records, equipment and evidence itemized in the attached Inventory, incorporated by reference:
>
>> [suspect] is satisfied that the backup or mirror image copies. made on _____, 2000, are complete and accurate copies of the entire contents of the systems searched as of that date. [suspect] will not contest the accuracy, reliability or source of any record copied, printed out or derived from those backups/mirror image copies. [suspect] waives any objection as to best evidence, authenticity or foundation as to any record copied, printed out or derived from those backups/mirror image copies.

b. What If the Computer Owner Is Not the Suspect?

But what if the person from whom the computer was seized, and who wants it back, is not the suspect. The suspect has no incentive to stipulate in this context and the owner of the computer can't stipulate to admissibility of evidence against the defendant. In this case try to reach a compromise with the owner. In most cases a mirror image on a different drive will be sufficient.

If the owner must have the original, and the suspect will not stipulate, so long as you have a valid mirror image and an expert who can testify as to its creation, you should be safe in returning the original even without a stipulation. The absence of a stipulation does not make your mirror image and evidence from that mirror inadmissible, it simply raises your proof hurdle.

c. Contraband on Computer

Unless a computer is forfeited, there will come a time when you must return the computer to its owner. That may be early in the case when you determine there is no useful evidence on the computer or when a court orders the return of non-evidentiary items. It may occur when you have mirrored the hard drive and are returning the original under a stipulation as described earlier. It may occur when you have seized a business computer or a third party computer and wish to get it back to a non-suspect owner.

But what if there is contraband on the computer? Must you return it? Must you destroy it?

(1) Obvious Contraband

There are certain items that are contraband *per se* and should never be returned. These include, for example, illegal narcotics, weapons that are illegal for anyone to possess, and child pornography. While these should not be returned, neither should they be destroyed arbitrarily. Often the "owner" of this contraband has the right to challenge your retention of this material and you face the possibility of civil liability for destroying the items without authority. Seek permission from the judge issuing the warrant (or your own legal advisor) before deleting this material.

(2) Suspected Stolen Property—No Irreversible Harm in Returning

Where there is a legitimate question as to ownership of property, you may have the right to withhold the property in question until a court has determined ownership. For example, if you have what appears to be pirated software, can you withhold the software from the person you seized it from until they prove their ownership. While this may vary from case to case, I would be very careful in presuming software to be pirated and withholding it from the purported owner. In these days of buying software online, there may be no books or documentation, no specially produced CD or floppy disk, and the software is still legitimate. If you have concerns you can contact the software company and alert them to what you've found. They have seizure remedies available to them under the Federal Copyright Act.

(3) Suspected Stolen Property—Irreversible Harm in Returning

But what if the property about which there is a dispute is proprietary information—information that if returned to the defendant could be copied or transmitted to others. Some after-the-fact remedy by the true property owner may be too late. In this instance the cautious approach is to hold on to the property until the warrant judge has directed what is to become of the property.

(4) Other Types of Contraband — Passwords, Hacking Programs

Often computer criminals have cybercrime related contraband on their computers — passwords of others, hacking programs, utilities for cracking password accounts, etc. What can/should you do with those? Passwords of others, under federal law and most state law, are "access devices." Access devices in the names of two or more different people besides the possessor are presumed, in many jurisdictions, to be stolen. You are, if your law is comparable, entitled to treat this like any other clearly identified stolen property. You keep it and return it to the lawful owner.

Hacking programs, like burglar tools, are different. Just like many non-criminals own crowbars, many non-criminals own hacking programs. Such tools and programs serve many legitimate purposes and cannot be considered contraband *per se*. In addition, most hacking programs can be easily found on the Internet. Deleting such a program simply delays its subsequent acquisition by a few minutes.

IV. Presentation of Evidence at Trial

A. Computer Printouts and Summaries

With proper foundation courts have routinely admitted computer printouts as evidence of computer contents.[99] Often the problem with computer printouts is not their admissibility but their volume. Evidence Rule 1006 allows summaries to be used in many circumstances. Summaries of computer records, if they meet the other requirements of the rule, as just as valid as other records.

B. Display Computer Contents on Screen/Demonstrations

Any "live" presentation of computer data is always fraught with peril. The data may not look like you want it to. The program may act differently

---

99. King v. Mississippi *ex rel.* Murdock Acceptance Corp., 222 So. 2d 393 (Miss. 1969); Washington v. Ben-Neth, 663 P.2d 156 (Wash. App. 1983).

in court than in your office. The hardware may not display the data correctly. The electrical outlets will be too far away, or not have enough plug-ins, or not be three pronged when all your equipment is. Murphy's law applies at least as well to live presentations as it does to other aspects of our lives. Glitches show up—even Bill Gate's attempt to do live presentations in front of Judge Jackson in the Microsoft antitrust trial was problematic.

Having said that, live demonstrations can be amazingly effective. Seeing the incriminating evidence on the defendant's own screen removes the evidence from the virtual world and makes it real and attached to the defendant. Seeing the evidence on the defendant's own screen tends to help validate your expert and your other theories of the case.

As with any live demonstration, however, it can be turned against you. If your live demonstration produces changes in the hard drive (a copy of the mirror image, of course, not the actual hard drive) that were not found on the actual hard drive, you will have to explain why (or why not.) If the hardware you use differs at all from the defendant's, have a witness prepared to explain why the differences don't affect the evidence.

One example of the problems that come from not thinking ahead. A deputy prosecutor had the entire contents of the defendant's computer put onto a CD-ROM. (It shows how long ago this was that the CD could contain all of the hard drive.) She was preparing to demonstrate where files downloaded from news groups were stored by default on the defendant's computer. But when she started Windows and downloaded a file, it did not appear in the defendant's default location. The problem, obvious in hindsight, was that she was booting and starting Windows from her presentation laptop, and even though the CD with the defendant's copy of Windows and the settings associated with that copy of Windows was in the drive, the laptop's default settings were the ones recognized, not the defendant's.

C. Animation

If I have learned anything as a parent, it is this—never underestimate the ability of cartoons to hold the interest of a three-year-old with an attention span of thirty seconds. If I have learned anything as a trial lawyer it is this—never expect a jury to have an attention span longer than a three-year-old, particularly when you are presenting crucial evidence.

It takes very little insight to realize that what will hold the attention of a three-year-old will also hold the attention of a jury. Not just graphics, not just charts and pictures, but *animation*. Mental images are perceived and retained far better than spoken words. With effective animation, a jury works with a visual image of the accident, the crime, and even the contract, rather than abstract concepts.

If your case turns on the jury understanding unfamiliar technology or a complex factual situation, I suggest you consider hiring an animator to present the technology or facts.

D. Experts

In a computer crime courtroom an expert serves three purposes:

- Education
- Legal validity
- Persuasion

1. Expert as Educator

When the matter can be explained with just a little background information this task is easy. The problem comes when the matter to be explained is complex.

How do you explain a complex matter? For truly complex matters accept that you will not be able to explain it sufficient for all to understand. What you can do is explain it in a way that makes sense — is not counterintuitive. Where possible an explanation should have analogies to the familiar. The problem is, not all parts of the electronic or virtual world have a sufficiently close real world counterpart for analogizing to be accurate or useful. David Weinberger, a commentator on NPR, described this as "framejacking" — hi-jacking our normal frames of reference:

> "We're using age old methods of... reasoning trying to evaluate an unfamiliar situation by finding analogy to a familiar one.... But applied to the web the analogies get so complex that the familiar turns into the unfamiliar.... To make the situation accurate you have to make it so weird that it doesn't help us figure things out."[100]

Nevertheless, analogizing from the familiar to the unfamiliar, from the simple to the complex, is a time proven method for learning new things.

---

100. David Weinberger, Commentator, *All Things Considered* (Nat'l Public Radio broadcast, May 2, 2000).

2. Expert for Legal Validity

There are many requirements that must be met before evidence can be admitted. A proper foundation must be laid. Authenticity and relevance must be shown. To introduce evidence that came from a computer you searched you have to demonstrate that the evidence you seek to introduce did in fact come from the computer you searched. If you have recreated evidence from deleted or partially deleted files, you must be able to demonstrate the reliability of your recovery. Admissibility issues are typically left to the sound discretion of the trial judge. Probably the most important criteria for determining admissibility of evidence that is neither clearly admissible nor clearly inadmissible, is the believability of your expert. When the law does not provide clear guidance, judges are much more likely to allow in evidence in which they believe as opposed to evidence about which they have doubts.

3. Expert for Persuasion

Unless there is only one interpretation of the facts and no disagreement about that interpretation, after an expert educates, and after an expert qualifies evidence as admissible, the expert must persuade the fact finder that her/his version of the facts or interpretation of the facts is the correct one. Expert witnesses are a special category of witness. Unlike other witnesses, an expert can give an opinion. But that opinion must be persuasive.

An effective expert is one who is not argumentative, demonstrates no bias, and is knowledgeable but human. If the issue is truly complex then all fact finders are looking for someone they can trust to explain it to them. If your expert comes across as trustworthy then your expert will be able to persuade.

In those cases where you think the fact finder would accept your version of the case if they only had a rudimentary level of knowledge, it might be useful to have two experts—one for education and the other for legal validity and persuasion.

V. Unique Issues

One of the paradoxes of computer searches is that Ockham's Razor[101] is both correct and incorrect. Often, in searching computer records, things are simpler than they seem. Directories and file names do describe their con-

---

101. Paraphrased, "the simplest explanation is most often the correct one."

tents. Incriminating files are neither hidden nor encrypted. File dates and times are accurate and can be relied upon.

And often simple explanations are not correct. Date and time stamps are inaccurate because the user's clock if off, or because a difference in time zones is involved, or because the user has changed the date and time.

What I describe in this catch-all section are some small issues that may arise in computer search cases, that although small, may be enough to render the evidence suspect if the issues are not understood.

A. Dates and Times

How does the operating system date files? What does the operating system consider to be "accessing" a file? What does the operating system consider to be "creating" a file? What does the operating system consider to be "modifying" or "writing" a file? Although specific answers to these questions are beyond the scope of this article,[102] you need to be sensitive to them as you prepare a computer-crime case.

Of course, the accuracy of the date and time stamped on a file is dependent upon the system's date and time itself being accurate. They system's date and time is kept current[103] when the system is on, but when the computer is turned off the system and time remain accurate only so long as the battery backed CMOS remains accurate. As the battery starts to wear out, the system date and time will slowly slip behind actual date and time.

If the frailties of the system itself weren't bad enough, the date and time can also be manually modified. This can be as simple as setting a different date and time for the system or the only moderately more complex act of modifying a file's own date and time stamp.

How, then, can you verify that the date and time shown as the file creation date, or last modified date, are accurate or that the system's internal

---

102. Information about this can be found in general books on the operating system involved. Detailed information can often be found at www.zdnet.com and other computer information sites on the Internet.

103. I learned with my own system that the date and time can be accurately stored in CMOS but get out of sync when the computer is on, if the system is overheating or otherwise causing the CPU to run slow. For several weeks earlier this year I was puzzled that my clock kept getting behind when the system was on, but immediately caught up if the system was turned off and then back on. The apparent culprit was a defective or failing fan which failed to adequately cool the CPU, causing the system itself to slow down. This is still a hypothesis, but since I replaced the fan the problem has not recurred.

date and time are accurate? To determine if the date and time shown on a file is accurate, you can:

- Compare any dates in the content of the file with its alleged creation date
- Compare the date and time header information in an e-mail file with the date and time stamp given that file (if it is a separate file) by the operating system
- If you have a known file date (you know when a stolen file was downloaded for example), you can compare that time to the date/time of the stolen file on the suspect's computer.

To determine if the date and time set on a computer is accurate, you can:

- If the computer is attached to a network, determine if the server sets the clock of each workstation each time the user logs on
- Look for patterns of file creation dates and times. See if any files are dated after the date the computer was seized. If so, either the computer's internal clock is off or you're going to have a major problem explaining to the judge and jury the apparent changes to files after the seizure date
- Experiment. Since the date and time comes from the values stored in the computer's CMOS, not the hard drive, you need to experiment using the suspect computer *but not* the hard drive containing evidence. Put a new hard drive in the system, create some files and see if the file creation date matches the actual date.

You may be able to prove the actual file date/time from dates/times that are ahead or behind their actual times (because the CMOS date/time is ahead or behind.) If you can demonstrate the CMOS is two hours behind, for example, you should be able to argue that increasing the shown file date/time by two hours produces the actual time the file was created. This is particularly true if you can independently show a particular file's date/time to be off by two hours, using one of the methods described earlier.

In one case from the early 1990s, *Washington v. Merillin Paris*,[104] we were attempting to reconstruct the sequence of events when an intruder physically went into a series of offices, turned on computers, created directories and files and copied a proprietary file. There were numerous time and date

---

104. King County Superior Court, No. 92-1-05560-7 SEA

stamps on the files and directories created, there were network login times when the computers were turned on, and there were records of the security company that showed when key card access was made to the office.

My concern about whether the date/times on the files and on the log records were accurate was relieved by the system administrator's explanation and demonstration to me that on their network as configured, whenever a computer logged on to the network, that computer's clock was synchronized to the server's clock. We were able to verify that the server's clock was accurate, and thus were able to demonstrate the accuracy of the workstation clocks.

B. Authenticity

How can you prove what you present in court is what was actually on the computer you seized? On its face, this seems like a chain-of-custody question. If you have witnesses who can identify the item and trace its location from when it was seized to when it was produced in court, then you can prove the item you produce is what was seized.

If all you're producing in court is the physical computer that's true. But when you're producing the contents of the computer, and claiming that those contents were on the computer when you seized it, your task is more difficult. This is especially true if what you're introducing is evidence from the erased file or slack space of the hard drive.

If you have a good protocol for how you handle the computer and how you recover data from the computer, you should have no problem. But remember, any time you start up the computer from the hard drive, any time you execute files on the hard drive, any time you start up windows on the hard drive, you modify file dates. Even when there is a simple answer that does not invalidate your evidence, it's always embarrassing to have the defense point out the files with written-to dates and times after the time the computer was seized. Knowledgeable judges and juries can distinguish between file alterations done by the system that do not impact the validity of the contents or date/time stamp of other files, but don't assume you'll have either in your crucial trial.

C. How to Prove Authorship of Computer File

In some cases the existence of the incriminating file on the suspect's computer, by itself or together with other evidence you have, may be sufficient. In some cases, however, you may need to tie the evidence to the defendant beyond showing that the evidence was found on the defendant's computer. Here are some ways that can be used to make this connection:

- Directory structure and location of the file within that directory structure
- Suspect file matches defendant's unique file-naming convention
- Common misspellings or grammar mistakes between suspect file and files known to have been authored by the defendant
- Common use of unique sentence structure, word choice, etc., between suspect file and files known to have been authored by the defendant.

D. Computer Trespass by Outsider Versus Exceeding Authority by Authorized User

Computer trespass statutes typically speak in terms of "unauthorized access" or "without authority." When the access at issue is made by someone with no authority to use the computer system there is usually little difficulty demonstrating that the access they made was unauthorized. When the access at issue was by someone who did have authority to access the system, but not all parts, or when their access is for an unauthorized purpose, proof of the "unauthorized" element of the offense can be more problematic.

Let's take three examples, all of which will involve a computerized data base of the Motor Vehicle Department of a state. In the first example, someone with no authority to access the database hacks into the system and gains access to the driving record of a candidate for political office. This is clearly unauthorized.

In the second example, an employee of the Department of Motor Vehicles whose job duties require access to the DMV computer system (for entry of payroll data, for example) but not to the driving record database, accesses the same data about the candidate. While this scenario presents some possible problems, the only real issues in this case are whether the employee knew the database was out-of-bounds, and whether the access was made intentionally. The first issue turns on what you can demonstrate the employee knew, such as the provisions in the employee manual, training materials, a screen banner before accessing the database, etc. The second issue turns on how clearly separated, the authorized and unauthorized areas are. Was the access accidental or innocent? Warning banners can be helpful here, also.

The third example is the most difficult. Suppose the employee in question is one whose work directly involves the database and they are clearly authorized to access the database, but they access it for a non-business reason—to embarrass a political candidate, for example.

This example presents two distinct problems. First, if our argument is that accessing the database for an unauthorized reason is unauthorized access, then we must prove the state of mind of the suspect when they initially accessed the database. If the employee came to work, logged on her/his computer, did their work, and in the middle of the afternoon, while still logged on, obtained the candidate's records for the purpose of providing them to the candidate's opponent, is there an unauthorized access? While semantically one could argue that the unauthorized access is not the access to the database but the access to the candidate's record, most observers would consider the initial access to the database to be the "access." Thus, we would have to prove that when the employee first accessed the protected database itself, it was her/his intent to get the candidate's records rather than some other legitimate task.

Second, is the real crime in this example the access to the candidate's data or the provision of that data to the candidate's opponent? Some courts have taken the position that the real crime in this instance is the provision of the data to the opponent, not the access to it in the first place. If you have not charged that crime—the crime of making unauthorized *use* of the data—or if that action is not illegal, your case may be dismissed. In *Washington v. Olson*,[105] the defendant was a police officer. As part of his job he had access to records maintained in the computer system of the state Department of Licensing. He obtained information about University of Washington co-eds using that system. This was not related to any investigation. He was charged and convicted of computer trespass under a statute which made criminal the intentional access to a computer system of another without authority. The court, in reversing the conviction, noted that the statute criminalizes the entry into the computer database, not the use of the information obtained. The court also noted that there was no evidence that permission to access the computer was conditioned on the uses made of the data. As a result, although the defendant had made unauthorized use of materials he had obtained from the computer system, he had not committed the crime with which he was charged. The court did note that there

---

105. 735 P.2d 1362 (Wash. App. 1987).

could be situations where there are conditions attached to computer access, but there were no such conditions in the case before them.

Computer trespass by an otherwise authorized user is difficult to prove. Clear warnings to authorized users about the scope of their authority, both as to areas of the computer they may access, and purpose for which they may access the computer, are essential to any prosecution of a qualified or limited access case.

E. Knowledge/Intent

One common issue in child pornography cases is proving the defendant knew that she/he had the offending items on her/his computer. While many news viewers allow you to view a file before your actually download it to your computer, many others require you to download a file before you can view it. Further, many news viewers allow you to download multiple files without previously seeing the contents of any of them. Thus it is quite plausible that someone downloading adult pornography might have what qualifies as child pornography on their computer without their knowledge.

How to you separate the innocent from the guilty? How do you prove that the presence of a file was done with knowledge or intent?

1. Directory Structure

One way is the directory structure. The directory structure can provide clues in at least two different ways.

Directories are files and directory creation date and time is stored with the directory just like file creation date and time is stored with a file. In fact, if the files are copied from one location to another, it is often the directory creation date on the target computer which shows the date/time the directory was created that is helpful rather than file creation date/time as that will usually show the original creation date of the file, not the date it was copied to the target system.

In addition, the names and organization of the files and directories can show knowledge and intent. In one case, *Washington v. Rosul*,[106] the defendant was accused of possession of child pornography. While an employee of Microsoft, the defendant had used Microsoft equipment to burn a CD-ROM containing sexually explicit images, including images of children. His defense was that he had downloaded the material from news groups and

---

106. No. 96-1-05106-0 SEA (Wash. Super. Ct., Jul. 24, 1997).

while he was aware it was sexually explicit material, he was unaware any of the images were of children.

The defendant acknowledged that he had created the directories both on his computer at Microsoft and on the CD-ROM. That directory structure contained a directory called E:\GIFS. Subdirectories included E:\GIFS\BOY and E:\GIFS\YOUNG. This last subdirectory was subdivided as follows: E:GIFS\YOUNG\BOY, E:GIFS\YOUNG\CLEAN, E:GIFS\YOUNG\YOUNG, and E:GIFS\YOUNG\GIRL. The E:GIFS\YOUNG\GIRL subdirectory was further subdivided: E:GIFS\YOUNG\GIRL\AA, E:GIFS\YOUNG\GIRL\NUDE, *E:GIFS\YOUNG\GIRL\SEX*, and E:GIFS\YOUNG\GIRL\SLYGS.

The images in issue were found in the E:GIFS\YOUNG\GIRL\SEX directory. That directory consisted of children under the age of 14 being sexually molested or otherwise sexually exploited. The other directories contained images consistent with the directory name. The state was able to successfully argue that the defendant was aware of the contents of the images by virtue of the sorting and directory naming in which he admitted engaging.

2. File Names

Another way to establish intent or knowledge is to examine the file names. If the file names describe their contents — "babyfuk.jpg" was one file in the *Rosul* case — there is at least circumstantial evidence that the defendant was aware of the file's contents. This is particularly true if the defendant named the file her/himself.

Often file names, when coupled with an inculpatory directory structure, will be sufficient to show intent or knowledge.

3. Date and Time

Sometimes a file's creation date, or the date/time shown on e-mail headers, can be coupled with file names and directory structure to produce an incriminating picture. In the *Rosul* case, there were system logs showing the defendant had accessed a Usenet site in the Netherlands several times. The log showed the defendant had downloaded several graphic files in the GIF format. One of the images at the site was found on Rosul's computer, converted to JPG format. The file creation date/time on the JPG file was consistent with the time the log showed Rosul had accessed that same file on the Internet. Producing an expert who testified that such a conversion requires viewing the file, the State was able to demonstrate the defendant's knowledge of the information on his computer.

VI. Conclusion

Searches of computers, whether because of cybercrimes or because the computer contains evidence of other crimes, is becoming common. The law in non-computer cases provides guidelines that can safely be used in most computer searches. The slowly increasing body of law specific to computer searches will help bridge the gap between non-computer search law and computer search law.

Computer searches are, in some ways, different from non-computer searches. Further, cases specific to computer searches are still rare. As computer search law evolves, there may well be different standards applied to searches of computers. Thus, practitioners—be they police officers, prosecutors, defense attorneys or judges—should remain alert to the development of the law in this evolving area.

Chapter Four

Defending Cybercrime Cases: Selected Statutes and Defenses

Joseph F. Savage, Jr. with Amanda J. Metts and Darlene DeMelo[*]

The computer is a necessity for virtually all in society, including criminals and those in law enforcement.[1] Computer-related criminal conduct — "computer crime" or "cybercrime" — is now a priority focus of law en-

---

[*] Joseph F. Savage, Jr. is a partner in the Boston law firm of Testa, Hurwitz & Thibeault, LLP where he heads the firm's White Collar Criminal Defense Group as well as representing clients in complex civil litigation. He is a former federal prosecutor in Boston, New York, West Virginia, Washington, D.C. and Missouri. Mr. Savage has lectured extensively, particularly on issues relating to the high tech economy and is the author of more than 30 articles on white collar crime issues.

Amanda J. Metts and Darlene DeMelo are associates in the Litigation Practice Group at Testa, Hurwitz & Thibeault, LLP.

1. D. Deneen Evans Cox, *Comment: Journey From Computer Security to the Millennium Bug*, 29 U. West. L.A. L. Rev. 257 (1998) (discussing society's heavy reliance on computers for conduct of daily activities). *See also* Joseph M. Olivenbaum, *Rethinking Federal Computer Crime Legislation*, 27 Seton Hall L. Rev. 574, 575 (1997) ("The greatly enhanced ease of access to, and large scale reproduction of, legally protectable materials presents new challenges to the law of intellectual property and copyright.") [hereinafter Olivenbaum, *Rethinking Federal Computer Crime*].

forcement.[2] This chapter addresses the elements of, and defenses to, some of the more significant crimes that fall under the realm of cybercrime, including the Computer Fraud and Abuse Act ["CFAA"], the Electronic Communications Privacy Act of 1986 ["ECPA"], the Economic Espionage Act ["EEA"] and the Copyright Act. The CFAA and ECPA deal directly with crimes relating to computer technology. The EEA and Copyright Act are intellectual property statutes that address efforts to steal intellectual property which frequently involve use of computers. Part one of this chapter discusses these statutes and certain potential defenses unique to each one. Part two of the chapter addresses some defenses that may be generally applicable in any computer crime prosecution.

I. COMPUTER RELATED OFFENSES IN THE NEW ECONOMY

A. Introduction

There is no universal definition of "cybercrime." Computer-related offenses are generally placed in one of three categories.[3] First, the computer may be the target of the crime.[4] Second, the computer may be the actual physical site of the crime.[5] Third, the computer can be the device used to commit the crime.[6] Actions included in this category may form the basis

---

2. *See id.* at 577 ("Computer-related criminal conduct presents a challenge to the criminal law, in significant part, precisely because it involves electronic impulses that cannot be seen, touched, moved, or copied as those terms have traditionally been defined, and that therefore seem to fall outside the idea of 'property' as defined over centuries of Anglo-American jurisprudence.").

3. These offenses can, however, span a wide array of activities. *See* Eric J. Sinrod & William P. Reilly, *Cyber-Crimes: A Practical Approach to the Application of Federal Computer Crime Laws*, 16 COMPUTER & HIGH TECH. L.J. 177, 179 (2000) ("computer crimes include not only hacking and cracking, but now also include extortion, child pornography, money laundering, fraud, software pirating, and corporate espionage, to name a few.") [hereinafter Sinrod, *Cyber-Crimes*]. *See also*, Michael Hatcher, Jay McDannell & Stacy Ostfeld, *Computer Crimes*, 36 AM. CRIM. L. REV. 397, 398–99 (1999) (narrow definition of computer crime unsustainable because of diversity of offenses) [hereinafter Hatcher, *Computer Crimes*].

4. *See* Hatcher, *Computer Crimes* at 401 (computer is object of crime when offense involves theft of computer time and services).

5. *Id.* (computer is the subject of the crime when a virus is released).

6. *Id.* ("computer may be an instrument used to commit traditional crimes").

for "traditional" crimes such as credit card fraud, but are often called computer crimes when the criminal conduct is on-line.[7]

As with computer crimes, there are also different brands of computer criminals. "Hackers" have been depicted as the typical computer criminal and described as "skilled computer users who penetrate computer systems to gain knowledge about computer systems and how they work."[8]

Pure hackers are outsiders who access systems, without any authorization, for their own interest and not for economic profit,[9] and traditionally lack the criminal intent to damage systems.[10] Another breed of computer criminal is the "cracker," who is described as "a hacker with criminal intent" because he or she intends to access a system to steal information or otherwise damage the system.[11]

While there is no single standard "computer crime," the most common computer-related criminal activity centers around the transmission of, or unauthorized access to, information stored on a computer.[12] Congress has responded to the increase in computer-related crimes by enacting statutes that specifically target computer criminals. With the passage of the Counterfeit Access Device and Computer Fraud and Abuse Law in 1984, Congress began handling computer-related crimes as discrete offenses.[13]

---

7. *See* Joe D. Whitley & William H. Jordan, *Computer Crime, White Collar Crime: Business and Regulatory Offenses* (Law Journal Seminar 1999), *reprinted in* WHITE COLLAR CRIME 2000 at E1 (computer used to facilitate traditional fraud crimes) [hereinafter Whitley, *Computer Crime*].

8. *See* Sinrod *Cyber-Crimes* at 181–83 (A significant challenge is presented due to the overlapping nature of many terms. For example, the individual who defeats the copyright protection of pirated software is called a "cracker." U.S. v. Rothberg, No. 00 CR 85 (N.D. Ill. Nov., 1999) (Special November 1999 Grand Jury Indictment of Rubin Rothberg). The term "hacker" appeared to have originated in the 1960s to describe the hacker "prankster" culture surrounding certain students at the Massachusetts Institute of Technology).

9. Haeji Hong, *Note: Hacking Through the Computer Fraud Abuse Act*, 31 U.C. DAVIS L. REV. 283, 289 (1997) ("[H]ackers access systems generally out of curiosity and to learn....") [hereinafter Hong, *Hacking*].

10. *See* Sinrod, *Cyber-Crimes* at 185 ("'Recreational hackers break into computer networks for the thrill of the challenge or for bragging rights in the hacking community.'").

11. *See id.* at 182.

12. *See* Olivenbaum, *Rethinking Federal Computer Crime* at 577 (noting computer criminal activity involves "distribution of information on one computer by means of software operating on another remote computer").

13. Pub. L. No. 98-473, Title II, Chapter XXI, § 2102(a), 98 Stat. 1837, 2190 (1984) (current version at 18 U.S.C. § 1030 (Supp. IV 1998)). This approach differs from that

B. The Computer Fraud and Abuse Act

The primary federal statute aimed specifically at combating computer crime is the Computer Fraud and Abuse Act ["CFAA"].[14] The CFAA was originally directed at individual theft of information from government computers.[15] Since its enactment, Congress has amended the statute twice, most recently in 1996, "to reflect the changes in technology and criminal techniques."[16] These amendments broadened the scope of the CFAA and also abolished some previously-available defenses.

The 1996 Amendments ["Amendments"] replaced the term "federal interest computer" with the term "protected computer."[17] The definition of a protected computer includes any computer "used in interstate or foreign commerce or communication."[18] This sweeping definition includes almost every computer because most computers today, whether for business or personal use, are connected to a network involving interstate communications. With the Amendments, Congress greatly expanded the coverage of the CFAA to punish unauthorized access to and/or theft of information from private computers, as well as government computers.

1. Substantive Prohibitions

The CFAA contains seven main subsections aimed at specific computer-related criminal conduct.[19]

The first of the CFAA's prohibitions, section 1030(a)(1), is the knowing access of a computer, without authorization or in excess of authorization,

---

taken by many states where traditional theft and trespass statutes are used to address such offenses.

14. *See* 18 U.S.C. § 1030(a)(1)–(a)(7) (1994 & Supp. IV 1998).
15. *See* Whitley, *Computer Crime* at E-4.
16. *See* Sinrod, *Cyber-Crimes* at 180.
17. Under 18 U.S.C. § 1030(e)(2) (Supp. IV 1998) "protected computer" is defined as:

> exclusively for the use of a financial institution or the United States Government, or, in the case of a computer not used exclusively for such use, used by or for a financial institution or the United States Government and the conduct constituting the offense affects that use by or for the financial institution or the Government; or which is used in interstate or foreign commerce or communication

18. *Id.*
19. *Id.* §§ 1030(a)(1)–(a)(7) (1994 & Supp IV 1998).

and the subsequent transmission of classified government information.[20] Relatively few computers are not covered because the statute protects computers used in interstate or foreign commerce or communications.[21] Information is protected if it *could be* used to injure the United States, eliminating a pre-1996 requirement that the offender have knowledge or belief that the information "is to be used" to injure the United States.[22]

Section 1030(a)(2) prohibits *obtaining*, without or in excess of authorization, information from a financial institution, the federal government, or a "protected computer" involved in interstate or foreign communication.[23] Merely reading the information is "obtaining," as this subsection does not require that the information be copied or altered.[24]

Under section 1030(a)(3), the CFAA also protects government computers and prohibits intentionally accessing a nonpublic computer of a U.S. department or agency without authorization.[25] The requirement that the access "adversely" affect the government's use was removed by the 1996 Amendments and, consequently, a possible defense that the access was harmless was also eradicated.

Section 1030(a)(4) prohibits access to a protected computer, without or in excess of authority, with the intent to defraud or obtain anything of value.[26] If the only thing obtained or taken is computer time, the value of the use obtained must exceed $5,000 in any one-year period to violate this section.[27]

Section 1030(a)(5) is the principal anti-hacking subsection in the CFAA. The statute makes it a crime to intentionally damage a protected computer through the "transmission of a program, information code, or command."[28] Whether the offender acted without authorization or in excess of autho-

---

20. *Id.* § 1030(a)(1) (Supp. IV 1998).
21. *Id.*
22. *Id. See* Hatcher, *Computer Crimes* at 404, n.38 (noting the scienter element in the 1994 Act was eliminated by the 1996 Act).
23. 18 U.S.C. §1030(a)(2) (Supp. IV 1998).
24. *See* Hatcher, *Computer Crimes* at 404 n.39 ("Since there is no requirement that information be transported or copied, merely reading the information may be considered 'obtaining'.... Merely reading information, however, is not considered 'obtaining something of value' for purposes of... 18 U.S.C.A. § 1030(a)(4) (Supp. 1998).").
25. 18 U.S.C. § 1030(a)(3) (Supp. IV 1998).
26. *Id.* § 1030 (a)(4).
27. *Id.*
28. *Id.* § 1030(a)(5).

rization is irrelevant.[29] Insiders with authority are responsible only for the intentional damage they cause.[30] Outsiders are culpable if they are reckless in causing damage or even if only negligent.[31] The lack of an intent requirement in section 1030(a)(5)(C) shows Congress' willingness to punish outside hackers who merely intend to access a system but cause damage in the process.

The statute prohibits trafficking in passwords that could be used to access a protected computer, where it is done knowingly and with intent to defraud, in section 1030(a)(6).[32] The transmission of any threats to cause damage to a protected computer with the intent to extort something of value is prohibited in section 1030(a)(7).[33]

The CFAA also prohibits any attempts to commit any of the offenses detailed in §1030(a).[34]

2. Defenses

The 1996 Amendments to the CFAA sought to greatly limit the defenses available under section 1030.

a. Jurisdiction

Before the Amendments, the statute required that a "federal interest" computer be accessed before a violation existed under section 1030(a)(4). Therefore, someone who, with intent to defraud, was accessing a private computer from within the same state was not in violation of the statute.[35] However, with the amendments, the term "federal interest computer" was

---

29. *Id.* § 1030(a)(5)(A).
30. *See Id.* (requiring intentional damage).
31. *See id.* § 1030(a)(5)(B)-(C) (requiring only reckless damage for a felony and no *mens rea* requirement for a misdemeanor). *See also* Hong, *Hacking* at 300 ("As to outside hackers, innocent or not, CFAA allows prosecution under the entire spectrum of mens rea levels. Therefore, any innocent hacker who stumbles into someone else's computer file or computer data by accident may be strictly liable.").
32. 18 U.S.C. § 1030(a)(6) (1994).
33. *Id.* § 1030(a)(7) (Supp. IV 1998).
34. *Id.* § 1030(b).
35. This was not true under § 1030(a)(5) as it did protect computers in interstate commerce. However, if intrastate government or financial institution computers were damaged, they were not necessarily covered by the statute. *See* Hatcher, *Computer Crimes* at 406.

replaced by "protected computer," expanding the CFAA to include every computer linked to an interstate communications line. Any remaining jurisdictional challenges are likely not case specific. A constitutional claim that the prohibition exceeds Congress' powers under the Commerce Clause may remain.[36]

b. Intent

Previous statutory ambiguities under section 1030(a)(5) allowed defendants to challenge the proof of intent requirement in the statute by claiming that an intent *to damage*, and not merely an intent to access, was required. In *United States v. Morris*,[37] the defendant was convicted for intentionally accessing a "federal interest computer" and thereby causing damage after releasing a destructive program onto the Internet. The defendant did not intend to cause any damage, but only to point out defects in the computer network's security.[38]

The defendant argued that the statute required an intent to cause damage and not merely an intent to access. The Second Circuit disagreed. While recognizing the ambiguity in the wording of the statute, the Court affirmed the defendant's felony conviction concluding that the "intentional" element only applied to accessing a system and not to causing damage.[39]

In 1994, this subsection was amended to require evidence of an "intent to damage" for a felony conviction while recklessly causing damage became a misdemeanor.[40] Congress amended the statute in 1996 and again redefined the different *mens rea* requirements for a felony and a misdemeanor.[41] Under the amended section 1030(a)(5)(C), recklessness no longer need be proven for a misdemeanor conviction. Instead, a defendant may be convicted of a misdemeanor even absent intent to damage if there is an intent to access.[42] Once it is shown that the defendant intentionally accessed a pro-

---

36. *See generally* U.S. v. Lopez, 514 U.S. 549 (1995) (invalidating a criminal statute as unconstitutional because it exceeded congressional power to regulate interstate commerce).
37. 928 F.2d 504 (2d Cir.), *cert. denied*, 502 U.S. 817 (1991).
38. *See id.* at 505.
39. *Id.* at 506–09.
40. Pub. L. 103-322, § 290001, 108 Stat 1796 (1994) (codified, as amended at 18 U.S.C. § 1030 (a)(5)(A)-(B) (Supp. IV 1998)).
41. *Id.* §§ 1030(a)(5)(A), (B) & (C).
42. *Id.* § 1030(a)(5)(C).

tected computer, it is no longer a viable defense that the damage caused was beyond the intent of the offender.[43]

c. "Obtain Anything of Value"

Before a defendant can be found guilty under section 1030(a)(4), the prosecution must demonstrate that the offender knowingly and with fraudulent intent accessed a protected computer without or in excess of authority, and *obtained anything of value*.[44] A defendant may raise the defense that she did not "obtain anything of value" when she only viewed the information on a computer screen, but did not actually take anything.[45] This defense was successfully raised in *United States v. Czubinski*.[46]

In *Czubinski*, the defendant was convicted on four counts of computer fraud under section 1030(a)(4) when he carried out unauthorized computer searches and viewed confidential taxpayer information.[47] On appeal to the First Circuit, the defendant argued that he had not violated section 1030(a)(4) because he merely viewed information and did not obtain anything of value.[48] The court agreed and reversed the conviction, emphasizing that "merely viewing information cannot be deemed the same as obtaining something of value for the purposes of this statute."[49] This defense is valid where a defendant has not in some way used, recorded or printed the information obtained.[50] Congress responded by amending the CFAA. Thus, a defendant now may be convicted under section 1030(a)(2) simply for obtaining information, which includes merely viewing the information, where the information is obtained from a financial record of a financial institution, from any department or agency of the United States or from a

---

43. *See* Hatcher, *Computer Crimes* at 407 ("[O]nce a prosecutor proves intentional access, courts will reject a defense claiming that the effects of a program exceeded the programmer's intentions.").

44. 18 U.S.C. § 1030(a)(4) (Supp. IV 1998).

45. *See* Whitley, *Computer Crime* at E-8 (stating defense is not available under 1030(a)(3), where mere access or access in excess of authority of a nonpublic computer is a violation).

46. 106 F.3d 1069 (1st Cir. 1997).

47. *See id.* at 1071 (defendant also convicted of nine counts of wire fraud under 18 U.S.C. §§ 1343 & 1346).

48. A defendant could not raise this argument under §1030(a)(2) where merely viewing is considered "obtaining" information. *See supra* note 26 with accompanying text.

49. 106 F.3d at 1078.

50. *Id.*

protected computer if the conduct involved an interstate or foreign communication.[51]

3. Lack of "Damage" Under the CFAA

Section 1030(e)(8) defines "damage" in part as "any impairment to the integrity or availability of data, a program, a system, or information" that causes a loss of at least $5,000 in a one-year period.[52] This provides a fact specific argument about the consequences of an intrusion. Courts have used different methods to calculate the aggregate losses. In *United States v. Sablan*, the court calculated damages by looking at losses "directly resulting" from the defendant's criminal conduct.[53] The court in *United States v. Middleton*, on the other hand, calculated damages in terms of the time employees expended in identifying, investigating and correcting the damage caused by the defendant.[54]

4. Penalties

The CFAA's sentencing provision is found at section 1030(c), which was also amended in 1996.

The main change to this subsection related to repeat offenders who, before the amendments, only received enhanced sentences if they violated the same subsection under which they were previously convicted. Today, a person convicted under the CFAA will receive an enhanced sentence if she subsequently violates *any* other 1030(a) subsection.[55]

The Federal Sentencing Guidelines ["Guidelines"] govern what sentence the defendant receives.[56] In 1996, Congress directed the U.S. Sentencing Commission ["U.S.S.C."] to amend the Guidelines and provide for a minimum six-month prison sentence for defendants convicted under the fraud

---

51. 18 U.S.C. § 1030(a)(2) (Supp. IV 1998).
52. Under 18 U.S.C. § 1030(e)(8) (Supp. IV 1998) the term "damage" means: any impairment to the integrity or availability of data, a program, a system, or information, that causes loss aggregating at least $5,000 in value during any 1 year period to one or more individuals; modifies or impairs, or potentially modifies or impairs, the medical examination, diagnosis, treatment, or care of one or more individuals; causes physical injury to any person; or threatens public health or safety.
53. 92 F.3d 865, 870 (9th Cir. 1996).
54. 35 F. Supp. 2d 1189 (N.D. Cal. 1999).
55. 18 U.S.C. § 1030(c) (Supp. IV 1998).
56. U.S. SENTENCING GUIDELINES MANUAL, ch. 3 (1999) [hereinafter U.S.S.G.]

and hacking provision, sections 1030(a)(4) and 1030(a)(5).[57] The U.S.S.C. complied[58] and the Guidelines were adopted in 1997.[59]

C. The Electronic Communications Privacy Act of 1986

The Electronic Communications Privacy Act ["ECPA"] was enacted in 1986 and extends privacy protections to electronic communications.[60] In general, the statute criminalizes the interception of electronic communications. The ECPA can be divided into two main chapters: the "wiretap statute"[61] and the Stored Wire and Electronic Communications and Transactional Records Act ["SWECTRA"].[62]

1. The Wiretap Statute — § 2511

The wiretap statute prohibits the interception and disclosure of wire, oral or electronic communications.[63] The broad definition of "electronic communication" catches within the statute electronic mail, voicemail, cellular phones and satellite communications. Interception of electronic communication can include anything from tapping telephones to intercepting

---

57. Antiterrorism and Effective Death Penalty Act of 1996, Pub. L. No. 104-132, Title VIII, § 805, 110 Stat. 1214, 1305 (1996).
58. United States Sentencing Commission, *Report to Congress: Adequacy of Federal Sentencing Guideline Penalties for Computer Fraud and Vandalism Offenses* (June 1996), http://www.ussc.gov.
59. U.S.S.G. app. C, amend. 551 (1998) (*codified at* U.S.S.G. § 2B1.3(d)(1) and § 2F1.1(c)(1)).
60. Pub. L. No. 99-508, 100 Stat. 1848 (1986), *codified as amended at* 18 U.S.C. §§ 2510-21, 2701-10 (1994).
61. 18 U.S.C. §§ 2510–22 (1994 & Supp. IV 1998).
62. *Id.* §§ 2701–11.
63. Under 18 U.S.C. § 2510(12) (Supp. IV 1998), "electronic communication" is defined as:
> any transfer of signs, signals, writing, images, sounds, data, or intelligence of any nature transmitted in whole or in part by a wire, radio, electromagnetic, photoelectronic or photooptical system that affects interstate or foreign commerce, but does not include—(A) any wire or oral communication; (B) any communication made through a tone-only paging device; (C) any communication from a tracking device (as defined in section 3117 of this title); or (D) electronic funds transfer information stored by a financial institution in a communications system used for the electronic storage and transfer of funds.

e-mails. Violations under this section can result in a fine, imprisonment for not more than five years, or both.[64]

For a person to be convicted under section 2511, the interception must occur as the communication is transmitted, or the conduct will instead be covered by SWECTRA, which prohibits access and disclosure of information stored electronically. However, it is difficult to determine when a communication is "in transit" because electronic communications, such as e-mails or voicemails, are only transmitted for milliseconds and stored on different servers as they are routed.[65]

The issue of whether a communication is in transmission was raised in *Lopez v. First Union Nat'l Bank*,[66] where the plaintiff claimed that the defendant bank improperly disclosed electronic funds transfer information to federal authorities in violation of section 2511. The court dismissed the allegation, stating that the defendants could not be held liable under the wiretap statute because the communications were not "in transmission" at the time they were disclosed, but were communications held in electronic storage because the fund transfers had already occurred.[67]

2. SWECTRA—§ 2701

SWECTRA prohibits access of electronic communications while they are in storage.[68] Section 2701 penalizes anyone who, without or in excess of authority, gains access to a facility through which an electronic communication service is provided and "thereby obtains, alters or prevents authorized access to" the communication while it is in storage.[69] The statute provides that an "electronic communication service" is any service that allows users to send or receive electronic communications.[70] Entities providing these services include an Internet Service Provider or even an employer who provides e-mail or voicemail services to its employees.

---

64. *See id.* § 2511(4)(a).
65. *See* Whitley, *Computer Crime* at E-9 ("For example, an e-mail message is typically typed on one computer, stored on the sender's e-mail server, transmitted over the Internet through a series of routers to the destination, stored on the recipient's e-mail server, delivered to that person's e-mail account at which time it may, depending on the configuration, be stored on the recipient's hard drive. Thus, there is only a fraction of a second when the e-mail is actually in transit between the sender and the recipient.").
66. 129 F.3d 1186 (11th Cir. 1997).
67. *Id.* at 1190.
68. *See* 18 U.S.C. § 2701(a) (1994).
69. *See id.* § 2701(a)-(b) (1994 & Supp. IV 1998).
70. *See id.* § 2510(16) (Supp. IV 1998).

Section 2701 exempts from its prohibitions conduct that is authorized by the entity providing the service or by the user of the service, where the communication was intended for that user.[71] As such, an employer who provides its employees with electronic communication services to be used in the course of employment cannot be liable for accessing the communications. In addition, where a governmental entity follows the procedures delineated in the statute for accessing such information, its conduct is exempted from section 2701.[72]

The criminal penalties under section 2701 include a fine or imprisonment of not more than one year, or both, if the offender obtains the unauthorized access for "commercial advantage, malicious destruction or damage, or private commercial gain."[73] Repeat offenders may also be fined, imprisoned for a maximum of two years, or both.[74] Other cases of unauthorized access are punishable by a fine, imprisonment for up to six months, or both.[75]

D. The Economic Espionage Act

1. Overview of the Statute

The Economic Espionage Act of 1996 ["EEA"][76] was drafted to protect information guarded by "reasonable" secrecy measures, valuable because of its secrecy, and "related to or included in a product" in interstate commerce.[77] President Clinton heralded the Act as crucial to preserve "the competitiveness of critical U.S. industries" and to protect the trade secrets of all businesses operating in the United States from economic espionage and trade secret theft.[78] At a time when twenty-six states did not have criminal trade secrets statutes in effect, the Act criminalized the theft of trade secrets and allowed the Federal Bureau of Investigation ["FBI"] and the United States Department of Justice ["DOJ"] to prosecute employees and businesses, and even to seize companies for stealing trade secrets.

---

71. *See id.* § 2701(c)(1)-(2) (1994).
72. *See id.* § 2701(c)(3) (1994) & § 2703 (1994 & Supp. IV 1998).
73. *See id.* § 2701(b)(1)(A) (Supp. IV 1998).
74. *See id.* § 2701(b)(1)(B) (1994).
75. *See id.* § 2701(b)(2) (Supp. IV 1998).
76. 18 U.S.C. §§ 1831–39 (Supp. IV 1998).
77. *See id.*
78. For further discussion of this topic, *see* Joseph F. Savage, Jr. & Carol E. Didget, *The Economic Espionage Act: A Promise Unfulfilled?*, CORPORATE LAW WEEKLY, Sept. 30, 1999.

Prior to the EEA's enactment, the only federal statute directed at economic espionage was the Trade Secrets Act, which did not apply to trade secret theft by private parties.[79] Private citizens handled trade secret theft through civil litigation, but in the criminal context, the government was forced to make creative use of other statutes.

The EEA filled that gap, and several cases prosecuted under the EEA contain examples of trade secret theft effected through the use of computers and, more specifically, e-mail. In *United States v. Ho*, an employee of one company sent an e-mail to an employee of a competitor's company, which outlined and requested information relating to the competitor's technology.[80] Unfortunately for the employee making the request, the competitor's employee cooperated with the FBI and provided information that ultimately led to the employee's arrest.[81]

More recently, the First Circuit affirmed an EEA conviction that arose "out of an electronic mail 'pen-pal' relationship between a dissatisfied Maine chemist...and a California scientist...."[82] Camp, a chemist in Maine, was interested in leaving her current employment. Accordingly, she sent a resume and began corresponding with a competitor, Martin.[83] In the course of correspondence, Camp repeatedly sent confidential company information to Martin (some at his urging).[84] On Camp's last day, she inadvertently sent a message to the global marketing manager of her current employer, discussing a package of confidential information that she had sent to Martin.[85] Martin was ultimately convicted by a jury of conspiracy to steal trade secrets under the EEA.[86]

Although Martin repeatedly told Camp that she should send him only public information, the jury concluded, and the appeals court refused to reverse their decision, that Martin's actions nevertheless constituted a tacit agreement to accept trade secret information from Camp.[87]

---

79. 18 U.S.C. § 1905 (Supp. IV 1998).
80. *See* 155 F.3d 189, 192 (3rd Cir. 1998).
81. *See id.* at 192–93.
82. U.S. v. Martin, 228 F.3d 1, at *6 (1st Cir. 2000).
83. *See id.* at *6–10.
84. *See id.* at *7–10. Although Martin told Camp only to send public information, he encouraged her to accumulate relevant knowledge and used the word "spy."
85. *See id.* at *10.
86. *See id.*
87. *See id.* at *12 ("Given the type of information that Martin had already received, a reasonable jury could have concluded that, whatever Martin's original intentions, as of July 21, Camp and Martin had reached a tacit agreement by which she would send

The EEA proscribes two types of trade secret theft: foreign economic espionage[88] and commercial theft of trade secrets.[89] Section 1832, the only

---

him items and information that potentially fell under the trade secret definition of 18 U.S.C. § 1839(3).").
88. See 18 U.S.C. § 1831 (Supp. IV 1998). Section 1831 provides in full:
(a) In General—Whoever, intending or knowing that the offense will benefit any foreign government, foreign instrumentality, or foreign agent, knowingly—
(1) steals, or without authorization appropriates, takes, carries away, or conceals, or by fraud, artifice, or deception obtains a trade secret;
(2) without authorization copies, duplicates, sketches, draws, photographs, downloads, uploads, alters, destroys, photocopies, replicates, transmits, delivers, sends, mails, communicates, or conveys a trade secret;
(3) receives, buys, or possesses a trade secret, knowing the same to have been stolen or appropriated, obtained, or converted without authorization;
(4) attempts to commit any offense described in any of paragraphs (1) through (3); or
(5) conspires with one or more other persons to commit any offense described in any of paragraphs (1) through (3), and one or more of such person do any act to effect the object of the conspiracy, shall, except as provided in subsection (b), be fined not more than $500,000 or imprisoned not more than 15 years, or both.
(b) Organizations—Any organization that commits any offense described in subsection (a) shall be fined not more than $10,000,000.
89. See id. § 1832. Section 1832 provides in full:
(a) Whoever, with intent to convert a trade secret, that is related to or included in a product that is produced for or placed in interstate or foreign commerce, to the economic benefit of anyone other than the owner thereof, and intending or knowing that the offense will injure any owner of that trade secret, knowingly—
(1) steals, or without authorization appropriates, takes, carries away, or conceals, or by fraud, artifice, or deception obtains such information;
(2) without authorization copies, duplicates, sketches, draws, photographs, downloads, uploads, alters, destroys, photocopies, replicates, transmits, delivers, sends, mails, communicates, or conveys such information;
(3) receives, buys, or possesses such information, knowing the same to have been stolen or appropriated, obtained, or converted without authorization;
(4) attempts to commit any offense described in paragraphs (1) through (3); or
(5) conspires with one or more other persons to commit any offense described in paragraphs (1) through (3), and one or more of such persons do any act to effect the object of the conspiracy, shall except as provided

provision used at trial to date, criminalizes commercial theft of trade secrets, regardless of who receives the benefits.

The EEA as drafted presents potential issues for those accused of criminal trade secret theft both because of its breadth and because the elements of the statute are not clearly defined. With computer use pervading the workplace, the implications of the Act are increased. An employee can more easily depart her workplace with a disk full of confidential information than with an armload of hard copies.

2. The Wide Expansion of Trade Secret Prosecution

Section 1832 of the EEA requires the government to establish that: (1) the defendant stole, or without authorization of the owner, obtained, destroyed or conveyed information; (2) the defendant knew that this information was proprietary; and (3) the information was in fact trade secret information.[90]

The EEA encompasses not only the removal of property from the owner's physical possession, but also less-traditional methods of misappropriation (often computer assisted). These include, among others, copying, duplicating, replicating, transmitting, delivering, sending, communicating, or conveying, thereby fulfilling Congress's intention "to ensure that the misappropriation of intangible information is prohibited in the same way that the theft of physical items are protected."[91]

The government must further prove that a defendant under the EEA acted "without authorization" from the owner of the property. Authorization is "the permission, approval, consent or sanction of the owner" to obtain, destroy or convey the trade secret.[92] The EEA only protects against knowing misappropriation of trade secrets.[93] The government must establish that the defendant was aware or substantially certain that he was misappropriating a trade secret.[94] Trade secrets have been traditionally limited

---

   in subsection (b), be fined under this title or imprisoned not more than 10 years, or both.

  (b) Any organization that commits any offense described in subsection (a) shall be fined not more than $5,000,000.

90. *See id.* §§ 1831, 1832.
91. S. Rep. No. 359, 104th Cong., 2d Sess. 16 (1996).
92. 142 CONG. REC. S12202, S12212 (daily ed. Oct. 2, 1996).
93. 18 U.S.C. § 1832(a) (Supp. IV 1998).
94. Computer Crime & Intellectual Property Section, Criminal Division, U.S. Dept. of Justice, *Federal Prosecution of Violations of Intellectual Property Rights (Copyrights, Trademarks and Trade Secrets)*, at 73, http://www.usdoj.gov:80/criminal/cybercrime/ip-

to scientific or technical information, but the EEA's definition of a "trade secret" is significantly broader than the scope of the Uniform Trade Secrets Act ["UTSA"], upon which many state criminal trade secrets statutes are based.[95] In addition, the government must show the defendant intended or knew the offense would injure the trade secret owner.[96]

Finally, the owner must have "taken reasonable measures to keep such information secret," and the information must derive economic value from not being generally known to or readily ascertainable by the public.[97]

The sponsors of the EEA stated that the Act does not criminalize the instance of employees leaving an employer and using general knowledge and skills developed while employed (which would, of course, include every employee who changed jobs within the same field). Instead, the legislative history expressed the intent to limit application of the EEA to employees who use a prior employer's knowledge about specific products to duplicate them or develop similar goods for themselves or their new employer.[98]

3. Defending Against Liability Under the EEA

Most EEA cases to date have involved theft by "insiders," that is, company employees stealing employee trade secrets. Several employment situations seem uniquely poised for scrutiny and potential liability for both a company and an employee under the EEA: (1) A company hires an employee who has substantial knowledge of his former employer's intellectual property; (2) a company buys a business that has employees who recently worked for another employer in the industry; (3) a company uses consultants who are privy to industry technical and marketing information because of their work with competitors. When a company hires a new employee who brings along her former employer's confidential information,

---

manual/05ipma.htm (Visited Jan. 30, 2001) [hereinafter U.S. D.O.J., *Prosecution of I.P. Crime*].

95. The UTSA covers "information, including a formula, pattern, compilation, program, device, method, technique, or process...." under 18 U.S.C. § 1839(3) (Supp. IV 1998). The EEA's definition of trade secrets includes:
> all forms and types of financial, business, scientific, technical, economic, or engineering information, including patterns, plans, compilations, program devices, formulas, designs, prototypes, methods, techniques, processes, procedures, programs, or codes, whether tangible or intangible, and whether or how stored, compiled, or memorialized physically, electronically, graphically, photographically or in writing.

96. 18 U.S.C. § 1832(a) (Supp. IV 1998).
97. *Id.* § 1839 (3)(A)-(B).
98. H. Rep. No. 788, 104th Cong., 2d Sess., *reprinted in* 1996 U.S.C.C.A.N. 4021.

the employee and employer are both at significant risk of criminal liability under the EEA, regardless of whether the employer is aware of the employee's inside information.

a. The Prosecutors' Perspective on Defenses

The Department of Justice has identified four categories of defenses which companies and employees may use to try to avoid liability under the EEA and the DOJ attempted to train prosecutors about how to respond to challenges: Parallel development, reverse engineering, general knowledge, and the First Amendment.

(1) Parallel Development

The Supreme Court has acknowledged that the owner of a trade secret does not have an absolute, sole right to possession of a trade secret. Other companies and individuals can discover or invent the same trade secret through their own research and work.[99] A defendant in an EEA prosecution can therefore assert as a defense that his possession of another's trade secret was derived through independent work. The government must disprove this possibility beyond a reasonable doubt as this defense is implicit in the statute's mens rea requirement.[100]

(2) Reverse Engineering

Reverse engineering refers to the practice of taking something apart to determine how it was made or manufactured.[101] The EEA itself does not mention reverse engineering, but the legislative history states: "[T]he important thing is to focus on whether the accused has committed one of the prohibited acts of this statute rather than whether he or she has reverse engineered. If someone has lawfully gained access to a trade secret and can replicate it without violating copyright, patent, or this law, then that form of 'reverse engineering' should be fine."[102]

Although the EEA suggests that reverse engineering can serve as a valid defense to the misappropriation of trade secrets (since no trade secret is

---

99. *See* Kewanee Oil Co. v. Bicron Corp., 416 U.S. 470, 490–91 (1974) ("If something is to be discovered at all, very likely it will be discovered by more than one person....").
100. *See* 18 U.S.C. § 1832(a) (Supp. IV 1998) (requiring that the defendant's actions were "knowing").
101. *See* Kewanee Oil Co., 416 U.S. at 476.
102. 142 Cong. Rec. S12201, S12212 (daily ed. Oct. 2, 1996).

being taken), it is not enough for a defendant to claim that the trade secret *could have been* discovered through reverse engineering.[103] The defense of reverse engineering therefore rests on the means actually used to develop the purported "trade secret."[104]

(3) General Knowledge

"The government can not prosecute an individual for taking advantage of the general knowledge and skills or experience that he or she obtains or comes by during his tenure with a company. Allowing such prosecutions to go forward and allowing the risk of such charges to be brought would unduly endanger legitimate and desirable economic behavior."[105] The defense of general knowledge applies particularly to the situation where an employee changes employers or starts his own company within the same industry. That employee cannot be prosecuted merely because he was exposed to the first employer's trade secret information, unless the government can establish that the employee stole or misappropriated a trade secret.[106]

(4) The First Amendment

Freedom of speech can serve as a defense to a claim of misappropriation of trade secrets if a defendant acts to serve or educate the public; however, if the government can establish the element of the EEA that a defendant intended his misappropriation to economically benefit a third party and harm the secret's owner, that defendant will not succeed with a claim of First Amendment protection for his actions.[107] The First Amendment does not protect speech made for economic gain with intent to harm another. In a related context, one court noted:

---

103. *See* Telerate Sys., Inc. v. Caro, 689 F. Supp. 221, 232 (S.D.N.Y. 1988).
104. *See id.*
105. 142 CONG. REC. S12201, S12213 (daily ed. Oct. 2, 1996).
106. U.S. D.O.J., *Prosecution of I.P. Crime*. Although the DOJ indicates that employers and employees will not face criminal liability for taking with them general knowledge from one employer to another, an employee may nevertheless be enjoined from working for a new employer in the same field. Specifically, the "inevitable disclosure doctrine" serves as the basis for enjoining employees from working for new employers in the same field where disclosure of a former employer's trade secrets is inevitable due to the nature of the new employment. Unlike the EEA, the doctrine of inevitable disclosure does not focus on the means by which an employee comes to learn a trade secret, but is concerned with the inevitability of that secret's disclosure to the employee's new employer. *See, e.g.,* Pepsico, Inc. v. Redmond, 54 F.3d 1262 (7th Cir. 1995).
107. *Id.*

[t]he defense is further unavailable if the speech itself is the vehicle of the crime. [T]he court finds no support for [defendant's] argument that the criminal activities with which he is charged... [are] protected by the First Amendment. Interpreting the First Amendment as shielding [defendant] from criminal liability would open a gaping hole in criminal law; individuals could violate criminal laws with impunity simply by engaging in criminal activities which involve speech-related activity. The First Amendment does not countenance that kind of end run around criminal law.[108]

The DOJ recommends that prosecutors seek an *in limine* order precluding the introduction of First Amendment protection when possible in these cases.[109]

b. Practical Conclusions

Often the most important time to "defend" a cybercrime case is before indictment. Some practical strategies both in dealing with the prosecution and in actively defending an EEA case can be deduced from experience, the case law and the DOJ's recent guidance on the EEA. At the pretrial stage, the defense attorney must:

- Focus the prosecutor on the standard of showing criminal intent beyond a reasonable doubt. The prosecutor will be looking primarily to civil case law in developing his or her theories and definitions of the case and may therefore forget that this is not a civil trade secret case.
- Challenge the trade secret status of the information at issue. If the defense can show the prosecution that the defendant made an effort to determine whether the information was a trade secret, and reasonably determined that it was not, then a jury may reach the same conclusion.
- Portray the information used by the client as "soft" business competitive information, as opposed to "hard" scientific data. The DOJ is more likely to prosecute theft of scientific information that is concrete and defined.
- Show, when possible, that the information is not of significant economic value.

---

108. U.S. v. Riggs, 743 F. Supp. 556, 560 (N.D. Ill. 1990).
109. See Note 106, *infra*.

- Suggest that the DOJ should be reluctant to thrust itself into business disputes that are being addressed by civil litigation.

E. The Copyright Act[110]

Copyright protection is as old as the Constitution itself,[111] yet is significantly challenged by computer technology. Criminal penalties for copyright infringement first appeared in 1909. In 1976, Congress preempted state law, making criminal copyright enforcement exclusively a federal function.[112] In the last twenty-five years, however, Congress has consistently expanded the scope of the copyright laws and dramatically increased the corresponding penalties.[113] Criminal sanctions for copyright violations are found in both Titles 17 and 18 of the United States Code.[114] Copyright infringement has recently become an even greater focus of law enforcement with increased use of computers and, more specifically, the Internet.[115]

1. Criminal Copyright Infringement and the NET Act

Title 17 U.S.C. § 506(a) is the principal criminal statute protecting copyrighted works. It provides: "Any person who infringes a copyright willfully and for purposes of commercial advantage or private financial gain shall be punished as provided in section 2319 of title 18."[116] Section 2319 in turn

---

110. *See* Joseph F. Savage, Jr., *Copyright Infringement, Trademark Counterfeiting and Intellectual Property Crime, in* 2 White Collar Crime: Business and Regulatory Offenses, Chapter 22 (Robert G. Morvillo & Betsy H. Turner eds. 2000 Update).
111. U.S. Const. art. I, § 8, cl. 8.
112. *See* 17 U.S.C. § 301 (1994 & Supp. IV 1998).
113. *See* 17 U.S.C. § 506(a) (Supp. IV 1998) (criminalizing copyright infringement), 506(c)-(e) (1994) (criminalizing conduct that undermines the integrity of the copyright system); 18 U.S.C. § 2319 (1994 & Supp. IV 1998) (outlawing unauthorized production of trafficking in sound recordings and musical videos of live performances, and computer theft of copyrighted works).
114. *See* previous note, *supra*.
115. MP3.com and Napster.com, both specializing in access to digital copies of CDs, made headlines when they were sued for copyright infringement by the Recording Industry Association of America (RIAA). Although civil disputes, the cases and the potential damages involved illustrate the need for companies to be aware of the reach of copyright laws in the age of computers. *See* UMG Recordings, Inc., v. MP3.Com, Inc., 109 F. Supp. 2d 223 (S.D.N.Y. 2000); A&M Records, Inc. v. Napster, Inc., 114 F. Supp. 2d 896 (N.D. Cal. 2000).
116. 17 U.S.C. § 506(a) (Supp. IV 1998).

provides for both imprisonment and a fine, both to be determined based on the amount and value of distribution in violation of section 506.[117] The NET Act was enacted in 1997, and amended section 506 to read:

> (a) Criminal infringement—Any person who infringes a copyright willfully either—
> (1) for purposes of commercial advantage or private financial gain, or
> (2) by the reproduction or distribution, including by electronic means, during any 180-day period, of 1 or more copies or phonorecords of 1 or more copyrighted works, which have a total retail value of more than $1,000, shall be punished as provided under section 2319 of title 18, United States Code. For purposes of this subsection, evidence of reproduction or distribution of a copyrighted work, by itself, shall not be sufficient to establish willful infringement.[118]

Section 2319 was also amended to provide additional penalties for offenses occurring on or after December 16, 1997.[119] After December 16, 1997, under the NET Act, copyright offenses that did not involve commercial or financial gain could be criminally prosecuted for the first time.

To prove copyright infringement after the enactment of the NET Act, the prosecution must show: (1) the existence of a valid copyright, (2) infringement of the copyright by the defendant, (3) that the defendant acted willfully, either (4) for purposes of commercial advantage or private financial gain, or by the reproduction or distribution, including by electronic means, during any 180-day period, of one or more copies or phonorecords

---

117. 18 U.S.C. § 2319(b) (1994 & Supp. IV 1998):
"Any person who commits an offense under Section 506(a)(1) of title 17—
(1) shall be imprisoned not more than 5 years, or fined in the amount set forth in this title, or both, if the offense consists of the reproduction or distribution, during any 180-day period, of at least 10 copies or phonorecords, of 1 or more copyrighted works, with a retain value of more than $2,500; (2) shall be imprisoned not more than 10 years, or fined in the amount set forth in this title, or both, if the offense is a second or subsequent offense under paragraph (1); and (3) shall be imprisoned not more than 1 year, or fined in the amount set forth in this title, or both, in any other case."
118. Subsection 506(a)(2) was added by amendment on December 16, 1997. Pub. L. No. 105-147, § 2(b), 111 Stat. 2678.
119. 18 U.S.C. § 2319 (1994 & Supp. IV 1998).

of "1 or more copyrighted works, which have a total retail value of more than $1,000."[120]

2. Defenses to Criminal Copyright Infringement

a. Invalidate the Copyright

A built-in defense to a claim of copyright infringement is that the copyright at issue is not valid. A defendant can attack the validity of a copyright in several ways. The copyright must first be registered, and infringement of an unregistered copyright is not generally criminally punishable.[121] The law does not require, however, that the copyright be registered at the time of infringement. A subsequent valid registration meeting the requirements of the Register of Copyrights is evidence of a valid copyright.[122]

A defendant can also invalidate a copyright by demonstrating fraud in obtaining the copyright. This requires proof that, but for the fraud, the copyright would not have been registered.[123] For example, the defendant could show that the entity that registered the copyright was not its author under the copyright act. When a defendant challenges a copyright's validity, the government must then independently prove validity.

b. No Infringement

The Copyright Act defines an infringer of a copyright as "[a]nyone who violates any of the exclusive rights" of the copyright as enumerated in the statute.[124] Sections 106 and 106A list the exclusive rights as the right to prepare derivative works, the right to public display or performance of the work, and the right to reproduce and distribute copies of the work.[125] To prove the element of infringement, the government must demonstrate that the defendant exercised these exclusive rights of the owner.

---

120. Additionally, the Sixth and Ninth Circuits require proof of the absence of a first sale. *See, e.g.,* U.S. v. Sachs, 801 F.2d 839 (6th Cir. 1986); U.S. v. Atherton, 561 F.2d 747, 749 (9th Cir. 1977).

121. *See* 17 U.S.C. §411(b) (1994 & Supp. IV 1998) (providing that owners of works of sounds or images, first fixed by transmission may institute an infringement action if they serve notice upon an infringer not less than 48 hours before transmission, and make registration for the work within three months).

122. A certificate of registration made within five years after the first publication of the work is *prima facie* evidence of the validity of the copyright under 17 U.S.C. §410(c) (1994).

123. *See* 15 U.S.C. §1115(b)(1) (1994).

124. 17 U.S.C. §501(a) (1994).

125. *Id.* §§106, 106A (1994 & Supp. IV 1998).

Defendants may avail themselves of a number of statutory exceptions to infringement and limitations on exclusive rights, including reproduction of a limited number of copies by libraries and archives, certain exempted performances or displays, secondary transmissions of certain performances or displays to a controlled group, transmissions or distribution of ephemeral recordings, secondary transmissions of works by satellite carriers and networks for private home viewing, and reproduction and distribution of copies for blind or disabled people.[126] A further specific exemption allowing copying of computer programs for adaptation in order to use the program "in connection with a machine" or "for archival purposes" is codified at 17 U.S.C. § 117.

c. First Sale Doctrine

An affirmative defense (in most circuits) limiting the exclusive rights associated with copyright is the "first sale doctrine," which provides that a sale of a lawfully-made copy terminates the copyright owner's authority to restrict subsequent sales or distributions of that particular copy.[127] The doctrine, however, does not permit a purchaser of a lawful copy to reproduce or distribute additional copies of the work, and is unavailable to anyone who has acquired only possession of the copy at issue without also acquiring ownership of the copyrighted work.[128]

d. Fair Use Doctrine

Another defense to a claim of copyright infringement is the "fair use" doctrine,[129] which exempts from prosecution certain activities that actually further the purpose of copyright law, although they would otherwise constitute copyright infringement.[130] Fair use has been codified in Title 17:

> [T]he fair use of a copyrighted work... for purposes such as criticism, comment, news reporting, teaching... scholarship, or re-

---

126. *See id.* §§ 108, 110-16, 118-19.
127. *Id.* § 109(a) (1994). The Sixth and Ninth Circuits interpret the Copyright Act to require proof of the absence of a first sale, thereby viewing it as an element of the crime rather than an affirmative defense. *See, e.g.,* U.S. v. Sachs, 801 F.2d 839 (6th Cir. 1986); U.S. v. Atherton, 561 F.2d 747, 749 (9th Cir. 1977).
128. *See* 17 U.S.C. § 109(d) (1994).
129. *See id.* § 107.
130. *See* Sony Corp. of America v. Universal City Studios, Inc., 464 U.S. 417, 477 ("There are situations... in which strict enforcement of this monopoly would inhibit the very [goal] that copyright [was] intended to promote.").

search, is not an infringement of copyright. In determining whether the use made of a work in any particular case is a fair use the factors to be considered shall include—
(1) the purpose and character of the use, including whether such use is of a commercial nature or is for nonprofit educational purposes;
(2) the nature of the copyrighted work;
(3) the amount and substantiality of the portion used in relation to the copyrighted work as a whole; and
(4) the effect of the use upon the potential market for or value of the copyrighted work. The fact that a work is unpublished shall not itself bar a finding of fair use if such finding is made upon consideration of all the above factors.[131]

The federal courts have considered these four factors in the context of alleged copyright infringement involving computers. The Ninth Circuit, for example, applied the fair use doctrine to a defendant's copying of a video game object code through reverse engineering because the defendant company had a legitimate interest in determining how to make its game cartridges compatible with another's video game console.[132] A First Circuit concurring opinion stated that defendant's use of Lotus' spreadsheet menu bar would constitute fair use even if such use otherwise constituted copyright infringement.[133]

e. Willfulness: The Use Was Authorized

Because the Copyright Act prohibits only unauthorized infringement, it is a defense to a claim of copyright infringement that the distribution, reproduction or other use of a copyright work was, in fact, "authorize[d]."[134] A clear-cut example of such a defense would be where the defendant possesses evidence of a license for distribution.

The Copyright Act does not define "authorization," however, and not all examples are so simple. Rather than asserting that the use at issue was actually authorized, a defendant may rely on "apparent authority." An exam-

---

131. 17 U.S.C. § 107 (1994).
132. *See* Sega Enterprises Ltd. v. Accolade, Inc., 977 F.2d 1510 (9th Cir. 1992).
133. *See* Lotus Dev. Corp. v. Borland Int'l, Inc., 49 F.3d 807, 821 (1st Cir. 1995) (Boudin, concurring), *aff'd*, 516 U.S. 233 (1996) (equally divided court).
134. *See* 17 U.S.C. § 106 (1994) (Both granting exclusive rights to the owner of the copyright and allowing the owner to "authorize" others to exercise these rights).

ple of apparent authority is a good faith belief that the reproduction or distribution at issue was within the scope of a license from the copyright holder. As revealed in the legislative history of the Copyright Act, Congress did not intend the criminal law to be the forum for resolving "the scope of licenses" or other private disputes between business.[135]

f. Copyright Misuse

A defendant may also raise the defense of copyright misuse to claims of copyright infringement involving computer software. When arguing copyright misuse, the defendant asserts that the owner is using the copyright in a manner violative of the public policy.[136] The defense, if successful, renders the copyright unenforceable, but does not invalidate the copyright.[137] Originally applied in patent cases, the misuse defense is generally raised in cases where a copyright owner attempts to extend the scope of his or her exclusive rights beyond those granted under the Copyright Act.[138]

The copyright misuse defense was successfully raised in *Qad. Inc. v. ALN Assoc. Inc.*,[139] where the defendants had copied part of plaintiffs' software. Defendants raised the affirmative defense of misuse, arguing that plaintiffs improperly extended their ownership rights because in creating their software, plaintiffs had copied another company's software program.[140] Agreeing with the defendants, the court allowed the defense and found that plaintiffs had misused their copyright in trying to assert ownership rights over portions of their software that had been copied from someone else.[141] The court stressed that it "...should not and will not offer its aid to a copyright holder whose actions run contrary to the purpose of the copyright itself."[142]

---

135. H.R. Rep. No. 997, 102 Cong., 2d Sess. at 5, reprinted in 6 U.S.C.C.A.N. 3573 (1992). For a more complete discussion of authority as a defense to copyright infringement, *see* Robert C. Kain, Jr., *Independent Contractors and Computer Crimes—The Impossible Prosecution?*, 1 B.U. J. Sci. & Tech. L. 13 (1995).

136. *See* Lasercomb Am., Inc. v. Reynolds, 911 F.2d 970, 978 (4th Cir. 1990). *See generally*, Ralph D. Clifford, *Simultaneous Copyright and Trade Secret Claims: Can the Copyright Misuse Defense Prevent Constitutional Doublethink?*, 104 Dick. L.R. 247, 252–71 (2000).

137. *See* Morton Salt Co. v. G.S. Suppiger Co., 314 U.S. 488, 492–94 (1942).

138. *See* 4 Melville B. Nimmer & David Nimmer, Nimmer on Copyright, §13.09[A], at 13–284 (2000).

139. 770 F. Supp. 1261 (N.D. Ill. 1991), *aff'd*, 974 F.2d 834 (7th Cir. 1992).

140. *Id.* at 1265–66.

141. *Id.* at 1270.

142. *Id.*

Generally, when applying the misuse defense, courts will analyze whether the copyright owner has in some way acted contrary to the public policy of copyright law or violated an anti-trust law. Where neither has occurred, courts will typically refuse to apply the misuse defense in cases involving computer software infringement. Further, since this defense only renders the copyright unenforceable rather than invalid, it is likely to be most useful at sentencing to show the limited harm from the defendant's conduct.

3. Pseudo-Copyright Infringement

Congress has enacted statutes imposing copyright-like criminal penalties and creating offenses that may be charged along with copyright infringement.

a. Trafficking in Counterfeit Labels or Computer Program Documentation or Packaging

Section 2318 of Title 18 prohibits two distinct offenses: (1) trafficking in counterfeit labels affixed or designed to be affixed to a phonorecord, a copy of a computer program, or documentation or packaging of a computer program, a copy of a motion picture or other audiovisual work; and (2) trafficking in counterfeit documentation or packaging of a computer program.[143] Violators may be subject to a fine or imprisonment of no more than five years, or both.[144]

For purposes of the statute, "trafficking" means transferring, transporting or otherwise disposing of the materials.[145] The label, documentation or packaging must be shown to be counterfeit, meaning that it is created to appear genuine but is not, as opposed to a pirated copy, which is not made to look legitimate.[146]

---

143. 18 U.S.C. § 2318(a) (Supp. IV 1998) provides:

(a) Whoever, in any of the circumstances described in subsection (c) of this section, knowingly traffics in a counterfeit label affixed or designed to be affixed to a phonorecord, or a copy of a computer program or documentation or packaging for a computer program, or a copy of a motion picture or other audiovisual work, and whoever, in any of the circumstances described in subsection (c) of this section, knowingly traffics in counterfeit documentation or packaging for a computer program, shall be fined under this title or imprisoned for not more than five years, or both.

144. *Id.*
145. *Id.* § 2318(b)(2) (1994).
146. *See* U.S. v. Schultz, 482 F.2d 1179, 1180–81 (6th Cir. 1973).

b. Unauthorized Fixation of and Trafficking in Sound Recordings and Music Videos of Live Performance

If a live performance is not "fixed in any tangible medium of expression," the unauthorized recording of a live performance may not violate the performer's copyright in the performance.[147] Section 2319A protects live performances and criminalizes the making of unauthorized "bootleg" recordings of live performances.[148]

The statute criminalizes the recording of sounds or images of a performance, transmitting the sounds or images, or distributing or offering to distribute or sell the sounds and images of a live musical performance.[149] The government must also show that the defendant acted knowingly, for purposes of commercial or financial gain, and without the consent of the performers.[150] Penalties under the statute for first time offenders include fines up to $250,000, five years imprisonment, or both and for repeat offenders include up to $250,000, ten years imprisonment, or both.[151]

c. Digital Millennium Copyright Act

The Digital Millennium Copyright Act[152] ["DMCA"] amended the Copyright Act to tackle copyright protection issues posed by digital information and the Internet. These amendments created two new criminal copyright offenses. Section 1201 protects against circumvention of technological measures used to protect copyright systems, which includes methods "to descramble a scrambled work, to decrypt an encrypted work, or otherwise to avoid, bypass, remove, deactivate, or impair a technological measure, without the authority of the copyright owner."[153] "Fair use" is a defense under section 1201.[154]

Section 1202 protects against the concealment of copyright infringement caused by tampering with copyright management information ["CMI"].

---

147. An unauthorized recording would likely infringe a copyright on the underlying musical work. *Cf.* Broadcast Music, Inc. v. Claire's Boutiques, Inc., 949 F.2d 1482, 1486 (7th Cir. 1991), *cert. denied*, 504 U.S. 911 (1992).
148. 18 U.S.C. § 2319A(a) (1994).
149. *Id.*
150. *See id.*
151. *See id.*
152. Pub. L. 105-304 §§ 101–05, 112 Stat. 2872 (1998), *codified at* 17 U.S.C. §§ 1201–05 (Supp. IV 1998).
153. 17 U.S.C. § 1201(a)(3)(A) (Supp. IV 1998).
154. *Id.* § 1201(c)(1).

CMI includes: (1) identifying information about the work, author, owner or performer of the work; (2) the terms and conditions for the use of the work; (3) identifying numbers or symbols referring to such information, or links to such information; and (4) other information as prescribed by the Register of Copyrights by regulation.[155] First time offenders of Section 1201 or 1202 can be fined up to $500,000 and/or imprisoned for not more than five years.[156] A repeat offender may be fined up to $1,000,000 and/or imprisoned for not more than ten years.[157] Where violations involve nonprofit libraries, archives or educational institutions, criminal penalties are not applied, but money damages may be awarded.[158]

d. Fraudulent Copyright Notice and Removal of Such Notices

Use of a notice of copyright informs the public of the copyright ownership and rights. Fraudulently using and/or removing such notices are distinct criminal offenses.[159] Violations of either section can lead to a fine of up to $2500.[160]

e. False Representation in Application to Register Copyright

In order to receive statutory damages for copyright infringement, a copyright owner must procure a registration of the copyright from the Library of Congress.[161] Section 506(e) prohibits the making of any false representations in an application to register a copyright.[162] The government must prove that the misstatement was material and that the defendant knowingly provided the erroneous information to the Copyright Office. Violations of this section can subject a defendant to a maximum fine of $2500.[163]

---

155. *Id.* § 1202(c).
156. *Id.* § 1204(a)(1).
157. *Id.* § 1204(a)(2).
158. *Id.* § 1203.
159. *Id.* § 506(c)-(d) (1994).
160. *Id.*
161. *Id.* § 411 (1994 & Supp. IV 1998).
162. *Id.* § 506(e) (1994).
163. *Id.*

II. General Defenses to Cybercrime Allegations

A. Search and Seizure Issues[164]

1. Introduction

The advances in computer technology and emergence of computer-related crimes have presented some complex legal questions in the areas of personal privacy. With the rise of the computer as a primary tool in many criminal schemes, law enforcement officials have recognized that any search for incriminating evidence must now include a search of computer files and data, in addition to the areas traditionally searched. Additional concerns arise as an increasing number of people use computers to store private information and transmit personal messages. There is a growing risk that the government will invade private lives through electronic surveillance.

The legislature has addressed these concerns with the enactment of statutes aimed at protecting the privacy of stored or transmitted computer data, such as the Electronic Communications Privacy Act ["ECPA"]. The Fourth Amendment also provides constitutional protection by prohibiting unreasonable government searches and seizures. Each of these will be discussed in turn.

2. Federal Statutory Protection

The Fourth Amendment protects individual privacy interests by limiting intrusions by the government, but does not apply to searches or monitoring by private citizens. Congress enacted the ECPA to extend privacy protections to invasions by both government entities and individuals not connected to the government.[165]

---

164. For further discussion on this topic *see generally* Raphael Winick, *Searches and Seizures of Computers and Computer Data*, 8 Harv. J.L. & Tech. 75 (1994) [hereinafter Winick, *Searches and Seizures*].

165. *See* 42 U.S.C. §§ 2000aa–2000aa-12 (1994). The PPA limits the government's ability to conduct intrusive searches of work product and documentary materials of those who disseminate public communications. The PPA restricts the government's ability to carry out searches or seizures of materials connected to the media and others conducting First Amendment activities. The statute requires that government authorities use subpoenas, not warrants, when searching documents, and computer systems of those who disseminate public communications. This prevents the government from

a. The ECPA — Interception of Electronic Communication

The ECPA protects wire and electronic communications affecting interstate commerce. In general, electronic communications within the language of the ECPA may be intercepted only by obtaining prior judicial approval upon showing probable cause that certain communications linking a defendant to a felony will be retrieved.[166] This requirement may be disregarded only in emergency situations, including cases of imminent physical harm to a person.[167]

The ECPA allows for the automatic suppression of unlawfully intercepted wire or oral communications, but does not make the same provision for the interception of electronic communications.[168] Even though suppression of such evidence is not automatic, a criminal defendant may argue for a suppression order.[169] In addition, if the interception also violates the Fourth Amendment, a criminal defendant may still exclude such evidence pursuant to the Fourth Amendment's exclusionary rule. The ECPA also allows for money damages, which may include punitive damages and attorneys' fees.[170]

b. SWECTRA — Accessing Stored Electronic Communications

As discussed, SWECTRA prohibits unauthorized access to stored electronic communications. SWECTRA delineates specific procedures for the government to follow before stored electronic communications may be accessed. Where a communication has been stored for less than 180 days, a valid warrant is required before the government can access the informa-

---

conducting surprise searches of newspapers, broadcasters or other corporations who disseminate books or magazines to the public. The PPA also prohibits government authorities from searching stand-alone computer systems that contain materials generated by the media or others disseminating public information, thereby eliminating a requirement under other privacy statutes that the computer be connected to a network affecting interstate commerce. Civil damages are the exclusive remedy for PPA violations, such that, evidence obtained in violation of the PPA will not be suppressed.

166. *See* 18 U.S.C. § 2518(3) (1994).
167. *See id.* § 2518(7).
168. *See id.* § 2518(10).
169. *See id.* § 2520(b)(1) (allowing "such preliminary and other equitable or declaratory relief as may be appropriate").
170. *See id.* § 2520.

tion.[171] Law enforcement officials may gain access to communications stored longer than 180 days through an administrative or grand jury subpoena, or through a court order executed after notice has been given to the user.[172] The owner of the computer system may seek to quash the order by demonstrating that the communications demanded are too voluminous in nature or that compliance with the order is unduly burdensome.[173]

A defendant may attempt to seek a suppression order as the ECPA provides for "preliminary and other equitable or declaratory relief as may be appropriate."[174] The contents of electronic communications acquired in violation of the statute, however, are not automatically excluded from judicial proceedings.

The statute also protects certain information from disclosure to the government, such as the identity of the sender or recipient of a message, or a user's location. Unless required by a court order, subpoena or warrant, an electronic communication service may not, without the user's consent, disclose such information to government authorities.[175] This restriction does not apply to a system operator, such as an employer, who unintentionally discovers communications relating to the commission of a crime.[176]

3. The Fourth Amendment

The Fourth Amendment protects citizens from unreasonable government searches and seizures. Most significantly, the Fourth Amendment requires that the government obtain a warrant before searching an area where an individual has a reasonable expectation of privacy. The warrant must be based on probable cause and particularly describe the place to be searched, and the persons or things to be seized.[177] Two exceptions to the warrant requirement that are particularly relevant to the area of computer searches and seizures are the "plain view" and consent exceptions.

---

171. See id. § 2703 (1994 & Supp. IV 1998).
172. See id. § 2703(b) (1994) (However, a warrant is still valid even if executed without prior notice).
173. See id. § 2703(d) (Supp. IV 1998).
174. Id. § 2707(b)(1) (1994).
175. See id. §§ 2703(a), (c)(1)(A). Ironically, no such prohibition applies when disclosing this information to private entities.
176. See id. § 2702(b)(6) (Supp. IV 1998).
177. U.S. CONST. amend. IV.

The Fourth Amendment remains the principal basis of protection of stand-alone computers and the data or information stored on an individual computer from searches by the government. Individuals may generally assume a high expectation of privacy in their personal computers.[178] An individual's Fourth Amendment right is personal, however, and one can only claim an expectation of privacy in property he or she owns, possesses or controls.[179]

a. Scope of Searches

An individual may challenge the search or seizure of a computer by arguing that the government exceeded the scope of the search. If the scope of a search is too broad, any evidence resulting from that search may be suppressed. Both the "particularity requirement" of warrants and the overbreadth doctrine work to ensure that searches and seizures do not exceed their permissible scope.

To meet the particularity requirement, a warrant must particularly describe the things to be searched and seized.[180] The particularity requirement is important in cases of computer searches because such searches can turn into sweeping examinations of a wide array of information. The particularity requirement safeguards personal privacy rights by ensuring that the government's search stays within the bounds of the items described in the warrant. Those bounds have differed by Court. While some courts have held that a search of hard disk space lacked particularity, others have found that warrants for seizure of all computer hardware and software were valid.[181]

The scope of a search may also be challenged for overbreadth, where a defendant argues that the scope of the search exceeded the specific things

---

178. Winick, *Searches and Seizures* at 103. (Home computers are exactly the sort of repositories of personal information that the Fourth Amendment protects most heavily).

179. *See* U.S. v. Taylor, No. 92 CR 322, 1992 WL 249969, at *19 (S.D.N.Y. Sept. 22, 1992) (One defendant attempted to challenge the search of a co-defendant's computer. The court found that because the defendant did not present evidence of any ownership or possessory interest in the computer searched, she lacked standing to challenge the search.).

180. *See* Maryland v. Garrison, 480 U.S. 79, 84 (1987).

181. *See* In re Grand Jury Subpoena Duces Tecum, 846 F. Supp. 11, 13–14 (S.D.N.Y. 1994). *See also* U.S. v. Hersch, CR-A-93-10339-2, 1994 WL 568728, at *1 (D. Mass. Sept. 27, 1994).

and area for which there was probable cause to search.[182] The overbreadth analysis is applied to subpoenas as well as warrants. In *In re Grand Jury Subpoena Duces Tecum*, the defendants challenged a grand jury subpoena requiring the production of computer disks that contained relevant, as well as irrelevant information.[183] The court quashed the subpoena as over broad, noting that because a keyword search could have identified the relevant files, there was no need to subpoena all of the computer disks.[184]

Other courts have interpreted warrants as allowing authorities to search and seize *all* computers and data where the warrant did not specify which records were to be searched.[185] In *United States v. Sissler*, authorities acting pursuant to a warrant allowing for the search and seizure of records of drug transactions were allowed to seize a personal computer and a large number of disks.[186] The court also concluded that the search could be performed off-site because breaking through the computer's security devices would involve greater effort.[187]

b. Intermingled Documents

The increasing focus of searches and seizures on computers and electronic data by authorities have increased the risk that a search will uncover not only information relevant to the investigation, but also personal information that is intermingled in the relevant documents. Preventing such widespread searches is precisely the purpose of the warrant requirement of the Fourth Amendment.

In *United States v. Tamura*, the Ninth Circuit announced a general rule to deal with the issues surrounding the search of intermingled documents.[188] The court held that when officers find relevant documents so intermingled with irrelevant documents, as they often are in computer directories, that they cannot reasonably be sorted at the site, they should seal

---

182. Maryland v. Garrison, 480 U.S. at 84.
183. In Re Grand Jury Subpoena Duces Tecum, 846 F. Supp. at 11.
184. *Id.* at 13.
185. *See* U.S. v. Musson, 650 F. Supp. 525, 531–32 (D. Colo. 1986) (allowing seizure of over 50 computer disks where warrant specified search of memoranda, correspondence, and any records or writings).
186. No. 90-CR-12, 1991 WL 239001 (W.D. Mich. Aug. 30, 1991), *aff'd*, 966 F.2d 1455, (6th Cir. 1992) (unpublished disposition), *cert. denied*, 506 U.S. 1079 (1993).
187. *Id.* at *4.
188. 694 F.2d 591 (9th Cir. 1982).

off or hold the documents until a magistrate can either sort them out or authorize a broader search.[189]

The *Tamura* rule has been applied to computer searches involving intermingled documents.[190] This rule allows authorities to remove the computer hardware and data before evidence can be altered or destroyed. At the same time, it accounts for individual privacy interests because once the authorities have control over the information, the files to be searched must be specified, preventing a widespread search of all the data seized. Once the computer data or hardware is lawfully seized, authorities may break passwords and defeat other security devices or encryption methods without obtaining another warrant. The government must return the equipment when the search of computer hardware, data or software is complete.[191] An individual may petition the court for return of the property, and where the government destroys or loses seized property, an aggrieved party may be entitled to damages.[192]

c. Plain View Doctrine

The "plain view" doctrine was first announced in *Coolidge v. New Hampshire*, and allows for the warrantless seizure of evidence of a crime if the officer lawfully obtained a plain view of the object, if the object's incriminating character was immediately apparent, and if the officer had lawful access to the object itself.[193] The doctrine has been applied in cases where the search of a computer pursuant to a valid warrant led to the discovery of other computer files not specified in the warrant.

In *United States v. Carey*, the court concluded that the "plain view" exception to the warrant requirement did not authorize a detective to open computer files that were not clearly specified in the warrant itself.[194] The police obtained a warrant to search the defendant's computer files for "documentary evidence pertaining to the sale and distribution of controlled substances."[195] While searching, a detective noticed image files with sexu-

---

189. *See id.* at 595–96.
190. *See* U.S. v. Carey, 172 F.3d 1268 (10th Cir. 1999) (applying the *Tamura* doctrine to computer search).
191. FED. R. CRIM. P. 41(d).
192. *Id.* 41(e).
193. 403 U.S. 443, 465 (1971).
194. 172 F.3d 1268, 1273 (10th Cir. 1999).
195. *Id.* at 1270.

ally suggestive titles.[196] Unable to find drug-related files, the detective continued to look by opening one of the image files, saw that it contained child pornography, and proceeded to download the rest of the child pornography files.[197]

Convicted of possessing child pornography, the defendant appealed, claiming that the detective exceeded the scope of the search because the warrant provided for the search of drug-related materials only. The government claimed that the "plain view" exception applied and compared the computer search to looking for drug-related documents in a file cabinet and finding child pornography instead.[198] The court disagreed and stated that the plain view exception did not apply because the *contents* of the files were seized, not the files themselves.[199] The court added that because the detective had originally obtained a warrant, he knew he was acting without judicial authority when he abandoned the search for drug-related evidence.[200]

The court limited its holding only to the image files opened *after* the inadvertent opening of the first file and stated that the image files in this case were closed and not in plain view. The court declined to answer the question as to what *would* constitute a plain view exception in the context of computer text files, where an officer might have to begin reading the files before determining their relevancy to the original search.

d. Consent Searches

A defendant may also challenge the validity of computer searches consented to by a business or an individual for exceeding the scope of the consent given. In *United States v. Turner*, the First Circuit held that a police search of the defendant's computer files exceeded the scope of the consent given, which objectively included only a search for incriminating objects in connection with the sexual assault of the defendant's neighbor.[201] In *Turner*, the defendant signed a consent authorizing police to search his apartment for evidence that the suspect of the assault had been inside the apartment.[202]

---

196. *See id.* at 1270–71.
197. *See id.*
198. *Id.* at 1272.
199. *Id.* at 1273.
200. *Id.*
201. 169 F.3d 84 (1st Cir. 1999).
202. *See id.* at 86.

While searching the apartment, the detective saw a photograph of a nude woman on the computer screen and, without obtaining a warrant, searched the computer hard drive and found evidence of child pornography.[203] Measuring the scope of consent by an "objective" reasonableness standard, the First Circuit affirmed the suppression of the computer files and held that the entire search was beyond the scope of the consent.[204]

The government in *Turner* also tried to argue that because the initial nude image was in "plain view," the rest of the files were "fair game" under the consensual search.[205] The court rejected this argument because the detectives did not tell the defendant the nature of the crime they were investigating. Therefore, the defendant could not have believed that his consent would include a search of evidence of a sexual nature.[206]

e. Privilege

Searches of business premises, and particularly business computers, can lead to the seizure of attorney-client material which is privileged. Law enforcement agencies have also recognized the potential consequences in court of obtaining privileged material when executing a search warrant and have in many cases implemented "taint" procedures to minimize such a risk. Common "taint" procedures contemplate that agents executing a search warrant should seize attorney-client materials, and then review those documents only to determine if they are potentially privileged. Potentially privileged documents are then to be segregated and delivered to an attorney (not involved in the investigation) who, in turn, reviews the contents of each potentially privileged document to determine if it is in fact protected by the attorney-client privilege.

These "taint" procedures are often insufficient to protect privileged materials because during the search, case agents are still reviewing and handling the most sensitive communications between counsel and clients relating to the underlying investigation. As such, defendants can challenge the search and demand the return of the documents or even disqualification of tainted case agents.

The court in *United States v. Lin Lyn Trading, Ltd.*,[207] supported the return of privileged documents and disqualification of tainted case agents. In

---

203. *See id.*
204. *See id.* at 88.
205. *See id.*
206. *See id.*
207. 149 F.3d 1112 (10th Cir. 1998).

that case, the government unlawfully seized a yellow notepad which contained privileged communications between the defendants and their attorney.[208] The notepad included incriminating statements and defenses relevant to the investigation. Defense counsel moved for a return of the notepad.[209] The district judge returned the notepad finding that it had been unlawfully seized and that the government's possession of it would cause irreparable injury.[210]

One month later, the defendants were indicted for various federal offenses and they moved to suppress the notepad and all evidence seized after that date claiming the illegally seized notepad provided a "roadmap" for the investigation.[211] The district court dismissed the indictment.[212] The Tenth Circuit recognized that the intentional seizure of privileged materials by government agents could violate the Fifth Amendment but adopted a remedy less drastic than dismissing the indictment.[213] That court held that there was "nothing to forbid the government from beginning a new investigation using the evidence legitimately acquired prior to [the seizure of the yellow notepad], and conducted by personnel—both investigatory and prosecutorial—untouched by the taint of the yellow notepad."[214]

B. Other Defenses

1. Anonymity

One of the issues in a computer crime case is that a network user can be anyone he or she wishes to be. The degree of anonymity that computers and the Internet provide is unparalleled.

A computer user's ability to be completely anonymous has significantly affected the criminal law. Prosecuting computer crime has become more difficult because computer users can easily hide behind false identities and screen names when carrying out illegal activity on a computer.[215] In fact, various services offered on the Internet guarantee anonymity.

---

208. *See id.* at 1113.
209. *See id.* at 1113–14.
210. *See id.* at 1114.
211. *See id.*
212. *See id.* at 1115.
213. *See id.* at 1117–18.
214. *See id.* at 1118.
215. *See* A. Michael Froomkin, *Flood Control on the Information Ocean: Living with Anonymity, Digital Cash, and Distributed Databases*, 15 J.L. & COM. 395, 398 (1996) ("...

Anonymous remailers are on-line systems designed to give a user an anonymous address to which people can send mail.[216] When the electronic mail is received at the anonymous address, it is then forwarded to the user's "real address." Anonymous remailers can also post or mail an individual's electronic messages without any trace of the sender's name or address.

A user's anonymity can be especially problematic in cases where a virus has been released on a system and law enforcement officials are looking for the author. In *United States v. Morris*,[217] the government faced this challenge with the investigation and prosecution of a Cornell University graduate student. In 1988, Morris released a "worm" from a computer at the Massachusetts Institute of Technology ["MIT"], intending to demonstrate the deficient security measures on the system and the ease with which the security could be bypassed.[218] The worm was released at MIT so as to disguise that it came from Morris at Cornell.[219] The worm spread quickly, causing severe damage to the computer networks.

The government's search for the author proved problematic because Morris had the advantage of anonymity. Once the defendant became a suspect, officials found copies of the worm that had been saved on the backup copies of his account. However, it was only when the defendant subsequently confessed, and the government was able to show that the defendant was logged on to his account at the time the worm was released, that the government was able to conclusively show that the defendant was the only author of the worm. In every case, "identity" thus becomes a crucial issue to pursue in the defense of an alleged cybercrime.

2. First Amendment as a Defense to Computer Crime

Computer use, including the Internet, has presented new challenges to the protections of the First Amendment. An attempt can be made to cast certain activities on the computer as constitutionally protected speech, not crime. "At the heart of the First Amendment lies the principle that each person should decide for him or herself the ideas and beliefs deserving of ex-

---

the availability of anonymous electronic communication directly affects the ability of governments to regulate electronic transactions over the Internet (both licit and illicit)").

216. One of the most famous anonymous servers on the Internet is Anon.penet.fi with over 500 users in the database.

217. 928 F.2d 504 (2d Cir.), *cert. denied*, 502 U.S. 817 (1991).

218. *Id.* at 506.

219. *Id.*

pression, consideration, and adherence. Our political system and cultural life rest upon this idea."[220]

Computer programs and encryption codes do not fit neatly under the traditional definition of protected speech, but those definitions are being expanded. The U.S. District Court for the Northern District of California, for example, held that the source code for a computer cryptography program was protectable speech under the First Amendment.[221] The State Department argued that the code was not entitled to protection because it was not intended to convey a particular message and was functional, not communicative.[222] The court nevertheless found the code to be language, which "is by definition speech, and the regulation of any language is the regulation of speech."[223]

Simply falling under the definition of speech, however, is not enough to warrant First Amendment Protection. Although not disputing that a computer program *may* constitute speech, in a criminal case, the Ninth Circuit denied First Amendment protection to a program because it was not *protected* speech.[224] The court required for protection "some evidence that the defendants' speech was information in a manner removed from immediate connection to the commission of a specific criminal act."[225] Because the computer program in question was not directed to any ideas or consequences other than committing a crime, the defendants' First Amendment claim was denied.[226] When appropriate, a defendant's conduct may be characterized as protected expression rather than criminal activity.

3. Entrapment

While the opportunity for anonymity on the Internet gives criminals the advantage of hiding behind pseudonyms, it also provides undercover officers with the same advantage in tracking criminals on the Internet.

Law enforcement officials are increasingly using undercover officers to "patrol" the Internet, especially in child pornography cases. Undercover of-

---

220. Turner Broadcasting Sys. v. F.C.C., 512 U.S. 622, 641 (1994).
221. *See* Bernstein v. U.S. Dept. of State, 922 F. Supp. 1426 (N.D. Cal. 1996), *aff'd*, 176 F.3d 1132 (9th Cir.), *opinion withdrawn & hearing en banc ordered*, 192 F.3d 1308 (9th Cir. 1999). *See also* Junger v. Daley, 209 F.3d 481 (6th Cir. 2000).
222. *See id.* at 1434.
223. *See id.* at 1435.
224. *See* U.S. v. Mendelsohn, 896 F.2d 1183, 1185 (9th Cir. 1990).
225. *See id.*
226. *See id.* at 1185–86.

ficers have entered chat rooms and posted messages feigning interest in child pornography with the intent to catch child molesters and other sexual offenders. When such tactics are successful, many defendants claim a defense of entrapment, at which point it is up to the government to show that the defendant was predisposed to commit the crime before the undercover agent entered the picture.

The Supreme Court has stated that "[i]n their zeal to enforce the law... Government agents may not originate a criminal design, implant in an innocent person's mind the disposition to commit a criminal act, and then induce commission of the crime so that the Government may prosecute."[227] On the other hand, "the fact that officers or employees of the Government merely afford opportunity or facilities for the commission of the offense does not defeat the prosecution."[228] The Ninth Circuit has applied this analysis to solicitation by the government through a computer.[229]

In *United States v. Poehlman*, the defendant, while searching "alternative lifestyle" Internet sites for adult companions, encountered a government agent posing as a mother seeking a "sexual mentor" for her three daughters. He was convicted of crossing state lines to engage in sex acts with a minor.[230] The defendant appealed, claiming that he was induced by the government to commit the crime and that he was not otherwise predisposed to do so.[231] Looking at the defendant's state of mind prior to his contact with the government agent, the Ninth Circuit found no evidence that the defendant was predisposed to engage in sexual relations with minors and reversed the conviction.[232]

III. Conclusion

Congressional reaction to the prevalence of computers in society has led to the enactment of several statutory schemes specifically aimed at punishing computer crimes as discrete offenses. With each new statute there are also both traditional criminal law defenses (lack of intent, alibi,

---

227. Jacobson v. U.S., 503 U.S. 540, 548 (1992).
228. *See id. quoting* Sorrells v. U.S., 287 U.S. 435, 441 (1932).
229. *See* U.S. v. Poehlman, 217 F.3d 692 (9th Cir. 2000).
230. *See id.* at 697.
231. *See id.* at 698.
232. *See id.* at 705.

entrapment, etc.) and new defenses to the government's proof of the specific statutory elements. As the technology changes, additional law enforcement efforts can be anticipated which will then be met by new defenses.

CHAPTER FIVE

INTERNATIONAL ASPECTS OF CYBERCRIME

JESSICA R. HERRERA[*]

I. INTRODUCTION

In 1986, an astronomer-turned-system manager at Lawrence Berkeley Laboratory in Berkeley, California was given the task of fixing a problem with the lab's accounting software. The lab ran two accounting programs that were responsible for tracking and billing computer users. Despite the fact that the programs tracked the same billing information, there existed a seventy-five cents discrepancy in their results. Clifford Stoll's job was to figure out why. He discovered a problem far more extensive than a mere accounting glitch.

Stoll determined that both software packages were functioning properly. Instead, what had occurred was an unauthorized user's attempts to penetrate the lab's systems without being detected. Stoll discovered that the user had created an account on the system without realizing that the bogus ac-

---

[*] Trial Attorney, Computer Crime and Intellectual Property Section, Criminal Division, Department of Justice. Member of the bars of Texas and D.C. The views expressed in this chapter are those of the author and do not necessarily represent the views of the United States. The author wishes to thank the following individuals for their insight and assistance with this chapter: Gloria Eldridge, Jennifer Martin, Christopher Painter, Betty Shave, Michael Sussmann and Martha Stansell-Gamm.

count's activity was only recorded by one software program. As detailed in the book *The Cuckoo's Egg*,[1] Stoll investigated further and uncovered an international spy ring that traced back to Markus Hess, a German hacker paid by the KGB to steal U.S. military secrets. Using a personal computer and modem, Hess connected to a German university and from there accessed Tymnet, an international data carrier, which then connected to various computers throughout the world, including U.S. military and educational computers. The seventy five cents discrepancy found at Berkeley demonstrated to law enforcement the threat that international computer crimes posed to U.S. national security, public safety and our critical infrastructures.

If the Berkeley hack did not make it clear to law enforcement that remotely-committed computer crimes should be taken seriously, the dissemination of the "Morris worm" two years later demonstrated the global and vulnerable nature of our interconnected computer systems. Robert Morris, Jr., a Cornell University student and the son of Robert Morris, a computer scientist with the National Security Agency, developed the "Morris worm," a program designed to attack networked computers.[2] The Morris worm replicated itself through the Internet, penetrating victim computers and, by taking up all available memory, shutting down the computers. The Morris worm spread quickly, crippling over 6,000 computers and causing over 98 million dollars in damage in just forty-eight hours. Large corporations and universities were shut down by the worm. Computer crime was no longer a theoretical problem.[3]

The Berkeley intrusion and Morris worm, as well as other early computer crime incidents, made it evident that the global nature of computer networks and the Internet[4] made it possible for criminals to know no national boundaries. As a result, law enforcement agencies were forced to re-

---

1. *See generally* CLIFF STOLL, THE CUCKOO'S EGG: TRACKING A SPY THROUGH THE MAZE OF COMPUTER ESPIONAGE (1989).
2. *See generally* KATIE HEFNER & JOHN MARKOFF, CYBERPUNK (1991).
3. While the mid-80s saw the Berkeley intrusion and Morris worm, there were earlier computer crime incidents of note. Phone phreakers, that is, individuals stealing service from telephone companies begin to appear and form groups in the 1970s. Hacking groups such as the "Legion of Doom" formed as early as 1984. For a chronology of hackers and the legal crackdown on them, *see* BRUCE STERLING, THE HACKER CRACKDOWN: LAW AND DISORDER ON THE ELECTRONIC FRONTIER (1992).
4. The Internet is a worldwide network of hundreds of thousands of computers that communicate with each other using a single standard protocol. The types of computers, communications links and software that are used vary widely.

formulate crime-fighting methods to facilitate multilateral international responses to cybercrime. Technology created new challenges that had to be addressed for nations to successfully combat cybercrimes such as computer intrusions, fraud, cyberstalking, child pornography and information warfare.[5] This chapter reviews the prevalent ways that computers are being used in criminal activity, the challenges created by the international aspects of cybercrimes and some of the unilateral and multilateral efforts countries are undertaking to overcome these challenges.

II. WHAT IS COMPUTER CRIME?

What is computer crime? Not every crime committed with a computer can be coined a "computer crime" or a "cybercrime." It would be impracticable to label every crime as such when almost every element of modern life involves some use of a computer. While it is very likely that computer security and information technology experts will continue to grapple with the definition of computer crime or cybercrime over the next several years, it is generally agreed that computers can be used in criminal activity in three ways.[6]

First, a computer can be the target of a criminal activity. This occurs when a criminal acts to illegally acquire information stored on the target system, to control the target system without authorization or payment, to alter the integrity of data, or to interfere with the availability of or damage the computer, server, or communications device. One way to think of this category is that it includes criminal attacks on the *confidentiality, integrity* or *availability* of a computer or network. Stoll's German hacker and the Morris worm both fit within this category. Over the years, the range of computer crimes fitting within this category have extended from defacement of websites by juveniles to distributed denial of service attacks to suspected computer intrusions conducted by foreign intelligence agencies. The individuals committing these crimes range from disgruntled insiders, hack-

---

5. *See generally* Robert J. Sciglimpaglia, Jr., Comment, *Computer Hacking: A Global Offense*, 3 PACE Y.B. INT'L L. 199 (1991).

6. The President's Working Group on Unlawful Conduct on the Internet, *The Electronic Frontier: The Challenge of Unlawful Conduct on the Internet*, http://www.usdoj.gov:80/criminal/cybercrime/unlawful.htm (2000) [hereinafter President's Working Group, *Unlawful Conduct Report*].

ers/crackers, hacktivists, virus disseminators, organized crime groups, cyberterrorists, foreign intelligence agencies and foreign militaries.[7]

By all accounts, these types of computer crimes will continue to increase and pose significant threats to the Internet, e-commerce and our critical infrastructure. According to Carnegie Mellon's CERT Coordination Center, the number of incidents reported each year has increased from six in 1988 to 21,756 in 2000[8] — an increase of over 100% from the 1999 total of 9,859.[9]

Second, a computer can be a tool that criminals use to commit offenses that often occur in the physical world. In this category are those crimes where the computer serves as the medium for undertaking conduct that is already illegal. These crimes include fraud, child pornography and sexual exploitation of children, intellectual property violations, distribution of narcotics and prescription drugs, illegal gambling, terrorism, financial crimes, extortion, cyberstalking, harassment and various other crimes. More information on this category can be found in *The Electronic Frontier: The Challenge of Unlawful Conduct on the Internet*, released March 2000, by the President's Working Group on Unlawful Conduct on the Internet.[10] In addition to raising serious concerns about the safety of our children and our society, the crimes fitting within this category are costing businesses millions of dollars. According to a study by Meridiem Research, credit card fraud alone cost merchants $400 million in 1999. The Business Software Alliance estimates that software piracy cost the United States some 109,000 jobs and $991 million in tax revenue in 1998.

Last, a computer can be an incidental accomplice that stores information that provide critical information related to criminal behavior. Computers are increasingly being used by criminals as "fancy" storage devices or filing cabinets. The evidence contained in these computers is often critical to a criminal investigation. For example, a drug dealer may store data on his customers on his personal data assistant. An individual that trades in false immigration papers may use a computer to create and store copies of those papers. A kidnapper may type a ransom note on his computer,

---

7. *Cybercrime: Hearing Before the Subcomm. on Crime of the House Comm. on the Judiciary and the Subcomm. on Criminal Oversight of the Senate Comm. on the Judiciary*, 106th Cong., 2d Sess. (Feb. 29, 2000) (statement of Michael A. Vatis, Director, National Infrastructure Protection Center, Federal Bureau of Investigation), http://www.cybercrime.gov/vatis.htm.

8. CERT Coordination Center, *CERT/CC Statistics 1988–2000*, http://www.cert.org/stats/cert_stats.html (visited Feb. 8, 2001).

9. *Id.*

10. *Id.*

leaving vital evidence behind. Law enforcement agencies around the world are finding that technology has changed the way they must investigate crimes and that evidence for just about any crime can may trace back to a computer or similar digital device.[11]

III. THE CHALLENGES OF CYBERCRIME

Transnational crime is not a new phenomenon. Nations with distinct and different legal frameworks have had to work together for centuries to combat dangerous international crimes such as terrorism, drug trafficking, forced slavery and organized crime. These crimes, however, still required the actor to have a physical presence within the country in which the crimes was committed. At the very least, law enforcement agencies could ascertain specific geographic locations where they expected to find evidence of criminal behavior.

The development of the Internet and other new technologies, however, has changed the nature of transnational crimes. Criminals no longer need a physical nexus with a particular country to commit a crime in that country. Individuals can commit crimes remotely and anonymously, operating across national borders, leaving evidence of their activities just about anywhere in the world. As a result, countries are reevaluating their legal structures and allocation of resources in order to meet the increasing demands to fight cybercrimes.

There are three types of challenges facing countries as they attempt to tackle cybercrime. First, technical challenges make it difficult to determine where evidence is located, whether it can be preserved and even whether the cybercriminal can be identified. Second, decision makers in countries throughout the world must decide how they will respond legally to the new threat, adopt adequate substantive and procedural laws, and enforce these laws meaningfully in the global Internet and network environment. Last, law enforcement agencies around the world are increasingly facing operational challenges, resulting from an increased demand for adequate resources, training and equipment to address cybercrime.

---

11. For the purposes of this chapter, the term "computer" includes the various digital and other high-technology devices that are used in criminal activities, including but not limited to, networks, personal and laptop computers, smart devices, personal data assistants, cellular phones, pagers and wireless and satellite services.

A. Technical Challenges

Cybercriminals are no longer hampered by national or international boundaries in conducting their illegal activities. Information and property can easily be transmitted through or stored in communications and data networks anywhere in the world within seconds. Criminals no longer need to be at the scene of the crime, or even on the same continent, for that matter, to find victims, exploit network vulnerabilities or find co-conspirators.

As a result, evidence of a local crime can now be located anywhere in the world. Take, for example, a hypothetical London resident who uses the e-mail address "stalker@US-ISP.com" to send threatening e-mails to a victim located a few blocks away or even next door. If US-ISP.com is an Internet service provider located in the United States, the London police must seek assistance from U.S. officials in obtaining information regarding the e-mails and the identity of the subscriber who uses "stalker@US-ISP.com." Even though the suspect and the victim are in the United Kingdom, the cybercrime has international consequences.

London law enforcement officials would face even more challenges if the stalker wanted to hide his or her identity, a task that is not impossible to do in today's Internet environment. The stalker could weave the communication through unfriendly countries that would not cooperate with the United Kingdom or through a series of anonymous remailers. Alternatively, the stalker could use "free-trial" accounts accessed from public computers, or create forged e-mail headers with point and click tools that are available on the Internet.[12]

If it were the case that London law enforcement officials had to find "stalker@US-ISP.com" immediately because he posed an immediate threat, the challenges become even more daunting. For example, if "stalker@US-ISP.com" stated that a bomb had been planted that would go off in hours, law enforcement officials would want to identify and locate "stalker" immediately. The current technical design of the Internet, as well as the legal regimes of many countries, hinders this ability. In some instances, the trail of a criminal may be impossible to trace once that individual terminates his connection, especially if a service provider or carrier does not keep traffic data or transmission information (i.e., connection times or source and destination logs). Complicating matters further is that a single communication often is handled by more than one carrier or ISP. For example, con-

---

12. See, e.g., *Cybercrime and Small Business, Hearing Before the House Comm. on Small Business*, 106th Cong. 2d Sess. (2000) (Statement of Scott Charney).

sider a typical route of an e-mail "packet."[13] The following, using traceroute on http://www.samspade.org, "traces" from AOL back to the IP address 63.36.40.168, the originating IP address of an e-mail received from an MSN e-mail account:[14]

    205.188.192.227 (ipt-fh04.proxy.aol.com)
    205.188.192.25 (tot2-dr5-G2-0.proxy.aol.com)
    205.188.168.29 (wc1-dtc-P6-1.aol.com)
    204.148.98.225 (pop1-dtc-P11-0.atdn.net)
    204.148.98.114 (gw1-iad2-P7-0.atdn.net)
    152.63.36.230 (133.at-5-0-0.XR2.DCA6.ALTER.NET)
    152.63.11.89 (0.so-3-0-0.TR2.DCA6.ALTER.NET)
    152.63.2.226 (121.at-5-0-0.TR2.SLT4.ALTER.NET)
    152.63.89.37 (290.at-1-0-0.XR2.SLT4.ALTER.NET)
    146.188.224.109 (186.ATM10-0-0.GW1.DEN1.ALTER.NET)
    137.39.68.201 (173.Serial2-0.AR1.DEN2.ALTER.NET)
    207.76.12.134 (dr1.den2.da.uu.net)
    204.177.252.66 (tnt1.denver2.co.da.uu.net)
    63.36.40.168 (1Cust168.tnt1.denver2.co.da.uu.net)
    63.36.40.168 (1Cust168.tnt1.denver2.co.da.uu.net)
    63.36.40.168 (1Cust168.tnt1.denver2.co.da.uu.net)

As this example demonstrates, a communication can pass through the systems of various different carriers before it reaches its destination. In some instances, the communication may also pass through carriers in a number of different countries, each in different time zones and subject to different legal systems.

In addition to locating and identifying criminals in a global connected environment, countries are also facing challenges related to preserving and gathering evidence related to cybercrime investigations. Information that previously could be found in paper form is now being kept in digital electronic formats on hard drives and networks. It is not uncommon for law enforcement investigators to come across computers with twenty and forty

---

13. An e-mail communications is divided into "packets" or pieces before it is sent over the Internet. The packets then travel different routes along the Internet and are recompiled into the final e-mail communication at their final destination to be viewed by the recipient.

14. Traceroute does not show the actual path taken by one of the received e-mail packets, but rather, routes three "new" packets from an IP address to a second IP address.

gigabyte drives, which can take computer forensic experts five to seven days to examine functionally. As the number of computers being seized and the amount of information being searched continues to grow, law enforcement agencies are finding that they cannot keep up with the volume of electronic evidence that is being produced.[15] Over the last decade, the FBI has gone from one computer forensic specialist to thirty in Washington and 140 others in field offices, handling 3,000 cases a year.[16]

On a related matter, there is a need for the standardization of forensic techniques both nationally and internationally to protect the integrity of evidence. Currently, the International Organisation of Computer Evidence has agreed to develop recommendations for standards, including the definition of terms, methods, and techniques for processing computer forensic requests. The Commission of the European Communities has recommended that the European Union be involved with this project.[17]

In addition, criminals are increasingly using encryption technologies to conceal their activities and thwart law enforcement efforts to collect critical evidence needed to solve and prosecute serious and often violent criminal activities.[18] The potential use of unbreakable encryption products by a vast array of criminals and terrorists, to conceal their criminal communications and information, poses an extremely serious threat to public safety and national security.

Other technical challenges are developing from emerging new technologies. Wireless, voice-over-IP and satellite communications are allowing consumers to stay connected practically anywhere in the world. While the benefits of these technologies are numerous, their use also raises national security and public safety concerns. Wireless and satellite communications systems can be configured in such a manner that the communications of a country's citizens are routed and processed entirely by foreign facilities. This occurrence hinders a country's ability to protect its citizens

---

15. *See e.g. Cybersleuths,* TEXAS MONTHLY, Aug. 1, 2000.

16. Greg Miller, *High-tech Snooping All in Day's Work Security: Some Firms Are Now Using Computer Investigators to Uncover Employee Wrongdoing,* LOS ANGELES TIMES, Oct. 29, 2000.

17. *See Communication from the Commission to the Council, The European Parliament, The Economic and Social Committee and the Committee of the Regions, Creating A Safer Information Society by Improving the Security of Information Infrastructures and Combating Computer Related Crime,* http://europa/eu/int/ISPO/eif/InternetPolicies-Site/Crime/CrimeCommEN.html (visited Feb. 14, 2001) [hereinafter *EU Communication*].

18. *See* President's Working Group, *Unlawful Conduct Report.*

privacy and its ability to protect against individuals who might use the systems to further criminal activities.[19]

B. Meaningfully Enforcing National Laws

> What we need is the rule of law at [an] international level, a universal legal framework equal to the worldwide reach of the Internet.
> —Jacques Chirac, President of France[20]

Law enforcement agencies increasingly are finding that existing legal structures are insufficient or, sometimes, non-existent for combating the increasing number cybercrimes. On the most basic level, countries need strong and consistent laws in place to protect their communities from cybercrime. Given the global nature of cybercrime, it is not enough for one country to enact cybercrime legislation if other countries remain havens for computer-related criminal activity. When one country criminalizes computer-related crime and another country does not, criminals are given opportunities to commit crimes remotely from "safe havens." Countries with strong laws find themselves unable to protect their citizens from high-tech crimes originating from elsewhere.

1. Differing Definitions of Cybercrimes

Currently, there exists a wide disparity in the laws governing cybercrime around the world.[21] Even in those countries with cybercrime statutes, the relevant laws often lag behind technological and social changes. A recent report by McConnell International LLC analyzing high-tech laws in fifty-two countries found that only nine countries had amended their laws to cover cybercrimes in four categories: data-related crimes (interception, modification and theft), network-related crimes (sabotage and interference), access crimes (hacking and virus distribution) and associated com-

---

19. *See e.g.* Neil King Jr. & David S. Cloud, *Global Phone Deals Get Scrutiny From New Source: FBI*, WALL STREET JOURNAL, Aug. 25, 2000.

20. ADDRESS BY JACQUES CHIRAC, PRESIDENT OF THE FRENCH REPUBLIC, AN ADDRESS TO THE G8 CONFERENCE ON SECURITY AND CONFIDENCE IN CYBERSPACE (2000), *reprinted in* http://www.elysee.fr/ang/disc/disc_.htm (visited Jan. 30, 2001).

21. *See e.g.*, Stein Schjolberg, *The Legal Framework—Unauthorized Access to Computer Systems: Penal Legislation in 37 Countries*, http://www.mossbyrett.of.no/info/legal.html (2001) [hereinafter Schjolberg, *Legal Framework*].

puter-related crimes (fraud, forgery, aiding and abetting cybercriminals).[22] The report found that only the Philippines—a country that this summer determined it could not prosecute the alleged disseminator of the Love Bug virus—had sufficiently updated its cybercrime laws.[23]

The progression of events in the Philippines regarding the Love Bug virus demonstrate the need for a coherent global approach to cybercrimes. While the Love Bug virus was traced back to the Philippines within days, inadequate Filipino law may have allowed the alleged disseminator of the virus, to escape prosecution. After the Philippine National Bureau of Investigation had gathered enough evidence to indict an individual, the case was dismissed because the Philippine Department of Justice determined that Filipino law had not been violated.[24]

Even if the majority of the world's countries enact substantive statutes to address cybercrime, some jurisdictions may decide intentionally that they do not need or want such laws. Some locales may hold themselves out purposefully to be "safe havens" from such laws. One such jurisdiction may be Sealand, an alleged "sovereign principality," established in 1967 on a former anti-aircraft military fortress located in waters a few miles from the coast of the United Kingdom. In the fall of 2000, a private company, HavenCo, announced that it would be locating its servers in Sealand so that it could offer secure and private networks that would be beyond the reach of legal process and law enforcement agencies. HavenCo and Sealand have publicly claimed that the only activities that will be prohibited on their servers will be child pornography and e-mail spam.[25] Obviously, an extrajudicial safe haven will pose serious threats to cybersecurity and to joint international efforts to combat cybercrimes.

Countries that are attempting to harmonize their substantive computer crime statutes are struggling with how to address differences in the morals and values of particular countries. In many European countries, for example, Neo-Nazi speech is prohibited. Countries such as Germany are com-

---

22. McConnell International, LLC, *Cybercrime...and Punishment? Archaic Laws Threaten Global Information*, http://www.mcconnellinternational.com/services/cybercrime.htm (2000).

23. *Id.*

24. The Philippines' cybercrime laws were not passed by the country's legislature until after the Love Bug virus had been released. The Department of Justice determined that the laws could not retroactively apply to De Guzman.

25. Edward Sherwin, *A Distant Sense of Data Security; "Havens" Promising Unparalleled Computer Protection Set Up Shop Offshore and Even Inside A Mountain*, THE WASHINGTON POST, September 20, 2000.

plaining that hate speech is readily available in their countries through U.S. websites. A dilemma arises in how to address this situation, when the U.S. Constitution protects its citizens' right to disseminate such speech. What is the appropriate response when U.S. citizens are prosecuted in foreign countries for websites or e-commerce businesses operated in the United States?[26] How should requests from other countries for assistance in gathering evidence or prosecuting U.S. citizens who conduct such activities over the Internet be handled?

The United States is also finding that certain of its laws that reflect its morals and values are being violated by foreigners using the Internet. Internet gambling provides a good example. It is illegal in the United States for a gambling business to use the Internet (or other wire communications) to transmit bets or wagers in interstate or foreign commerce.[27] In an attempt to circumvent these laws, individuals are setting up foreign online gambling businesses that accept bets and wagers from U.S. locales. This violates U.S. law, but prosecuting them in the U.S. can be difficult if they are located in countries where Internet gambling is legal.[28]

2. *Differing Procedural Hurdles*

In addition to disparity in substantive cybercrime laws, there are differences in the procedural laws that allow law enforcement agencies to investigate cybercrimes in various countries. Even with traces entirely within the United States, for example, the procedural laws that allow a law enforcement agency to employ a trap and trace device to trace a communications back to an individual suspected of criminal behavior requires the agency to obtain an order from a court located within the district in which the agency intends to install the device.[29] Such a requirement makes little sense in today's networked world, where a single communications may trace back through several providers in several jurisdictions and requires law enforce-

---

26. In May 2000, hate speech on the Internet took center stage when a French court ordered Yahoo Inc. to block French web surfers from Yahoo.com's English auction sites which included Nazi memorabilia. The judge found that Yahoo, which already had banned Nazi auction sites from its French portal, had violated French laws prohibiting the sale of objects that incite racial hatred. *See* Lee Dembart, *Boundaries on Nazi Sites Remain Unsettled in Internet's Global Village*, INT'L HERALD TRIB., May 29, 2000.

27. *See* 18 U.S.C. § 1084(a) (1994).

28. *See e.g. Jay Cohen Convicted of Operating an Off-shore Sports Betting Business That Accepted Bets from Americans over the Internet*, http://www.cybercrime.gov/cohen.htm (Feb. 28, 2000).

29. *See* 18 U.S.C. § 2518(3) (1994).

ment to obtain separate orders in multiple districts for the same communications. The problem of tracing is only compounded when a communication travels multiple countries.

Among the most serious procedural legal challenges facing nations are the following: (1) the ability to preserve stored data in a expeditious manner; (2) the procedures for searching, seizing and compelling the production of stored computer data, including stored traffic data and content and (3) the ability to collect critical traffic data in real time.

The preservation of stored data in an expeditious manner is critical to ensuring that important perishable electronic evidence is not lost. As noted above, this type of data is highly perishable and easily can be deleted or changed if it is not preserved in an appropriate manner. The United States addressed this need for preservation in 18 U.S.C. § 2703(f), which requires a provider, "upon a request of a government entity [to] take all necessary steps to preserve records and other evidence in its possession pending the issuance of a court order or other process."[30]

At the same time, some countries have laws that require service providers to routinely delete data that may be critical to an investigation. For example, EU directives issued in 1995 and 1997 require the deletion of transaction data at the end of a transmission, except if such data is needed for billing purposes or to further national security or certain law enforcement needs.[31] As Internet services are most typically sold on a flat or by-the-hour fee, thereby not requiring traffic data for billing purposes, these directives essentially require Internet service providers to delete transaction data. Without a business reason for keeping such data in the online world, the EU directives require their destruction thus limiting law enforcement's ability to investigate cybercrime.

Even in those countries that do not require mandatory destruction of data, there may be issues regarding the searching and seizing computer data, especially when such data is held by third-parties.[32] Many countries lack

---

30. 18 U.S.C. § 2703(f) (Supp. IV 1998).

31. Directive 95/46/EC of the European Parliament and of the Council of 24 October 1995 on the Protection of Individuals with Regard to the Processing of Personal Data and on the Free Movement of Such Data, 1995 O.J. (L. 281) 31; Directive 97/66/EC of the European Parliament and of the Council of December 15, 1997 Concerning the Processing of Personal Data and the Protection of Privacy in the Telecommunications Sector, 1997 O.J. (L 24) 1.

32. In the United States, The Electronic Communications Protection Act, 18 U.S.C. §§ 2701–11 (1994 & Supp. IV 1998) [hereinafter ECPA] sets forth a complex set of rules as to how and when the U.S. government can obtain stored data from third parties.

standards for obtaining electronic evidence, which can be transferred, altered or destroyed at the push of a key.[33] The challenge facing these countries is the enactment of procedures for searching, seizing and compelling the production of stored computer data.

Of course, beyond these issues in individual countries, there remains the issue of how countries should treat transborder searches and seizures. A transborder search and seizure is one where electronic evidence needed in the victim's country is stored remotely on computers located in another country, but law enforcement in the victim's country has the technical capability to access the remote computers to collect evidence. If the victim's country issues a domestic warrant that allows for such activity, should the international transborder search be accepted under international law? Currently, cybercrime experts in the G-8 and the Council of Europe have not reached consensus on what is an acceptable practice in this area.[34]

The third procedural legal issue is the tracing, in real time, of communications as some countries do not have the legal regimes in place that allow for it. As noted earlier, the technical tracing of a communications can be complicated, especially when multiple providers (and countries) are involved. In computer crime cases, where evidence sometimes can only be gathered as the crime is being committed via a communications network, the lack of real-time tracing can be detrimental to efforts to the investigation of misconduct on the Internet. Indeed, even in those countries where wiretap and real-time tracing laws are in place, there is often controversy over the methods used by law enforcement as real-time tracing can have privacy implications.[35]

ECPA distinguishes between subscriber information, transactional data and electronic communications content, information that is less than or greater than 180 days old and e-mails that have been opened by their recipients.

33. Michael A. Sussmann, *The Critical Challenges from International High-Tech and Computer-Related Crime at the Millennium*, 9 DUKE J. OF COMP. & INT'L L. 451, 451–489 (1999) [hereinafter Sussman, *Critical Challenges*].

34. In the United States, there may be some guidance on the issue in how the courts have treated overseas data in other circumstances. For example, in *U.S. v. Bank of Nova Scotia*, 691 F.2d 1384 (11th Cir. 1982), *cert. denied*, 462 U.S. 1119 (1983), the 11th Circuit enforced a grand jury *subpoena duces tecum* in a tax and narcotics investigation of a U.S. citizen. The subpoena required the production of records in a branch office in the Bahamas. Compliance would have required the bank to violate Bahamian bank secrecy laws.

35. *Compare* EPIC, *Comment on Carnivore System*, http://www.epic.org/privacy/carnivore/review_comments.html (Dec. 1, 2000) *with* "Carnivore" and the Fourth Amend-

C. Operational Challenges

> We need an adequate number of prosecutors and agents—at the federal, state and local level—trained with the necessary skills and properly equipped to effectively fight all types of cybercrime.
>
> —Eric Holder, Deputy Attorney General, United State Department of Justice[36]

Countries are facing significant operational challenges in their efforts to combat and reduce cybercrime. In their fight against cybercrime, countries must have available to them a team of professionals, including investigators, forensic experts and prosecutors, all of whom have technical expertise. Unlike law enforcement agents fighting more traditional crimes, these individuals not only need to know how to investigate or prosecute a crime in general, but also must have specialized skills and training in computer technology. Cybercrime investigators must do more than run investigations—they must be versed in the intricacies of technology to insure that evidence is not lost or overlooked. Forensic experts need to know how to recover, analyze, protect and handle digital evidence that is often perishable and easily altered. Prosecutors must know more than standard evidentiary and procedure rules; they must understand the jargon and complexities of high-technology crimes and be able to translate the evidence of these complex matters in a manner understandable to a judge and jury.

Even if governments successfully recruit high-tech investigators, prosecutors and forensic scientists, there is still a need for up-to-date training and sophisticated high-tech equipment. Technologies are quickly evolving. As a technology become archaic, so does the usefulness of experts in that technology. Continual training in cutting-edge technology, therefore, is critical in the cybercrime-fighting world.

---

ment: *Hearing before the Subcomm. on the Constitution of the House Comm. on the Judiciary,* 106th Cong., 2d Sess. (July 24, 2000) (statement of Kevin V. DiGregory, Deputy Assistant Attorney General of the United States), http://www.usdoj.gov/criminal/cybercrime/carnivore.htm.

36. *Internet Denial of Service Attacks and the Federal Response: Hearing Before the Subcomm. on Crime of the House Comm. on the Judiciary and the Subcomm. on Criminal Oversight of the Senate Comm. on the Judiciary,* 106th Cong., 2d Sess. (Feb. 29, 2000) (statement of Eric Holder, Deputy Attorney General of the United States), http://www.cybercrime.gov/dag0229.htm.

In addition, it is no longer true that a police officer only needs a gun, flashlight and a notepad as his or her basic issued equipment. As more crimes go online, police officers will need computer equipment to be able to investigate them. Further, constant upgrades in technology and training are necessary to insure that the police have adequate investigative tools to help keep pace with the new technologies that are used to commit crimes.

IV. Leadership and Education in the Private Sector

Even if governments and law enforcement agencies could overcome the challenges discussed earlier in this chapter, cybercrime would still exist. Perhaps the greatest weapon against cybercrime is not in the hands of any government, but instead, with the private sector and consumers.

The private sector, at least in the United States, owns and operates the majority of the technological infrastructure. Private companies are responsible for expanding the existing infrastructure, creating the programs that run it and give it increased capabilities and, most importantly, inventing the security measures are needed to safeguard it. The first line of attack against cybercriminals, therefore, must rest with these private companies.

The responsibilities that companies have with regards to protecting our infrastructures and the Internet are many. First, companies—whatever business they may be in—have a responsibility to employ network security systems to protect their own systems from attack and to keep those systems from being used by cybercriminals to attack others. In February 2000, several online services and businesses, including CNN, Yahoo! and Amazon.com were paralyzed by denial of service attacks that eventually were determined to have been caused by a teenager in Canada. This denial of service attack was not a sophisticated one. Indeed, both CERT and the National Infrastructure Protection Center had issued warnings regarding the vulnerabilities that allowed computers to become unwilling assistants in a denial of service attack several months before the February attack occurred. This attack showed how an individual or a group of individuals can break into hundreds of inadequately secure computers around the world and direct them to flood a targeted site with millions of phony data requests.[37] To

---

37. *See e.g.* Greg Miller, *Hacker Held in Web Attacks, Sources Say*, Los Angeles Times, Apr. 19, 2000.

avoid expensive repeat occurrences of this type of cybercrime, companies are facing pressure from internal business executives, insurance companies and auditors to secure their networks against being used to launch such attacks.

Second, companies should educate their employees regarding best practices and responsible online use. Many companies teach their employees that they should keep valuables locked in drawers and should not let strangers into their workplaces. These same companies, however, do not necessarily transfer lessons to the online world. An employee who opens a virus-infected e-mail attachment can do as much, or more, damage to an employer's network as would result from the employee allowing unauthorized individuals access to the employer's physical premises.

Third, companies should take the lead in condemning the activities of cybercriminals. A recent employment ad in the Washington Post proclaimed "HACKERS WANTED." The company posting the ad made no apologies that it was searching for hackers to help develop the company's online government procurement business. This type of practice encourages illegal activity and glorifies cybercrime. Fortunately, other companies have recognized this responsibility and have made it clear that they will not hire hackers or former hackers. Sending such a message is important to the overall effort to reduce attacks on the Internet, our infrastructure and our computers.

Fourth, companies should report cybercrimes to law enforcement agencies more readily. According to the *Issues and Trends: 2000 CSI/FBI Computer Crime and Security Survey*, only 25% of the companies polled reported to law enforcement intrusions and other cybercrimes on their systems.[38] If cybercrime is to be adequately addressed, industry must report crimes to law enforcement agencies. At the same time, law enforcement agencies must continue to build their trustworthiness with companies and recognize the sensitivities that keep many companies from reporting crimes. These sensitivities include fear of media coverage, customer flight and distrust and lack of adequate attention from law enforcement.

Last, companies should consider including in their business plans procedures and practices that facilitate efforts against cybercrime. As noted earlier in this chapter, there are no statutes in the United States that require manda-

---

38. *See* Computer Security Institute, *Ninety Percent of Survey Respondents Detect Cyber Attacks, 273 Organizations Report $265,589,940 in Financial Losses,* http://www.gocsi.com/prelea_000321.htm (Mar. 22, 2000).

tory data retention or tracing capabilities on particular networks. Companies have the critical responsibility of developing business plans that take into account the public interest. Given the U.S. government's largely hands-off approach to regulating the Internet, businesses are in the unique position of determining the value of public safety and welfare and the creation of a safe online environment, in relation to their revenues and business ventures. It is unclear at this point how companies will handle this responsibility.

Consumers also have responsibilities in efforts to combat cybercrime. As users of the infrastructure, computers and the Internet, they must take the precautions necessary to protect themselves and their equipment against cybercriminals. An individual living in an area with a high-crime rate is not likely to leave his or her front door unlocked and open. Yet, individuals with cable and DSL modems are essentially doing just this—leaving their computers online, opened and unlocked to be victimized by cybercriminals. Individuals must recognize that technologies such as firewalls and routine e-mail virus screens are as important to them as an adequate lock on the door of their home.

At the same time that consumers are protecting themselves online, they also should be practicing responsible online behavior and teaching their children the same practices. This especially is important as we now have a generation of new computer users, whose ability to employ powerful technology is not necessarily matched by their understanding of the responsibilities that come with such power. For example, in March of 1999, the Department of Justice and the Information Technology Association of America created a joint government-private sector initiative to address this phenomenon. The Cybercitizen Partnership focuses attention on appropriate social behavior in cyberspace and the importance of teaching young computer users to recognize that, in addition to protecting themselves while on the Internet, they are also responsible for their own actions and that these actions have consequences both for themselves and others.[39]

The development of the new cyber-technology requires society to establish proper rules to protect itself from the misuse of the technology. All parties that participate in the technology—government, private sector and consumer—must equally participate in the creation and implementation of the rules.

---

39. More information on the Cybercitizen Partnership can be found at http://www.cybercrime.gov (visited Jan. 29, 2001) and http://www.itaa.org (visited Jan. 29, 2001). Also, a website to assist parents and teachers with cyberethics was unveiled in September 2000 and can be found at http://www.cybercitizenship.org (visited Jan. 29, 2001).

V. INTERNATIONAL MULTILATERAL EFFORTS

Governments have been and are working together to combat cybercrime and the challenges discussed in this chapter. This section reviews some of the activities of some of the more active international organizations. It does not cover all international activity; instead, it focuses mostly on government-to-government efforts.

A. Organisation for Economic Cooperation and Development

The Organisation for Economic Cooperation and Development ["OECD"] was one of the first groups to take seriously transnational computer crime issues. In 1980, the OECD adopted *Guidelines on the Protection of Privacy and Transborder Flows of Personal Data*.[40] In May of 1983, the OECD gathered in Paris a group of experts representing France, the United Kingdom, Norway, Belgium and Germany to discuss the harmonization of European computer crime legislation. These experts recommended that OECD member countries revise their penal codes to ensure that certain categories of cybercrime were covered.[41] Subsequently, in 1992, the OECD issued the *Guidelines for the Security of Information Systems* which discussed the protection and reliability of information systems.[42] In recent years, the OECD has issued policy guidelines on cryptography[43] and e-commerce.[44]

B. The Group of Eight Nations

In 1996, the Group of Eight Nations ["G-8"][45] brought together a group of experts to formulate recommendations for fighting international crime.

---

40. http://www.oecd.org/dsti/sti/it/secur/prod/PRIV-EN.HTM (1980).
41. *See* Schjolberg, *Legal Framework*.
42. *See* http://www.oecd.org/dsti/sti/it/secur/prod/e_secur.htm (1992).
43. *See Cryptography Policy: The Guidelines and the Issues—The OECD Cryptography Policy Guidelines and the Report on Background and Issues of Cryptography Policy*, http://www.oecd.org/dsti/sti/it/secur/prod/E-CRYPTO.HTM (1997).
44. *See e.g.*, Andrea Goldstein & David O'Connor, *E-Commerce for Development: Prospects and Policy Issues*, http://www.oecd.org/dev/ENGLISH/NEW/documents/tokyo 2.pdf (2000).
45. Canada, France, Germany, Italy, Japan, Russia, United Kingdom and the United States. *See What is G8?*, http://birmingham.g8summit.gov.uk/brief0398/what.is.g8.shtml (1998).

One of the recommendations made by the experts was that the G-8 countries "review their laws in order to ensure that abuses of modern technology that are deserving of criminal sanctions are criminalized."[46] As a result of this recommendation, the G-8 created the "G-8 Subgroup on High-tech Crime" in 1997. Also in 1997, the U.S. Department of Justice hosted the first-ever ministerial meeting of G-8 countries on transnational organized crime. The meeting focusing on combating high-tech and computer-related crime. In all, sixteen Ministers and Deputy Ministers of Justice and Interior from the G-8 counties attended. On December 10, 1997, the ministers adopted a communique which contained ten principles and ten action items related to high-tech crime.

The ten principles adopted by the G-8 were as follows:

I. There must be no safe havens for those who abuse information technologies.

II. Investigation and prosecution of international high-tech crimes must be coordinated among all concerned States, regardless of where harm has occurred.

III. Law enforcement personnel must be trained and equipped to address high-tech crimes.

IV. Legal systems must protect the confidentiality, integrity and availability of data and systems from unauthorized impairment and ensure that serious abuse is penalized.

V. Legal systems should permit the preservation of and quick access to electronic data, which are often critical to the successful investigation of crime.

VI. Mutual assistance regimes must ensure the timely gathering and exchange of evidence in cases involving international high-tech crime.

VII. Transborder electronic access by law enforcement to publicly available (open source) information does not require authorization from the State where the data resides.

VIII. Forensic standards for retrieving and authenticating electronic data for use in criminal investigations and prosecutions must be developed and employed.

IX. To the extent practicable, information and telecommunications systems should be designed to help prevent and detect network abuse, and should also facilitate the tracing of criminals and the collection of evidence.

---

46. Sussman, *Critical Challenges* at 482.

X. Work in this area should be coordinated with the work of other relevant international fora to ensure against duplication of efforts.[47]

In support of these principles, the ministers requested their agencies to implement ten action items to combat high-tech crimes.[48] These ten action items indicate that the members will:

1. Use our established network of knowledgeable personnel to ensure a timely, effective response to transnational high-tech cases and designate a point-of-contact who is available on a twenty-four hour basis.[49]
2. Take appropriate steps to ensure that a sufficient number of trained and equipped law enforcement personnel are allocated to the task of combating high-tech crime and assisting law enforcement agencies of other States.
3. Review our legal systems to ensure that they appropriately criminalize abuses of telecommunications and computer systems and promote the investigation of high-tech crimes.
4. Consider issues raised by high-tech crimes, where relevant, when negotiating mutual assistance agreements or arrangements.
5. Continue to examine and develop workable solutions regarding the preservation of evidence prior to the execution of a request for mutual assistance, transborder searches, and computer searches of data where the location of that data is unknown.
6. Develop expedited procedures for obtaining traffic data from all communications carriers in the chain of a communication and to study ways to expedite the passing of this data internationally.
7. Work jointly with industry to ensure that new technologies facilitate our effort to combat high-tech crime by preserving and collecting critical evidence.
8. Ensure that we can, in urgent and appropriate cases, accept and respond to mutual assistance requests relating to high-tech crime by

---

47. *Communique Annex: Principles to Combat High-tech Crime*, http://www.cybercrime.gov/principles.htm (Feb. 18, 1998).
48. *Communique Annex: Action Plan to Combat High-tech Crime*, http://www.cybercrime.gov/action.htm (Feb. 18, 1998).
49. This network is commonly referred to as the "G-8 24/7 Network" and now includes over twenty participating countries. James K. Robinson, *Internet as the Scene of Crime*, International Computer Crime Conference, Oslo, Norway, http://www.cybercrime.gov/roboslo.htm (May 29, 2000).

expedited but reliable means of communications, including voice, fax, or e-mail, with written confirmation to follow where required.
9. Encourage internationally-recognized standards-making bodies in the fields of telecommunications and information technologies to continue providing the public and private sectors with standards for reliable and secure telecommunications and data processing technologies.
10. Develop and employ compatible forensic standards for retrieving and authenticating electronic data for use in criminal investigations and prosecutions.[50]

In 1998, the Heads of State of the G-8 countries endorsed and agreed to implement the principles and action plans.[51] Since then, the G-8 High-tech Subgroup has met numerous times to discuss how countries can work together and with industry to curb, investigate and prosecute computer crimes.

C. Council of Europe

In 1989 and 1995, the Council of Europe produced recommendations to its member states that governments adopt laws to meet the challenges created by computer crime.[52] The Council recognized, however, that there was a need for a more binding legal document that addressed the harmonization of computer crime laws, international cooperation between governments and the technical issues involved in high-tech investigations. In February, 1997, the Council created a Committee of Experts on Crime in Cyberspace to examine these issues.[53] Given the international aspects of the proposed treaty, several non-member States, including Canada, Japan, South Africa and the United States, attended meetings and actively participated in the expert discussion meetings.

---

50. *Communique Annex: Action Plan to Combat High-tech Crime*, http://www.cybercrime.gov/action.htm (Feb. 18, 1998).
51. *See The Birmingham Summit: Final Communique*, ¶ 21, http://birmingham.g8summit.gov.uk/docs/final.shtml (May 17, 1998).
52. *See* Peter Csonka, *Council of Europe Activities Related to Information Technology, Data Protection and Computer Crime*, 5 INFO & COMM. TECH. LAW 177, 179–180 & 186 (1996).
53. *See Council of Europe's Fight Against Corruption and Organised Crime*, http://www.coe.fr/corruption/epccy.htm (1997).

On April 27, 2000, the Committee released its draft Convention on Cybercrime. This convention is the first known multilateral instrument intended to address many of the challenges posed by computer crime.[54] The latest public draft of the Convention was released on December 22, 2000.[55] The draft Convention is in the process of being finalized and could be adopted by the Committee of Ministers and open for signature as early as September, 2001.

The Convention essentially covers three areas:

1. The harmonization of substantive computer crime laws between countries;
2. The development of procedural authorities to obtain and preserve evidence; and
3. The development of mechanisms for expedited international legal assistance in investigating and prosecuting computer crimes.

1. Substantive Laws

The Convention contains provisions to ensure that incidents that affect the "confidentiality, integrity, and availability" of a computer are criminalized.[56] Parties to the Convention are also obligated to criminalize the trafficking and possession of "hacker" tools where such conduct is (1) intentional, (2) "without right" and (3) done with the intent to commit and offense that constitutes illegal access, illegal interception, data interference and system interference.[57] Each of these offenses are defined in the treaty. The Convention has been carefully drafted to make clear that legitimate scientific research and system security practices, for example, are not criminal.[58] The other substantive legal area covered by the Convention involves the establishment of minimum standards in the areas of fraud, intellectual

---

54. European Committee on Crime Problems & Committee of Experts on Crime in Cyber-space, *Draft Convention on Cyber-crime* (Apr. 27, 2000).

55. European Committee on Crime Problems & Committee of Experts on Crime in Cyber-space, *Draft Convention on Cyber-crime (Draft No. 25 Rev.)*, http://conventions.coe.int/treaty/EN/cadreprojets.htm (Dec. 22, 2000) [hereinafter *COE Draft Convention of Cyber-crime*].

56. *Id.* preamble.

57. *Id.* art. 6.

58. *See e.g. Frequently Asked Questions and Answers About the Council of Europe Convention on Cybercrime (Draft 24REV2)*, http://www.cybercrime.gov/COEFAQs.htm (2000).

property and child pornography.⁵⁹ It is expected that these standards will make it easier to seek international assistance.

2. Procedural Laws

The procedural law sections of the Convention are designed to respect the various countries' jurisdiction and choices regarding legal processes. This area of the treaty is intended to insure that legal authority to collect electronic evidence exists in each country. For example, the Convention calls for the development of procedures for expedited preservation of data, much akin to the United States' 18 U.S.C. § 2703(f) (Supp. IV 1998).⁶⁰ The treaty also requires countries to establish rules for searching, seizing and compelling the turnover of evidence and for the development of rule for collecting critical traffic data in "realtime." ⁶¹ There has been some concerns raised by the Convention by civil libertarians and industry groups.⁶² In particular, there have been concerns raised that Internet Service Providers will have to collect and retain data on their customers, as well as build certain technical capabilities into their structures. The treaty, however, does not contain mandatory data retention requirements. The data preservation requirement would only require service providers to set aside specified data already in its possession when requested to do so by law enforcement authorities during a criminal investigation.⁶³ The Convention also does not require any particular architecture or capability.

3. International Cooperation

In the Convention, the Council of Europe has adopted the 24/7 network of the G-8.⁶⁴ The Convention would also require a country to provide the expedited preservation of data when another country approaches the first country with such a request.⁶⁵ The first country would preserve such data in accordance with its own preservation mechanisms. For example, if the United States was a party to the Convention and Canada requested the preservation of evidence from a U.S. service provider, United States law en-

---

59. *See COE Draft Convention of Cyber-crime*, art. 8–10.
60. *See id.*, art. 16–17.
61. *Id.*
62. *See* Vivienne Walt, *Civil Liberties Groups Criticize Proposed Internet Use Laws; ISPs Would Have to Keep Records on Customers,* USA TODAY, Nov. 20, 2000.
63. *See COE Draft Convention of Cyber-crime*, art. 16.
64. *Id.* art. 35.
65. *Id.* art. 29.

forcement officials would serve a letter on that U.S. service provider under 18 U.S.C. § 2703(f) (Supp. IV 1998). The evidence would be preserved and the Canadian officials would then work with the U.S. under international legal processes to obtain that data from the U.S. service provider.

With regards to transborder searches, the Convention adopts two principles. First, when the data is stored in a site that is publicly available, there is no required authorization from the searched state.[66] Second, when there is fully-sufficient legal consent to access by the police agency, a search would be acceptable without any additional authorization.[67]

D. United Nations

On December 4, 2000, the United Nations General Assembly passed a resolution entitled "Combating the Criminal Misuse of Information Technologies" that addressed computer crime issues.[68] The resolution recognized the work of organizations such as the G-8 and the Council of Europe to address the complex challenges of cybercrime. The resolution "took note" of the following steps that member nations should be taking:

a. States should ensure that their laws and practice eliminate safe havens for those who criminally misuse information technologies.

b. Law enforcement cooperation in the investigation and prosecution of international cases of criminal misuse of information technologies should be coordinated among all concerned States.

c. Information should be exchanged between States regarding the problems that they face in combating the criminal misuse of information technologies.

d. Law enforcement personnel should be trained and equipped to address the criminal misuse of information technologies.

e. Legal systems should protect the confidentiality, integrity and availability of data and computer systems from unauthorized impairment and ensure that criminal abuse is penalized.

f. Legal systems should permit the preservation of and quick access to electronic data pertaining to particular criminal investigations.

---

66. *Id.* art. 32(a).
67. *Id.* art. 32(b).
68. G.A. Res. A/RES/55/63, U.N. GAOR, 3d Sess., http://www.un.org/Depts/dhl/resguide/r55all1.htm (2000).

g. Mutual assistance regimes should ensure the timely investigation of the criminal misuse of information technologies and the timely gathering and exchange of evidence in such cases.
h. The general public should be made aware of the need to prevent and combat the criminal misuse of information technologies.
i. To the extent practicable, information technologies should be designed to help prevent and detect criminal misuse, trace criminals and collect evidence.
j. The fight against the criminal misuse of information technologies requires the development of solutions taking into account both the protection of individual freedoms and privacy and the preservation of governments' capacity to fight such criminal misuse.[69]

E. European Union

The European Union has taken various steps to fight cybercrime. In April 1998, the Commission of the European Communities presented to the European Council the results of a computer-related study. In October 1999, the Tampere Summit of the European Council determined that high-tech crime should be included in efforts to agree on common definitions and sanctions.[70] The Council of the European Union has adopted a Common Position on the Council of Europe cybercrime convention negotiations. Most recently, the Commission of the European Communities issued a Communication that discusses the need for a comprehensive policy initiative for improving the security of information infrastructures and combating cybercrime.[71]

VI. Conclusion

The Internet and other network technologies have given us the ability to communicate with one another or with masses of others, to conduct commerce virtually and to get information that only a few years ago would be

---

69. *Id.*
70. 1999 O.J. (C 118) 116.
71. *See EU Communication*; Communication from the Commission to the Council and European Parliament—The eEurope 2002 update prepared by the European Commission for the European Council in Nice, COM(00) 783 final.

inaccessible to many people. At the same time, the global nature of the Internet that has made it such a powerful tool has also created difficult and complex challenges for governments, consumers and companies. Criminals have discovered the virtues of networked computers and are increasingly using them to conduct their unlawful activities.

The legal, technical and operational challenges facing governments in their efforts to combat computer crimes cannot be addressed by government action alone. Without consumer and company participation, cybercrime is intractable. At the same time, the government's role is critical as the best efforts of companies and consumers to protect themselves from cybercrime will sometimes fail. Government must be prepared and equipped to respond to the crime should this happen.

Some have described the Internet and cyberspace as the new frontier where criminals run rampant, citizens are helpless, and sheriffs do not serve. This is not the case, however. Countries are devoting resources to combating cybercrime and to addressing the international aspects associated with this new type of crime. Governments, consumers and companies must continue to work together to construct solutions that allow the Internet to thrive while controlling the activities of wrongdoers.

INDEX

24/7 network, 187
access device fraud, 58–62
  penalties, 61–62
  requisites, 58–61
anonymity, 50, 55, 159–61
authenticity, 116
bulletin board, 50, 57, 75, 93–94
CERT Coordination Center, 168
child pornography, 15, 17, 42–48, 62, 64–65, 68, 72–73, 91–93, 109, 119, 124,157–58, 161–62, 167–68, 174, 187
  defenses, 46–47
  penalties, 47
Child Pornography Protection Act, 42
Committee of Experts on Crime in Cyberspace, 185–86
Communications Decency Act, 51–53
Computer Fraud & Abuse Act, 17, 32–39, 124, 126–32
  defenses, 128–31
  penalties, 38–39, 131–32
  scope, 35–38, 126–28
computers of third parties, 73
confirming computer dates & times, 114–16
consent to search, 84–88, 157–58
  advising consentor, 87–88
  by co-user, 86
  by employer, 85–86
  by parent, 86
  by spouse, 86
  limited, 88
  withdrawing, 88
conspiracy, 25, 30–31, 38, 41, 62, 135–36
Copyright Act, 18–25, 27, 77, 109, 124, 142–49
  defenses, 23–24, 144–48
  penalties, 19, 21–23
  scope, 18–21, 142–44
copyright management information, 26, 149–50
cost of cybercrime, 168
Council of Europe, 177, 185–89
Counterfeit Access Device & Computer Fraud & Abuse Law, 17, 32, 125
cracking, 13–14, 17, 32–33, 62–63, 110, 124–25, 168
  definition, 13, 125
crimes against government, 68
cyber-terrorism, 7, 69, 168
Cybercitizen Partnership, 181
cyberstalking, 50, 55–56, 65–66, 69, 167–68
definition of cybercrime, 1, 5–8, 11–16, 124–25, 167–69, 173–74
  computer as instrument, 14, 124–25, 168
  computer as target, 13, 124, 167–68
  computer being incidental, 16, 124–25, 168–69
  international, 173–74

Index

origin of the term, 5–6
denial of service attack, 14, 64, 179
Digital Millennium Copyright Act, 25, 27, 149–50
Economic Espionage Act, 30, 32, 124, 134–42
   defenses, 139–42
   scope, 136–39
Electronic Communications Privacy Act, 73, 82, 94, 96–98, 124, 132, 151–52
   defenses, 98
   exceptions, 96–97
   penalties, 97–98, 152
   scope, 96, 152
embezzlement, 15, 66
employee, 3, 13, 30, 33, 37, 61, 75, 85, 95, 117–19, 135, 137–40, 172, 180
encryption, 156, 161, 172
entrapment, 161–63
EU Draft Convention on Cybercrime, 186–87
   international cooperation, 187
   procedural laws, 187
European Union, 172, 189
exigent circumstances, 89–90
false copyright application, 24, 150
false information, 59, 63
FBI, 1, 5, 13, 15, 76, 79, 135, 172–73, 180
First Amendment, 7, 43, 46, 48, 52–55, 57, 93, 139–41, 151, 160–61, 175
forgery, 2, 15, 67, 174
Fourth Amendment, 73–74, 81, 83, 91, 98, 151–55, 177
fraud, 2, 4, 14–15, 17, 24, 30–33, 36, 39–42, 58, 60, 66, 69, 71, 124–26, 130–32, 136, 144, 167–68, 174, 186
fraudulent copyright notice, 150
FTP, 75
G-8, 177, 183–85, 187–88
   Ten Action Items, 184–85
   Ten Principles, 183–84
gambling, 168, 175
global nature of cybercrime, 173

hacking, 13–14, 17, 32–33, 62–63, 110, 124–25, 127–28, 132, 166–68, 173
   definition, 13, 125
harassing communications, 50–51, 56–57, 170
HavenCo, 174
history of cybercrime, 2–5
   Internet, 4–5
   World Wide Web, 5
international cybercrime safe havens, 174
International Organisation of Computer Evidence, 172
international procedural hurdles, 175–77, 187–88
   operational challenges, 178–79
   preserving evidence, 176–77, 187–88
   tracing communications, 177
interstate transportation of stolen property, 25
invasion of privacy, 64
inventory search, 90
ISP, 27–29, 78–79, 170
laptop computers, 75, 169
locating the cybercrime, 170
mail and wire fraud, 24, 39–42, 174
   penalties, 42
McConnell International LLC, 173
Morris worm, 166–67
Morris, Robert Jr., 166
National Infrastructure Protection Center, 168, 179
neo-Nazi speech, 174
number of cybercrimes, 168
obscene communications, 50–52
off-site computer search, 83, 105–07
   accurate pristine mirror, 105–06
   protocol, 106–07
Online Copyright Infringement Liability Limitation Act, 27
Organisation for Economic Cooperation and Development, 182
plain view doctrine, 72, 82, 85, 91–92, 104, 156–57
Privacy Protection Act, 73, 82, 92–95

civil liability, 95
good faith, 95
suppression, 94
private activities, 179–81, 190
protected computer, 33, 35–38, 126–28, 130–31
proving authorship, 116–17
proving knowledge or intent, 119–20
reasonable expectation of privacy, 74–75, 84–85, 153
Sealand, 174
search & seizure
   computers of third parties, 73
   consent to search, 84–85, 157–58
      advising consentor, 87–88
      by co-user, 86
      by employer, 85–86
      by parent, 86
      by spouse, 86
      limited, 88
      withdrawing, 88
   contraband on computer, 109–10
   court rules, 98–99
   exigent circumstances, 89–90
   expert accompanying officers, 100
   intermingled documents, 155–56
   international, 188
   inventory search, 90
   knock and announce, 81–82
   laptop computers, 75, 169
   magistrate imposed restrictions, 99–100
   mobility exigency, 90–91
   need for additional warrant, 104–05
   off-site computer search, 83, 105
      accurate pristine mirror, 105–06
      protocol, 106–07
   overbreadth doctrine, 154–55
   particularity requirement, 154
   plain view doctrine, 72, 82, 85, 91–92, 104, 156–57
   private dwelling, 75, 89
   privilege against seizure, 158–59
   property seized, 103–04
   return, 107
   return to non-suspect, 108
   scope, 154
   search by private party, 77, 151
   search incident to arrest, 88, 90
   silver platter doctrine, 75–77
   state constitutional search limitations, 92
   stipulation, 108
   stop and frisk, 90
   transborder search, 177
   unexpected computer, 71–72
   victim accompanying officers, 101–03
   victim's computer, 73
smuggling, 24
stalking, 170
state constitutional search limitations, 92
state cybercrime, 62–68
Stoll, Clifford, 165–66
SWECTRA, 133–34, 152–53
   exceptions, 134
   penalties, 134
   scope, 133
theft, 2–4, 12, 15–16, 18, 30–31, 41, 66–67, 124–26, 134–38, 141–42, 173
tracing an Internet communication, 78–79, 170–71, 177
trade secret, 30–32, 134–41, 147
trademark, 18, 22, 29–30, 142
trafficking, 24–25, 30, 33, 37–38, 61, 128, 142, 148–49, 169, 186
   trafficking in counterfeit labels, 148
transborder search, 177
transmitting information about a minor, 55
transnational crime, 169
transporting stolen property, 49
trap and trace device, 175
trial, 110–13
   evidence — animations, 111–12
   evidence — demonstrations, 110–11
   evidence — printouts, 110
   experts, 112–13
unauthorized access, 37, 49, 58, 60, 118, 125–26, 134, 152, 173

unauthorized fixation of sound
  recordings, 149
Uniform Trade Secrets Act, 138
United Nations, 188–89
virus dissemination, 17, 32–33, 63,
  168
warrant, 77–83
  description of items, 80–81
  evidence of a crime, 77
  found in place to be searched, 78
  good faith exception, 82
  knock and announce, 81–82
  magistrate, 79
  presence of computer unknown, 81
  probable cause, 77
  prompt execution, 83
  when not needed, 83
wiretap, 96, 132–33, 177